# Japanese FDI Flows in Asia

*The book is dedicated to*
*Dr. Johzen Takeuchi, Professor, School of Economics, Nagoya University, Japan – A great human, an eminent scholar, and my mentor – who initiated me in this area and has been instrumental for the completion of this study.*

# Japanese FDI Flows in Asia

## Perspectives and Challenges

Mohan L. Lakhera

palgrave
macmillan

First published 2008 by
PALGRAVE MACMILLAN
Houndmills, Basingstoke, Hampshire RG21 6XS and
175 Fifth Avenue, New York, N.Y. 10010
Companies and representatives throughout the world

PALGRAVE MACMILLAN is the global academic imprint of the Palgrave Macmillan division of St. Martin's Press, LLC and of Palgrave Macmillan Ltd. Macmillan® is a registered trademark in the United States, United Kingdom and other countries. Palgrave is a registered trademark in the European Union and other countries.

ISBN-13: 978–0–230–20155–2 hardback
ISBN-10: 0–230–20155–5 hardback

This book is printed on paper suitable for recycling and made from fully managed and sustained forest sources. Logging, pulping and manufacturing processes are expected to conform to the environmental regulations of the country of origin.

A catalogue record for this book is available from the British Library.

Library of Congress Cataloging-in-Publication Data

Lakhera, Mohan L., 1936–
Japanese FDI flows in Asia : perspectives and challenges / Mohan L. Lakhera.
p. cm.
Includes bibliographical references and index.
ISBN 0–230–20155–5 (alk. paper)
1. Investments, Japanese—Asia. 2. Investments, Foreign—Asia. I. Title.
HG5702.L35 2008
332.67'35205—dc22

2008015143

10 9 8 7 6 5 4 3 2 1
17 16 15 14 13 12 11 10 09 08

Printed and bound in Great Britain by
CPI Antony Rowe, Chippenham and Eastbourne

# Contents

# List of Figures

# List of Tables

*End note tables*



*Technical Annex Tables*

# List of Abbreviations

| | |
|---|---|
| ADB | Asian Development Bank |
| AFTA | ASEAN free trade area |
| AIA | ASEAN investment area |
| ASEAN | Association of Southeast Asian Nations |
| BUGTDEF | Budget deficit to GDP |
| CSA | Country-specific advantages |
| EPZ | Export processing zones |
| EXRATE | Real effective exchange rate |
| FEM | Fixed effects model |
| FDI | Foreign direct investment |
| FTJGDP | Ratio of trade with Japan to GDP |
| FSA | Firm-specific advantages |
| GDP | Gross domestic product |
| GDCF/GDP | Ratio of Gross domestic capital formation to Gross domestic product |
| INVINFRA | Investment in infrastructure |
| IPR | Intellectual property rights |
| JBIC | Japan Bank for International Cooperation |
| JETRO | Japan External Trade Organization |
| JIT | Just-in-time |
| JMT | Japanese Management Technique |
| JV | Joint ventures |
| MNEs | Multinational enterprises |
| MoF | Ministry of Finance |
| NIEs | Newly industrializing economies |
| ODA | Official Development Assistance |
| OLI | Ownership, Location and Internalization |
| PCINVEDU | Per capita expenditure on education |
| REM | Random effects model |
| SME | Small and medium-sized enterprises |
| SEZs | Special Economic Zones |
| TQC | Total quality control |
| UN | United Nations |
| UNCTAD | United Nations Conference on Trade and Development |
| WTO | World Trade Organization |
| XRTY | Change in exchange rate of yen |

# Preface

Japan, the greatest economic success story in the world's economic history, performed miracles for almost four decades since the postwar period turning into a leading economic power. Emulating Japan and with its assistance the Asian four tigers – the so-called newly industrializing economies (NIEs) – also transformed themselves into major economic powers. Joining the race, the ASEAN-4, the second generation newly industrializing powers, also successfully displayed high levels of economic performance. The latest to join this Asian growth club with a bang is China. And now with the emergence of India, along with China, in the global scene recording impressively higher economic growth implies that over 40 per cent of the world population is potentially engaged in the global economy. There are no historical antecedents for such a development process as is happening in Asia.

Forces of globalization are compelling the countries to act. The economic environment is undergoing a sea change in terms of investment flows, trade and technology transfers. Foreign direct investment (FDI) has emerged as a potent factor in the spillovers of knowledge and promotion of growth. The globalization of competition, the localization of competitive advantages and technological changes are affecting the multinational enterprises (MNEs) across the world. MNEs, the principal source of FDI, are facing a variety of challenges and sharpening their strategies with multiple motivations. The host countries are also competing for FDI along multiple dimensions – for superior technology and for increasing their competitiveness, augmenting domestic investment, gaining market access abroad, to bridge foreign exchange gap and so forth. This integrated international dynamics has become a part of the larger picture leading into the present century. The fast-changing paradigms, alliances, economic networking between nations have become vital instruments in facilitating the diffusion and increasing the speed of change – economic as well as technological. In addition, for the same reasons such changes have increased the instability of technical and economic conditions. It would be critical to disentangle the forces that are currently shaping the global patterns of FDI. An important dimension of FDI, that it could also work as a catalyst in the economic development process and enhance structural adjustment process providing an attractive option as part of the future dynamics of the economic development strategy, makes this even more critically important.

The remarkable expansion in FDI in recent years has been the result of many significant developments which include: First, regional integration, diffusion of production techniques, standardization of product designs, and reduction in barriers owing to World Trade Organization (WTO) regulations, have all tended to spur FDI. Secondly, the increasing importance of intra-firm trade – instead of arm's-length transactions – has created comparative advantages due to domestic sourcing, economies of scale, transfer pricing and captive markets. These considerations have augmented the incentives for FDI. Thirdly, the diminishing amount of overseas development assistance (ODA) on the one hand and dramatic performance by the FDI has led the economies to its increased competitive bidding. And, finally, the economic reforms have augured well for FDI.

## Japan – a lead country

Japan – the second largest economy in the world and one of the most important sources of FDI, technology, and trade – has been playing an important role in providing capital and technology for greater reorientation and improving the economic linkages which have made technology transfer possible, apart from larger FDI flows and access to larger and more sophisticated markets. Despite prolonged recession and notwithstanding the present down-trend in its FDI outflows, it has still both the capacity and resources that can maintain the supply of 'public goods', and become the 'lender of the last resort' and provider of investment and technology to developing countries.

## NIEs and the ASEAN-4

Japan ranks topmost among NIEs and ASEAN's partners in investment, trade and aid. Much of the economic growth of these countries has been fuelled by Japanese investment and is induced by its trade. Following shortly after the Japanese economy's decade of rapid economic development during the 1970s and 1980s, the Asian economies – starting with the NIEs, then the ASEAN countries and now China – have emerged from the pack of developing countries to what one may call the 'miracle' of economic growth. The Japanese MNEs, in particular, implemented the transfer of their technologies to the host countries through FDI. This generated an FDI-led sequential process of economic development also referred to as 'staged development' or 'tandem growth' paradigm and so forth. Greatly facilitated by Japanese FDI, changes in the industrial restructuring and trade flows, has enabled the countries of this region to move upward on the ladder of industrialization while maintaining an international division of labour. In this process, the region has become increasingly intertwined through linkages of FDI, technology and trade.

## China and India

With over 40 per cent of the world's population, the experience of China and India, their striking similarities and contrasts, underscores the need to understand the political economy of policy making in these countries in the context of attracting Japanese FDI. The year 1978 marks a paradigm shift in China. The 'emancipation of thought', after the fall of the Gang of Four – throwing off the dogmatic shackles of the Mao period – released a great burst of energy and enthusiasm, and signalled radical departures from the earlier system by bringing openness in a command economy which began the first reform decade and has moved fast ever since then.

India, which can also be described as a command economy model, had a fairly restrictive foreign private investment policy until 1991. After remaining a closed and heavily regulated market economy for almost four decades, in July 1991, it initiated changes in its economic policies broadly on the lines of the World Bank's Structural Adjustment Program, involving a major shift towards greater integration with the world economy and the liberalization of market transactions and private economic activities. India is now seeking to consciously 'benchmark' its policies against those of the rapidly growing Chinese and East Asian economies in order to attract a greater share of Japanese FDI flows.

China and India, wide apart in terms of political beliefs, institutions, traditions and culture, are grappling with the challenges of globalization in their own ways, thereby providing similarities and contrasts for enticing FDI. China's growth is manufacturing-led while that of India is service-led; the former has strong infrastructure and high R&D, whereas the latter has weaker infrastructure and relatively poor R&D. Likewise, while India has a very high export orientation in software, China is equally strong in hardware. It is clear from this that both countries have different orientations towards globalization.

## India – Japan

In the 1950s it was believed that India would succeed economically, because of its experience in manufacturing, entrepreneurship, and its relatively developed rail network. It was also endowed with rich resources and Japan was keen to invest in establishing greater trade relations. As long ago as February 1958 a Bilateral Trade Agreement was signed with Japan. This provided for a 'Most Favored Nation' treatment, yet India has continued to remain lowest on the ladder while China, which established itself as a potential market much later, has taken the lead. Japan could have emerged a major player in promoting India's development programmes and policy if there had been an eagerness to work in cooperation, a better understanding of Japan and an improvement in the realities on the ground. India did not learn from its missed opportunities. Now many countries are in competitive bidding through 'reform competition' to attract Japanese FDI. Although India has introduced numerous policy measures, many of these remain largely on paper and many more have yet to be introduced.

# About the Book

## The need for this study

There is a large amount of literature on FDI and also on Japanese FDI. There are also country studies testing the impact of one or two variables – mostly 'market' or 'appreciation in Japanese yen', or else 'decline in effective exchange rates' on Japanese FDI, but this is the first attempt when Japanese FDI has been investigated country-group wise – NIEs, ASEAN-4, China and India – taking into account a comprehensive set of economic variables. Using Hendry's approach we started with a large number of variables and successively reduced the number to a smaller set, depending upon the economic reasoning and level of significance, which was ultimately used to explain the Japanese FDI location choice in the current global scenario.

The present study also adds to the existing literature by directly collecting primary data from the investors that influence their decision choice to invest in a particular country, interviewing the leading MNEs and holding discussions with all the leading chambers of commerce and industry in Japan. The study adopts a combination of different mythological approaches which distinguish it from other contributions. Thus, the study attempts to fill an important gap.

The book provides insight to policy makers on how to design policies to attract Japanese FDI; to the researchers on methodological aspects; and to the general readers on various facets of Japanese investment.

## Title of the book and chapter planning

This book is entitled *Japanese FDI Flows in Asia: Perspectives and Challenges*, and focuses especially on the NIEs-4, ASEAN-4 China and India. The study has been organized into six chapters.

Chapter 1 introduces the subject by first presenting a brief taxonomy of different FDI theories and hypotheses in order to provide the analytical framework for much of the analysis attempted in the study. This is followed by providing some empirical evidence of Japanese FDI flows in developing and developed countries. Having provided the backdrop, the chapter next presents the motivation, goals, design and methodology adopted in the study.

Chapter 2 assesses the globalization of Japanese FDI, and traces different waves. It examines the trends in size, growth and developments in Japanese FDI over the decades providing a perspective on its changing geography in NIEs, ASEAN–4, China and India. There is also an examination of the role of the factors that have shaped the distribution of Japanese FDI in these countries. Data have been compiled and time series constructed from different sources.

Chapter 3 examines the perception of Japanese investors to invest in these countries. Based on an intensive survey and collection of primary data directly from the investors, it gives the ratings in respect of the critical variables considered essential by Japanese investors for the location of their investment.

Chapter 4 extends the presentation by first tracing the international orientation of Japanese companies; it then investigates the factors involved in their internationalization and through collection of primary data assesses the perception of the domestic-oriented companies to internationalize – to stimulate new and sequential investments across borders.

Chapter 5 takes up the drivers of Japanese FDI. It deals with an econometric estimation of the determinants for attracting Japanese FDI to country-groups – NIEs, ASEAN-4, China, India and also for all ten countries making use of long, balanced panel data. We have also examined the important policy factors in the host countries. Models constructed for the country-groups are analysed and the significance of a set of economic determinants in attracting Japanese FDI is assessed.

Chapter 6 presents the main results. The basic aim is to provide inputs for the host country's policy formulation.

References are given at the end at the book. In the text, we have mainly presented the analysis and the results. Explanatory notes are given at the end of the book.

# Acknowledgements

The study is mainly the outcome of research carried out by me as a Visiting Fellow at the Economic Research Center (ERC), School of Economics, Nagoya University, Japan, wherein I also gave a Seminar on the 'Declining Share of Japanese FDI in India'. I am extremely grateful to the ERC for providing me the fellowship and other financial support and facilities to carry out the study.

I owe a special debt to Professor Johzen Takeuchi – a great human and my mentor – who recommended my visit to the ERC, and encouraged, helped and guided me in a number of ways during my stay in the ERC. Together we visited the Chambers of Commerce and Industry of Hiroshima, Nagoya, Osaka, Tokyo and Yokohama for discussion. He was also instrumental in translating the questionnaires from English to Japanese and back again to English. He has gone through the study and given me a lot of insight. He has been my support throughout the study.

I am extremely grateful to Professor Atsushi Kitahara, then Director of the Center, now Dean of the School of Economics, for his encouragement, cooperation and for giving me every support at the Center. He has been so good that I have no words to express my gratitude to him.

I am deeply indebted to Mr. Fumihide Toyooka, Chief of the ERC, for his support from day one. He was always extremely generous in giving me his time in solving my problems. Even after I left the ERC he has been helpful.

Ms. Mami Masuoka, a staff member of the Center, helped me at every stage of my work. The Office of General Administration has been very helpful to me. And so was the Library staff. I am indebted to all of them. I am also grateful to Ms. Miyoko Uchida, a student at the school, for translating the questionnaires' replies from Japanese into English

I owe my special gratitude to the multinational enterprises (MNEs) for the time and the effort in replying the questionnaires in a candid manner and, later, for giving personal interviews despite busy schedule. The domestic companies have also been highly cooperative. I owe the completion of this study to them.

The Chambers of Commerce and Industry of Hiroshima, Nagoya, Osaka, Tokyo and Yokohama gave me their full support and cooperation. I am extremely indebted to them. In fact, no word is adequate enough to express my gratitude to them.

Following my return to India from Nagoya, JETRO's office in Delhi was extremely helpful. In particular, I must thank Mr. Yuji Hashimoto, then Director-General and on his transfer to Tokyo, Mr. Hirotoshi Ito, Director, in the organization, for helping me constantly by way of giving the requisite data on Japanese FDI and other related material.

Professor K.L. Krishna, former Director and Professor of Econometrics, Delhi School of Economics has been extremely helpful in discussing all of the econometrical and methodological aspects and also in going through the manuscript. He saw through the entire evolution of this work to its present form, always listened to my questions which makes me owe him a great deal of intellectual debt.

Professor B.N. Golder, Institute of Economic Growth (IEG), Delhi, helped from time to time by way of giving valuable suggestions on the draft. I have also had the benefit of discussions with Prof. T.A. Bhavani, IEG, Delhi. I thank Mr. P.K. Jain, Librarian-in-charge, IEG, Delhi, and Mr. Parveen Babbar, Assistant Librarian, Indira Gandhi National Open University, New Delhi for their help.

I would like to thank the Managing Editor, *Review of World Economics*, for granting permission to adopt a table from the *Review* (1981) which gives the main vehicles of foreign involvement by enterprises, and to Mr. Junko Tazawa, Japan External Trade Organization (JETRO), for giving permission to use the data relating to monthly wages paid by the Japanese companies from the study: *The 15th Survey of Investment-Related Cost Comparison in Major Cities and Regions in Asia* (2005).

Special thanks go to the reviewer at Palgrave Macmillan, for providing many constructive suggestions, including chapter planning, which has led to significant improvements throughout the text.

I gratefully acknowledge the professionalism of Alec Dubber at Palgrave Macmillan, whose tireless efforts has turned this manuscript into an accessible product. Mr. Nick Brock, Consultant, Palgrave Macmillan, edited the final manuscript with dexterity and fineness. Nick is a professional *par excellence*. It was a great pleasure to work with him.

Finally, I take full responsibility for the opinions expressed.

Mohan L. Lakhera

# 1
# Introduction

This chapter provides a perspective of the issues involved in this study by way of a brief taxonomy of foreign direct investment (FDI) theories and hypotheses. It also offers a discussion of the current international environment, an examination of Japanese FDI outflows and an outline of the context and motivation of the present study, including its design, methodology and goals.

## 1.1 The overview

The central issue in the theory of foreign direct investment (FDI) has been the nature of firm-specific advantages (FSA), which relate primarily to the possession of superior 'knowledge' and other 'intangible assets' giving them a competitive edge – be it in the form of technology, production, innovation, product diversification, marketing or other activities – and their transfer across borders through a process of internalization rather than arm's-length transactions.[1] This 'knowledge' has the character of a 'public good' – being difficult to hold and protect – that can be easily transferred, with the additional point that the market for the sale of this 'knowledge' is imperfect. Multinational enterprises (MNEs) arise due to an internalization failure in the market for 'knowledge' and information, that is, any type of externality in the goods and factor markets. FDI is, thus, the means of internalizing the externalities which constitutes a general theory of FDI and a factor for the emergence of MNEs. FSA and country-specific advantages (CSA) are linked by the MNEs either to extend their knowledge base or to reduce their level of risk. It is precisely the nature of a company's FSAs and the type of CSAs and the configuration that determines whether or not a particular production activity is likely to be located in a foreign country through FDI, that is, whether internalization will occur. Needless to say, in a world of perfect markets for 'knowledge', MNEs would not exist and there would be no FDI. Alternatively, FDI and MNEs may arise because of shortcomings in the arm's-length markets for intangible assets (Caves 1996). Firms undertake FDI because the alternatives (trade, licensing) are less efficient. FDI provides the means to internalize any firm-specific advantage (FSA) of the MNEs.

In the dynamic context, the growth of firms is dependent on their ability to create new knowledge and replicate this knowledge in order to expand their market, keeping in view the stream of net benefits that will accrue during the product life cycle – the limiting factors being market demand, the competitiveness of other firms and the replication of knowledge ahead of the competitors. The process of internalization, and the ability to create new knowledge, is efficiency-based helping competitiveness both at home and in the host country (that is, factor conditions, demand conditions, related and supporting industries, the firms' strategy, structure and rivalry in a specific industry) and are fundamental for a firm to become successfully multinational.

There are both weak and strong location advantages at firm, industry and country levels. At the cross-country level, a country's relative attractiveness *vis-à-vis* other countries is described by a set of general location parameters. These relate mainly to the accessibility to output markets – both domestic and foreign; accessibility to inputs – intermediate and raw materials; labour – its cost, productivity and skills; infrastructure in all its aspects; and taxes, tariffs and subsidies. These induce the investor to produce in that country rather than serve it by exports either from their home country or from an 'export' base. Obviously, these should lead the firm to buy or create a foreign subsidiary rather than to engage in non-equity arrangements.

## 1.2 FDI theories and hypotheses: a brief taxonomy

This section will contain a discussion of some of the main and most relevant theories of FDI from the viewpoint of this study.

### 1.2.1 Market imperfections hypothesis

The foremost is the market imperfections hypothesis for the existence of FDI. Hymer–Kindleberger (Kindleberger 1969; Hymer 1976) postulated that FDI is the direct result of an imperfect global market.[2] They identified two main types of market imperfections: one to do with the structural imperfections of the market, and the other related to transaction costs. This theory of FDI asserts that the basis for such investments lies in the transactions costs of transferring technical and other knowledge and market imperfections. According to the Hymer–Kindleberger theory, the foreign-owned firm would make an investment in the host country only if it possesses some compensating advantage over local firms, which allows it to compete on equal terms with indigenous firms, and the market for the sale of this advantage is imperfect. The taxonomy suggested by Kindleberger (1969) in the 'market imperfection paradigm' is as follows: imperfections in the goods market, imperfections in factor markets, scale economies and government-imposed disruptions.[3] Since the firm still has the option of licensing the advantage (technology) to an indigenous producer or exporting the product to the host country, clearly, certain other conditions have to be satisfied in order for FDI to occur. Three such conditions are:

(i) The advantage is internally transferable (it can be exploited by a subsidiary of the parent firm with no additional cost to the parent firm or to the subsidiaries that are already exploiting it);
(ii) It is more profitable for the foreign-owned firm to exploit the advantage itself than to license it to an indigenous producer (because of imperfections in the market for knowledge and the heavy firm-to-firm transfer costs of the advantage); and
(iii) Exporting the product to the host country is impossible or unprofitable due to tariff or transport cost barriers.

Hymer's theory has evolved, with the contribution of, among others, Vernon (1966); Caves (1974, 1996); Dunning (1993); Rugman (1980); Teece (1977, 1986); Williamson (1989); and Hennart (1982, 1986 and 1991).

### 1.2.2 The internalization hypothesis

The market for the sale of intangible assets – research, information and knowledge – is imperfect. The internalization theory draws from the paradigm of market failure for intangible assets – be it structural, transactional or one of information asymmetry. These could also be in response to exogenously induced regulations and controls being in the way of trade and investment. However, the markets for these firm-specific assets suffer from a number of hazards and infirmities in transferring this knowledge across boundaries which lead to high transaction costs. These infirmities arise from the characteristics of the intangible assets. *First,* knowledge, which is an intermediate product, paradoxically has the property of being a 'public good' – that is, it can be transferred at zero marginal cost. Johnson (1970) has shown that knowledge is a public good with a zero social price but a non-zero private cost. As a result, the firm that is responsible for its creation and development faces the difficulty of appropriating a return to its use. Hence, these are inefficiently priced (Magee 1977; Caves 1996). MNEs internalize these in their structure as an intermediate product and appropriate a fair return for such costly knowledge expenditures. *Secondly*, a severe information asymmetry may exist due to the dynamic nature of technology and the inability of the seller to make any disclosure of the stage of development of its intangible assets. Williamson (1981) and Buckley and Casson (1976) have stressed the importance of information. The size of the firm expands because of the internalization of information produced. *Thirdly*, there may be a failure to recognize the productive potential of the intangible assets (Williamson 1981). Or else there may be buyer's uncertainty about the potential value of the intangible asset (Caves 1996). *Fourthly*, certain kinds of knowledge may be embodied in the skills of personnel or may have a high 'tacit' component (Teece 1981, 1983). All of these are interdependent factors and are related through a flow of intermediate products – mostly in the form of knowledge and expertise (Buckley and Casson 1976). *Finally*, the arm's-length market may fail to ensure uniform quality standards, particularly in cases relating to the transfer of goodwill assets, brand names and the like (Giddy 1978; Giddy and Rugman 1979).

These infirmities lead to a high cost of market transactions which the MNEs avoid by internalizing their transactions and hence their transaction costs. Firms that internalize transactions across national boundaries through FDI become multinationals. However, internalization also has costs and therefore the presence of significant transaction costs in international markets is not a sufficient condition for internalization by multinational firms. The firm will only make a decision after comparing the market transaction costs to those of internal organizational or any other associated costs it expects to experience. The net economies arising out of this will represent the advantages of internalization. Furthermore, propensities to internalize vary between industries, being dependent on the costs of the market transaction of intangible assets involved (Dunning 1981a). FDI may be high in areas where location and internalization incentives are important. In short, multinationals are creatures of internalization, replacing external markets with more efficient internal ones. This is a necessary and sufficient condition for the existence of MNEs. Thus, as a refinement of the market imperfections approach, this hypothesis gives a synthesizing explanation of the motives for FDI, envisaging that FDI takes place as a result of the internalizing the externalities.

A more general theory tracing the emergence of the internalization of markets (Buckley and Casson 1976, 1981) is based on the following simple postulates:

- Maximize profit in the world of imperfect markets;
- When markets in intermediate products are imperfect, there is an incentive to bypass them by creating internal markets (within the firm); and
- Internalization of markets across national boundaries generates MNEs.

The link between direct investment and the transfer of firm-specific intangible assets as an intermediate good was made explicit in an important article by Caves (1971), which emphasized the ability to differentiate goods. He observed: 'Here is the link to the basis for direct investment: the successful firm producing a differentiated product controls knowledge about serving the market that can be transferred to other national markets for its product at little or no cost'.

One of the most influential studies on market imperfection and externalities is that of Caves (1971) who suggests that the reason for a parent company establishing overseas subsidiaries is to produce a similar product and to benefit from the managerial and technical advantages acquired in the original development of that product. These are the externalities involved in the horizontal integration. One may say that the 'Caves economies' of product differentiation and horizontal integration contrasted with 'Coase economies' of information constitutes the essence of internalization.

It is argued that the location strategy of a firm is determined by the interplay of comparative advantage, barriers to trade, and incentives to internalize; the firm will be multinational whenever these factors make it optimal to locate different stages of production in different countries. Another prediction of this theory is that unless transport costs are very low and returns to scale at the plant level are high, or the comparative advantage of one location is very significant, the international acquisition and exploitation of knowledge will normally involve international production through a world-wide network of basically similar plants.

### 1.2.3 Vernon's (1966, 1979) product cycle

Knowledge is not a universal free good. In addition, there is a large gap between the knowledge of a scientific principle and its embodiment in a marketable product entailing risks. A powerful generalization of the process of FDI emphasizing the factors in influencing the origin of the competitive advantages of the firms is given by Vernon. The product life cycle theory divides the life cycle of a product into a sequence of well-defined stages that differ from one another in respect of technology, the rate of growth of sales and market characteristics. During the initial stages of the cycle, when the product is new, technology is evolving and not standardized, and there is little threat that competing firms will copy the new product. The innovating firm that has succeeded in introducing the new product during this stage will have a monopoly advantage and this advantage is best exploited through exports rather than through FDI. This stage is characterized by exports, high R&D expenditure and rapid technological change. The second stage denotes the process of stabilizing the new technology. In this stage, technology and investment flows are more likely to be between two developed countries because the threat of copying is likely to come mainly from another advanced country. However, investment flows to developing countries are likely to materialize during the later part of the second stage of the product cycle, when technology has not yet stabilized but is known to a group of firms confined to a few countries. Here, there will be limited competition between the MNEs to invest in the developing countries in order to capture markets. The third stage of the product cycle represents one in which the product becomes standardized and the technology is well known. During this period the multinational investments will be governed by considerations of the comparative costs and factor endowments of the countries.

Thus, Vernon emphasized the role of product innovation and the standardization of production methodologies over time as well as the gain and loss of comparative advantage of particular countries in both the product and the maturation process. He identified different stages in the life cycle of a product, each with a different implication for the internationalization of production of the innovating company. The first stage is domestic in nature, the home country being the major market. As the production process comes to be better understood, the firm moves to the second stage. Production is transferred to other countries. Later again, in the mature stage, the production process becomes fully standardized and the market entry very competitive. This is the consequence of the production technology diffusing to rival firms, while manufacturing is transferred to countries with lower labour costs. Vernon's model brings exporting and foreign production into a single explanation of foreign market entry and offers a developmental view on the relocation of production activities.

Vernon focuses on the symbiosis between home country location advantage in technological innovation and the resulting proprietary assets at the MNE level. He links MNEs and location advantages – predicting both the point of origin for MNEs and something about the pattern of their international spread. From a dynamic perspective, MNEs are observed to be capable of linking their firm-specific advantages (FSAs) to the specific-location advantages of host countries as the standardization of products occurs (see Rugman 1980, 2002).

### 1.2.4 The Kojima trade-complementing hypothesis (1973, 1978, 1982 and 1985)

The market imperfections and internalization theories – discussed above – seek to explain FDI in a microeconomic behavioural context without making a distinction with regard to the country of origin. Kojima developed a macroeconomic framework, integrating trade theory with FDI making a distinction with regard to the country of origin. His theory of FDI has led to a wide-ranging debate comparing various aspects of the nature and impact of FDI from Japan and the USA (for instance, Dunning 1988, 1992a, 1995; Doyle, Saunders and Wong 1992; Yamamura 1994; Schroath, Hu and Chen 1993; Encarnation 1999; Ravenhill 1999).

Kojima argued that there is an inherent difference between FDI originating in the West from that which originates in Japan and draws a contrast between the 'Japanese-type' foreign investments and the 'American style'. In his theoretical framework, he shows that while Japanese foreign investment is pro-trade oriented, US FDI is not. This framework makes it possible for him to contrast 'Japan-style' foreign investment with the 'American style'. In the Japanese case, the host country's production frontier expands in such a direction that those industries which have a comparative advantage expand while those with disadvantages contract, thus enhancing the basis for trade. He points out that Japanese FDI tends to congregate towards export-oriented and labour-intensive industries in developing economies that have a comparative advantage in these industries. It is argued that Japanese FDI represents a search for location-specific inputs to complement the skills developed by Japanese enterprise, and this makes it different from the FDI originating in the West. It should be pointed out here that the

'Kojima theory' was developed in the first, early wave of Japanese FDI in the 1960s and 1970s, when most of the host countries in Asia adopted the import substitution industrialization policy with the inflow of foreign investment. One of the core arguments of the 'Kojima theory' is that Japanese-type FDI would upgrade the industrial structures of both Japan and the host country, or play the role of initiator and tutor in the industrialization of less-developed countries. Many Japanese small and medium-sized firms in the host countries were expected to provide production and technological linkages with local firms. Thus, the theory presents the triple effect of Japanese-style FDI, trade and industrial restructuring with mutual benefit for both sides. The triad effect was typically seen in the textiles industry and to a lesser extent in the automobiles and electrical appliances industries, which contributed to upgrading local industry and also, to a lesser extent, to the exports of these manufactures. The dramatic rise of Japanese FDI to Asian countries in the latter half of the 1980s was characterized by different features. The 'investment rush' forced Japanese firms either to bring group vendor firms to the host countries or to start a new transaction in the host country with non-group Japanese vendor firms. There was quick setting up of new manufacturing lines that kept to quality, and a timely delivery of goods for exports of the same volume/standard as that of Japan to the US and other developed countries. In other words, the new investing firms were more self-contained. Although new investment from Japan in the late 1980s helped to bring about a considerable increase in the host countries' exports, it contributed little in terms of industrial restructuring/up-gradation of local supporting (vendor) industries. The 'Asian economic crises' reinforced the fundamental weakness in these countries, viz., that their own industrial structure lacked a strong base of local supporting industry. Dunning (1993) points out that Kojima's trade-complementing hypothesis is an extension of the neo-classical theory to embrace cross-border transactions of intermediate products (for instance, technology, management, skills, and so on) but in the static framework.

### 1.2.5 The eclectic paradigm

Dunning's eclectic approach (1958, 1980, 1988, 1991, 1993 and 1995) integrates the structural imperfections and transaction-cost perspectives and adds a third perspective – the location aspect. The eclectic theory of international production – which is also a microeconomic explanation – explains the ways in which the firms decide to invest abroad. According to this theory, a firm will make a direct investment in a foreign country if it possesses:

(i) Some ownership of core competencies or specific intangible assets that enhance competitive advantage;
(ii) Location advantages that would derive from a transfer of operations onto the new region;
(iii) Internalization advantages that may accrue to the investing firms.

The greater the ownership advantage of the enterprise the greater will be the incentive to exploit this. The more the economies of production and marketing favour a foreign location, the greater is the inducement for FDI. The eclectic paradigm, incorporating ownership, location and internalization (OLI) variables, provides an analytical framework fundamental to the understanding of international production (see Table 1.1). If exploited optimally, the ownership-specific advantages (for example, the proprietary technology) of a firm can compensate for the additional costs of establishing production facilities in a foreign environment and can overcome the firm's disadvantages *vis-à-vis* local firms. The investor will benefit if both ownership-specific and location advantages – such as large markets or lower costs of resources – are internalized. While the first and third conditions are firm-specific determinants of FDI, the second is location-specific and has a crucial bearing on the host country's inflow of FDI.

Within the framework of the OLI approach, the above-mentioned advantages explain all three internalization strategies – exporting, licensing and direct investment. Dunning (1981b) states that the importance and configuration of the three advantages differ according to the country, industry and firm involved. Dunning's eclectic theory of

*Table 1.1* Ownership, location and internalization (OLI) approach

| **Ownership-specific advantages (FSA) – internal factors** | **Location-specific advantages – external factors: country-specific factors (CSF)** | **Internalization advantages** | **Route of serving market** |
|---|---|---|---|
| Yes | Yes | Yes | ⇒ FDI |
| Yes | No | Yes | ⇒ Exports |
| Yes | No | No | ⇒ Contractual resource |

*Source*: Dunning (1981b).

international production explains the ways in which overseas markets are served by enterprises of different nationalities as well as the industrial and geographical composition of such activities.

The theory suggests that all forms of international production can be explained by reference to the above conditions. Location-specific or country-specific advantages have an important bearing on FDI. Such advantages of particular host countries make them preferable not only for FDI as compared to other potential host countries, but also for domestic investment. It needs to be recognized that one important determinant of FDI is the ability of the firm to generate ownership advantages which are best exploited by the firm in a foreign rather than a domestic location. In this way, the eclectic theory is able to provide an explanation for differences in the industrial pattern of outward FDI of different industrialized countries. At any given moment of time, the more a country's enterprises possess 'O' advantages relative to those of another, the greater the incentive they have to internalize rather than externalize their use. In addition, the more they find it in their interest to exploit this from a foreign location, then the more likely they are to engage in outbound production. In the opposite case, a country is likely to attract investment by foreign MNEs when the reverse conditions apply.

In a dynamic perspective changes in the outward or inward direct investment position of a particular country can be explained in terms of the following: changes in the O advantages of its enterprises relative to those of other nations; changes in its L assets relative to those of other countries; changes in the extent to which firms perceive that these assets (and any others it may acquire) are best organized internally rather than by the market; and changes in the strategy of firms which may affect their reaction to any given OLI configuration (Dunning 1992, 1993, 1998a).

While the eclectic paradigm provides the conceptual framework for an analysis of the international expansion pattern of business and a good explanation for the decision to invest abroad, it is evident that the theory does not cover the competitive FDI induced by trade restrictions. When a country imposes restrictions on the imports of a particular industrial product, there is obviously an inducement to multinational firms of the country to invest in that country. If one or two firms invest, the others must also do so in order to counter competition and ensure their market share even if the returns to investment are negligible or negative, particularly for late entrants. Some of the FDI in the USA and Europe is of this variety. In addition, multinationals may enter a market today even if it is not profitable to do so, because they foresee future growth and want to corner the first entrant's advantage. Finally, the configuration of

OLI advantages changes as the country traverses along the development path (Dunning 1981b, 1986, 1988 and 1998b) moving thus to a new configuration of OLI.

### 1.2.6 Internationalization process school

In the 1970s and 1980s, an important stream of literature emerged – popularly known as the internationalization process school – which explains FDI not as an act but as a process focusing on the long-term, sequential nature of internationalization. Of these, Vernon's (1966) product life cycle model and the internationalization (Uppsala) model are the most prominent. The internationalization process school postulates a sequential or incremental approach explaining model choice on the basis of a firm's knowledge gained through experience in the international market, and retains considerable influence based on empirical studies. The model postulates that firms would begin by entering the foreign markets that they were most familiar with and then capitalizing on the knowledge acquired move on to less familiar ones. This posits that the internationalization occurs in stages, beginning with irregular export activity (Johanson and Wiedersheim-Paul 1975; Johanson and Vahlne 1990). Businesses move from irregular exporting, through exporting via an independent agent, sales subsidiary and eventually to full production in foreign markets. Progression through the stages is driven by experiential knowledge accumulation. Each stage calls for more commitment to international markets and enables firms to gain in knowledge, skill, and confidence. Because the knowledge gained relates to the existing mode of operation, firms tend to move gradually, adopting new modes, which make the most of their previous experience. There are, however, exceptions to this process (Johanson and Vahlne 1990; Anderson 1993). First, large firms can take larger internationalization steps. Secondly, when market conditions are stable, knowledge can be gained in ways other than through experience. Thirdly, experience in similar markets may allow a firm to generalize this experience. These exceptions may allow firms to jump stages. Technology and the creation of other firm-specific knowledge also play a central role in the evolution of national firms into international or multinational enterprises. MNEs may also arise when an enterprise finds opportunities to start or link up with an establishment in another country endowed to support these. National qualities have a direct influence on the prevalence of MNEs. For instance, real resource endowments or cultural affinity provide an efficient environment for the development of potential MNEs.

The internationalization model suggests that the location pattern of FDI is influenced by 'psychic distance' – which is defined as the cost of acquiring and internalizing relevant information about business conditions in other countries, the perception of risk and uncertainty involved in foreign operations, and the resources required to gain access to foreign networks (Johanson and Vahlne 1977). It is argued that the costs involved in overcoming psychic distance decline over time as a function of the experience gained by the firm in each market. Firms are thus expected to enter familiar, probably neighbouring markets first because of their historical familiarity and then to fan out into progressively more remote territory. This is based on behavioural theories, with assumptions about the lack of information and the importance of perceived risk and uncertainty. In this view, the internationalization process is not seen as a sequence of deliberately planned steps founded on rational analysis. Instead, it is the sequential or the incremental nature of successive stages of deepening of the commitment of firms to foreign markets that is the main characteristic of the process school. According to Johanson and Vahlne (1990) firms will gradually increase their international involvement whether strategic decisions are made in this direction or not. The model is deterministic in nature and limited in its applicability to the early stages of internationalization when a lack of market knowledge and market resources are constraining forces (Forsgren 1989; Melin 1992; Anderson 1993; Calof and Beamish 1995). Firms in many countries have skipped the initial 'domestic only' or primary stage in the Upsalla model and graduated very quickly to full-scale FDI. 'Born global' behaviour has been observed in many countries (Welch and Luostarinen 1988). A study by Nordstrom (1991) found that, while psychic distance played a role, market potential was the most important explanatory factor in locational choice. Nevertheless, the Uppsala model's staging and psychic distance constructs retain widespread acceptance (Melin 1992; Anderson 1993; Calof and Beamish 1995).

Historical evidence confirms the incremental approach that companies have taken to become foreign investors. Technology and the creation of other firm-specific knowledge also play central roles in the evolution of national firms into international or multinational enterprises. MNEs may also arise when an enterprise finds itself with opportunities to start or link up with an establishment in another country endowed to support these. National qualities directly influence the prevalence of MNEs. For instance, real resource endowments or cultural affinity provide an efficient environment for the development of potential MNEs. There are three possible hierarchical entry mode choices:

full equity control through greenfield investment; full equity control through acquisition/merger; and joint ventures, either greenfield investment or acquisition. The theory of entry mode choice is rarely specified in empirical work, although most of the empirical literature focuses on market entry choices and not on forms of involvement. The different approaches explaining the foreign production of firms as a market failure replacing activity argue that this would occur whenever and wherever firms perceived that the net benefits of using cross-border markets to organize the transactions of intermediate goods and services were lower than those of hierarchical control, i.e., their own internal administrative mechanism.

To sum up, in the vast literature on FDI, the most important focus consists in the firm-specific factors of the MNEs – which internalize the gains from market imperfection – and the location factors. The relative importance of the determinants changes as the economic environment changes. Mere ownership of intangible assets and the presence of location advantages though necessary are not sufficient conditions for FDI. These advantages needed to be complemented by some incentives for the internalization of the markets for intangible assets. Important location advantages include the technological status of a country, the brand name and goodwill enjoyed by the local firm, the openness of the economy, trade and macro policies, and intellectual property protection granted by the government. Furthermore, there are also non-economic variables which may play an important role in FDI decisions.

## 1.3 Motives

Traditionally, FDI is classified according to its motives, for example: (i) resources, (ii) markets, (iii) efficiency, and (iv) strategic assets-seeking (Dunning 1988) with different location selection criteria being applied to projects with different motivations.[4] Historically, natural resource-seeking FDI has been most important in countries lacking in capital, skills, know-how, and infrastructure required for the extraction of natural resources and sale to the rest of the world. Market-seeking investments are attracted by the size of the market – in other words, the income of the country and its growth rate. High-income countries have an obvious advantage in terms of attracting FDI. Even if a country is not large in terms of the size of its market, it can, by belonging to a regional union, attract market-seeking investments. In fact, FDI for market access is a typical objective of investment by MNEs. The rapid economic growth of Asia's developing countries has made it a more attractive market for final products. As a result, Japanese companies have been building marketing networks and facilities in this region. This has led to increased FDI flows, given the prospects of rising demand and other savings. FDI for outsourcing is also an important objective in these Asian countries. Dunning (1973) has identified thirty location advantages viewed as determinants of especially market-seeking FDI, including host country market characteristics, trade barriers, cost factors and investment climate components. Efficiency-seeking FDI is usually trade-creating investments and depends on a host of considerations, such as good infrastructure facilities, a low-cost, but educated workforce, productivity, skill intensity, R&D base, technological capabilities, liberal trading regime and such other variables (see also Zhao and Gangti 2000; Ferrantino 1993). Strategic-seeking FDI aims to promote long-term strategic objectives – especially those of sustaining or advancing their international competitiveness.

In this scenario, a new social contract and cooperative alliances are taking place. While the efficiency and strategic-seeking FDI are providing greater motivation to the MNEs, they want strategic access seeking and technology markets where they can build their own identities. This is affecting the country-specific advantages which emphasize the economic fundamentals and enabling investment climate of the host countries as important determinants of FDI. The location-specific advantages include an investment climate suitable to the culture of the country, a supportive environment – important elements of which include macroeconomic stability and liberal policy framework of the host countries to promote and facilitate such investments. In addition, characteristics of the economy such as adequate physical infrastructure facilities like ports, the availability of cheap and dependable electricity, and the availability of extensive road and rail links, apart from legal and administrative infrastructure facilities that reduce the transaction costs and bureaucratic delays and a trained labour force are the other attractive factors. Host countries cannot capture positive externalities (such as developing forward and backward linkages, promoting technology and entrepreneurial diffusion) and try to reach higher stages of the product cycle without supplying a trained stock of human capital. Good governance is also emphasized as being one of the factors affecting the decisions of MNEs about where they will locate their investments. The presence of controls on investments, regulations on the import of goods, including capital goods and components, and restrictions on foreign exchange are also mentioned as factors adversely affecting location advantages.

These determinants essentially influence the firms' decision to invest and produce abroad rather than supplying foreign markets through exports. The firms' decision is also influenced by the host countries' characteristics including elements of public policies, the proactive measures adopted to promote and facilitate the location of foreign direct investment. Thus, the location of FDI would depend upon the foreign investors' perception of the conditions in the host countries that influence the maximization of the firms' objectives. Inter-temporal variations in FDI flows to a country over time take place as a result of policy changes and macroeconomic performance variables. This literature is in line with Dunning's eclectic paradigm (1993), which suggests that it is the location advantages of the host countries that determine the cross-country pattern of FDI.

Furthermore, location advantages are comparative in nature. When deciding on a location, MNEs tend to grade the advantages among comparable countries. For example, the location advantages of India are not comparable with those of the USA and Western Europe, but are comparable with those of China and East Asia. It is important to keep this factor in mind while discussing Japanese FDI to different locations.

## 1.4 The current international economic environment

In the pre-WTO regimes, one of the important drivers of FDI was to seek and exploit the host markets, as the option of exporting to third countries was made difficult due to the presence of high tariff and non-tariff barriers erected by these countries. Under the conditions dominated by protectionist measures, multinational enterprises (MNEs) principally aimed to exploit their intangible assets such as new technology, knowledge base and brand name in a foreign location through FDI (Caves 1996; Dunning 1993, 1998 and 1998b).

In the current liberalized WTO regime, results from empirical work conducted during the pre-WTO regime might not be useful in predicting the current FDI pattern (Aoki 1984, 1988; Aoki and Dore 1994; Barrell and Pain 1999; Bayoumi and Lipworth 1997; Belderbos 2001; Tan and Vertinsky 1996; Chen 1996; Cheng and Kwan 2000; Cleeve 2000; Kuemmerle 1999; Ozawa 1979; Phongpaichit 1990; Ramstetter 1991; Sazanami 1992). In the present environment, the character of foreign direct investment (FDI) inflows is likely to undergo a significant change (Caves 1996). In the WTO regime, with the drastic reduction of tariff rates and the virtual disappearance of non-tariff barriers, MNEs can exploit their ownership of intangible assets in third countries through exports. Therefore, efficiency-seeking investments are likely to dominate over host country market-seeking investments. For example, one of the drivers of FDI was the exploitation of intangible assets in a foreign location and this could change to the augmentation of intangible assets. MNEs could be motivated to go where knowledge is found (Belderbos 2001; Kuemmerle 1999; Florida 1997). Here, traditional factor endowments play a less important role in influencing FDI, while 'created' competences and capabilities, the availability and quality of supporting industries, the characteristics of the local competition, the nature of consumer demand and the macro-micro policies of governments play a more important role. Once a firm realizes it has a capability that could be used to satisfy demand in a foreign country, it will evaluate different options for exploiting this capability. The firm will generally face a choice between setting up its own subsidiary in the foreign country, and contracting out the activity in question. Rivoli and Salorio (1996) show that the decision between FDI and contractual agreements to exploit firm-specific capabilities should evaluate not only the direct benefits of FDI, but also the option value of deferring an FDI commitment under conditions of high uncertainty.[5]

However, the new competitive environment has raised new challenges for both governments and MNEs. Ownership advantages are changing and MNEs are seeking to enhance their own competitiveness in an international context, the vital part of which is to improve through higher value-added activities in line with logistic and market demands. The magnitude of FDI – which is now occupying centre stage in the growth policies of developing countries – is to a considerable extent determined by the relative advantages of the host countries as a location for MNEs value-adding activities. The location-specific advantages are determined by the host country's structural characteristics, and also its policy regime. National governments are meeting these challenges through policy intervention and by improving location advantages through various strategic and the adoption of structural adjustment policy measures. However, the relative importance of these variables from the perception of MNEs has not been studied. Most of the inferences have been drawn indirectly from secondary data collected during the pre-WTO regime. In the recent past, regional economic integration has increased the propensity of MNEs to internalize trade flows. Hence, the nature of CSAs has changed. In the 1980s and 1990s three important changes have occurred. The first is the emergence of knowledge as the 'key wealth creating asset'. As a result, MNEs now attach more importance to locations with excellent infrastructure and institutional facilities, rather than conventional location advantages such as low labour costs or easy access to raw materials.

Second is the rise of 'transactional benefits' of spatial proximity in the knowledge-development process between the non-location-bound FSAs and the location-bound immobile clusters of complementary assets in host countries. And third is the emergence of 'alliance capitalism', especially in knowledge creation (see Dunning 1998). Localized networks are acting as an agglomerative magnet on FDI yielding potential benefits from the cluster spill over effects.

## 1.5 Japanese FDI flows

### 1.5.1 Japanese-type FDI

Japanese FDI, though a comparatively late development, has immensely intrigued the world by its role, strategy and performance. Some consider this to be the result of a 'vintage' effect as Japanese FDI is of more recent origin than US FDI, while others attribute the differences to the unique institutional set up of the country. While some economists (Reich 1990, 1991) feel that nationality of FDI should not matter but many others like Tyson (1991), Hu (1992) and Ravenhill (1999) suggest that nationality matters.

Kojima's framework, discussed earlier, highlights that the 'American-style' FDI eliminates the basis for trade while 'Japanese-type' FDI is export-oriented. Kojima (1985) compares the FDI from Japan and the USA in Asian countries – NIEs 4 and ASEAN-4 – and found in most cases FDI from USA followed a uniform pattern across countries and across time while Japanese FDI differed between resource-abundant countries and resource-scarce countries in line with the host country's development enabling them to expand in such a direction where they had comparative advantage. Studies comparing Japanese and US investments in Asian countries include those attempted by Schroath, Hu and Chen (1993); Encarnation (1999) and Ravenhill (1999). Dunning (1988) explains the management styles, structures, objectives, and stages of product cycles between Anglo-Japanese and Anglo-American enterprises. While comparing the Japanese ownership pattern with that of the USA he has highlighted that Japanese investors exercise closer control over the managerial philosophy, possess more efficient work organizations, quality control techniques, and a committed workforce.

From the literature certain stylized facts about the Japanese and US foreign direct investment are worth mentioning. These are: (a) Japanese FDI is identified as the main vehicle for the introduction of production technology and modern management techniques with an emphasis on just-in-time delivery, quality circles and total quality control;

(b) Japanese FDI is more export-oriented in nature as compared to US foreign direct investment which is relatively more domestic-market oriented; (c) Japanese subsidiaries have a higher proportion of imported components and capital goods since they have established production networks in different countries. Japanese firms rely more on their home country or third country for sourcing of their components and capital goods as compared to the USA which source more often from the host country; (d) Japanese firms have larger networking and a higher proportion of a two-way trade of output and inputs through intra-company shipments that link the parent company to their subsidiaries. Having close, long-term business relationships between large corporations and a number of selected smaller firms they have been seen as rational effective systems, and as a factor in its economic success. The US firms, however, are less networked, are horizontally integrated and stand as independent units; (e) Japanese investors are relatively more market-oriented – concentrating on market share, market segmentation, and positioning strategies, goodwill, and long-term profitability – in contrast to US firms that are oriented towards short-term profits with an emphasis on product range and technology; (f) Japanese investors are more sensitive to geographical and cultural proximity than their western counterparts, given that other factors are equal; (g) differential managerial practices are adopted by the Japanese affiliates compared to others which lead to vital differences with respect to their presence, conduct and performance. Japanese investors maintain a stable and a relatively longer-term subcontracting relationship with their vendors and encourage the local firms to invest in new machinery for modernization and introduction of more advanced technology, research and development activities and greater consciousness of product quality. These factors have their impact and lead to greater microeconomic contribution in terms of income and productivity (see also Aoki 1990 for a literature survey; for studies comparing Japanese and US investments see Dunning 1988, 1992a, 1995; Doyle, Saunders and Wong 1992; Eaton and Tamura 1996).

### 1.5.2 Empirical evidence of the determinants

Japanese FDI has responded to a variety of motivations over time and these have differed according to the host country. It is important to make a brief assessment of the determinants of Japanese FDI, taking into account the characteristics of the host countries. To begin with, we will cite some existing studies on Japanese FDI outflows – inter-temporal, inter-country, or inter-industry – that throw light on its determinants, even though these have limited relevance for our purposes. Most of these studies are limited to one or two variables using some case studies. To illustrate, in the case of the UK, the choice of location for Japanese FDI was found to be driven by transaction costs and the need to seek markets (Cleeve 2000). In the case of France, the location advantage in logistics and a large domestic market, together with liberalization and deregulation of the financial market, appear to be the main reasons responsible for an increase in Japanese FDI (Sazanami 1992). In the case of Latin America, market size, economic adjustment policies and political stability have influenced Japanese FDI (Tuman and Craig 1999). In the case of East Asia, Japanese FDI is explained in terms of FDI promotion policies, better conditions for efficient production (Mody *et al.* 1999) and a market-friendly approach. Ford and Strange (1999) investigated the factors that Japanese firms have taken into account in Western Europe. The data set used in the study comprised the seven most popular host countries – the United Kingdom, France, Germany, the Netherlands, Italy, Spain, and Belgium. Their results show that the per capita gross domestic product has a significant positive effect upon choice of location, notwithstanding European integration.

Some studies have emphasized the role of existing Japanese firms in attracting other Japanese firms to the same location. Using data for the 1980s, Head and Ries (1996) found the presence of Japanese firms positively effecting the location of other Japanese firms in the sectors and regions. Statistical results from several studies strongly buttress the argument that foreign investors are inclined to favour such locations that could minimize information costs and offer a variety of agglomeration economies.[6]

Jianping (1999), He Canfei (2002) and Belderbos *et al.* (2001) analysed the location choices by Japanese firms in China's regions during the period 1990–95 and confirmed a major impact of *keiretsu*-specific agglomeration benefits. Export-oriented plants are more responsive than local-market-oriented plants to Japanese (*keiretsu*) agglomeration and the presence of seaports, but appear less responsive to regional demand and region-specific incentives. Tuan and Linda (2003) found that with given distance from the core, firms prefer sites with higher firm agglomeration. Empirical results show that agglomerations of the core–periphery relation have affected FDI flow patterns. It may also influence the sectoral pattern of FDI across countries or inter-country distribution of a particular sector's FDI flows (Eaton, Lipsey and Safarian 1994). Wei *et al.* (1999) analysed the determinants of the distribution of foreign direct investment (FDI) within China and found that there exists a long-run relationship between the spatial distribution of FDI and a number of regional characteristics. Those provinces with higher levels of international trade, more R&D manpower, higher GDP growth rates, quicker improvements in infrastructure, more rapid advances in agglomeration, more preferential policies and closer ethnic links with overseas Chinese attract relatively more FDI.

For Indonesia, Syamwil *et al.* (2000) analysed changes in the pattern of Japanese firms and the effect of deregulation of foreign investment during the period 1984–94. The results of this study indicate continuous regional concentration in the core region of Java with markets and infrastructure being seen as the main reasons for the location of Japanese industries in the region.

The initial FDI flows were principally determined by factors, such as the desire to exploit economies of scale, to secure access to raw materials, or to penetrate and reap other benefits by investment in neighbouring Asian countries. This allowed Japanese companies to move production abroad in a sector in which it was losing comparative advantage. Trade frictions also stimulated flows of Japanese FDI to the United States and may have encouraged Japanese firms to invest in Asia in order to build 'export platforms' for the US market.

In the 1970s and 1980s, Japanese investors had ownership advantages based primarily on their ability to innovate new products and production processes, devise appropriate organizational structures, and coordinate and manage resources to minimize their transaction costs. The rapid expansion of Japanese FDI in the 1980s changed the nature of the competition. More recently, increases in FDI have been associated with the rapid growth of spending on research and development by Japanese firms. Some Japanese FDI has also been triggered by policy actions that make it advisable to move the production of certain goods to other countries.

The dynamics of the Japanese FDI outflows over the period is broadly outlined in Table 1.2. The table presents an overview of the evolutionary path in the nature of the Japanese FDI over time – from non-manufacturing and natural resource-seeking sectors to efficiency-seeking investment – which in part is a reflection of the landmark changes in the world economic environment and in the economic fundamentals of the Japanese economy. Japanese FDI during the pre-1970s was directed primarily to facilitating trade in commodities, focusing on developing countries, particularly the Asian neighbours. These, along with the trade-related financial services, were the leaders helping Japanese manufacturers to set up operations abroad. But the 1970s is identified as an important turning point in the multinational spread of Japanese companies. However, it is the 1980s which marks the phase of

*Table 1.2* Dynamics of Japanese FDI flows

| Period | Driving force | Sectors/industries | Facilitating factors |
|---|---|---|---|
| Prior to 1970 | Non-manufacturing | Investment in trade and commerce | Investment for Japanese trade |
| First phase – 1970s | Natural resource-seeking, trade supportive and labour-intensive FDI | Textile, steel, iron ore, raw materials, extractive and service sectors and trading | Natural endowments |
| Second phase – 1980s | Market-seeking and service-driven FDI | Electrical-electronics, automobile, chemicals and service sector | Large and protected markets, proximity to customers and production facilities |
| Third phase – 1990s | Market-seeking, skill-intensive, efficiency-seeking and service-driven FDI | Microelectronics, automobile and service sector | Skills, improved infrastructure |
| Present phase – 2000s | High value added service sector, technology-intensive, efficiency-seeking and innovation-driven | Microelectronics, service sector | R&D, skills, technology development, appropriate infrastructure, supporting institutions |

ownership-specific advantages and Japanese firms' ability to forge competitive edge over others. There was both acceleration and diversification in the Japanese FDI. It is in this period, that the export-oriented firms took the center stage.

## 1.6 The present study: context and motivation

Asia holds the key to the global future and the major players are NIEs-4, ASEAN-4 China and India. The last two are emerging rapidly as the leading forces in the region. Japan occupies a central place in Asia and the Japanese investment pattern to these countries is often described as the 'flying-geese' pattern in which Japan is seen as the first-tier industrial power, with NIEs as the second-tier economies and the ASEAN countries forming the third tier. This form of investment enabled Japanese companies to establish effective regional production and sales networks serving Japan and the third country markets. Japan provided the regional economic band that linked these economies into a dynamic and sustainable growth pattern for more than two decades.[7] The 'Asian Miracle' and the conscious emulation of Japan by Southeast Asian countries is attributed to the pivotal role played by Japan through FDI, trade and technology which purports to explain investment in terms of the so-called Vernon product cycle (Terry 1996; Vernon and Wells 1981; Yuan (ed.) 1991). The economic linkages between Japan and the countries of this region of East Asia – Japan, Asian NIEs, and ASEAN countries – have been growing as a natural process.[8] Rapid economic growth and trade expansion has occurred mainly due to the Japanese role. Japanese investors also implemented the transfer of their management systems and production technologies to local economies throughout East Asia, producing a unique form of region-based development through FDI. The close coordination between Japanese business and government in promoting FDI in East Asia extended and deepened the regional division of labour. These Asian countries are the most dynamic and open economies, in varying degrees, having witnessed an impressive growth performance, with average rates falling broadly in the range 5 to 9 per cent.

These countries together have successfully netted the bulk of Japanese FDI flowing to developing countries. This, along with the rise of their MNEs, constitutes an important landmark and represents in many ways a turnaround in the case of these countries. At the same time the flows exhibit a contrasting picture of wide inter-period and inter-country differences in the scale of Japanese FDI flows both within and between the country-groups – NIEs, ASEAN-4, China and India. This is also a group of economies representing somewhat diverse investment regimes, economic trends, ownership structures and policy reforms and general asymmetries in their macroeconomic fundamentals which are also evident in the FDI activities of NIEs, ASEAN countries, China and India.

To analyse Japanese FDI in these countries we have broadly divided and examined the ten countries into the following groups, namely: Asian NIEs, ASEAN-4, and China–India, as these are marked by many similarities notwithstanding their differences.

*Asian NIEs* – Korea, Singapore, Taiwan and Hong Kong – the high-income economies, rapidly followed in the wake of Japanese economic success and are regarded as the most successful of East Asia's 'four dragons', notable for their success. They had two interrelated policy goals: First, to retain their macroeconomic stability; and secondly, maintain their competitiveness, which sustained their outward-oriented growth.

*ASEAN-4 countries* – namely, Indonesia, Malaysia, the Philippines and Thailand – the middle-income countries, which came to the Asian 'miracle' relatively late, present a regional model of attracting FDI by enhancing individual country and regional competitiveness through cooperation. These countries remain significant competitors for Japanese FDI and as markets for the developed world. Japanese MNEs have gradually increased direct investments into Asian countries – a trend which began with the NIEs but later extended to the ASEAN.

*China and India,* the former being a low middle-income country and the latter a low-income one – are both late reformers, marked by great dissimilarities as well as by some common traits. They are both highly populated countries, with large domestic markets; have remained closed economies for long, with trade centrally controlled; have grown under very restrictive regimes with a high degree of protection; have followed almost similar economic models of import-substitution strategies; have regarded the state as promoter of growth; and began to change their economic orientation only in the last quarter of the past century, adopting a *controlled liberal policy* towards FDI. Both are now considered important new players, with a big gap in terms of their comparative attractiveness as host country for Japanese investment. Since joining the WTO – India in 1995 and China in 2001 – both have accelerated neo-liberal reform programmes and prioritized two tasks: market liberalization and globalization. In their post-liberation period, changes appear to be far deeper in China than in India – the former also achieving significant gains than the latter. India's current regulatory environment is already considered comparable with most Asian countries. The operating environment, policies and practices are claimed to be generally conducive to investment and trade. Both are set to undergo further significant reshaping in the years to come.

The different levels of Japanese FDI involvement and economic successes do not suggest the relative strength of their state apparatus or that of their social matrix. There are relative rather than absolute location advantages and economic differences of one in comparison with others which is determining the country choice. Cross-country differences in country-specific location advantages may be at the core of this. The economic fundamentals and FDI policies of the host countries influence the ability of the Japanese MNEs to internalize their operations for as far as the regional bias is concerned; it applies equally to all these countries and so do the investor's 'ownership' advantages. In addition, different location selection criteria apply to projects of different motivation – that is, whether meant for export platform or for the domestic market. Broadly, the configuration of OLI advantages (Dunning 1981a, b, 1993), stages of competitive development of the host countries (Porter 1990) and host government policies (Brewer 1993) provide motivations that influence the ability of the MNEs to internalize their operations. Over the past few decades, the complex nature of the location advantage concept has substantially broadened its analytical scope because of its in-depth focus on the actual behaviour of MNEs and the dynamics of the current international environment.[9]

The present study aims to posit the underlying logic and identifies the causes of inter-country differences in Japanese FDI outflows in the countries of East Asia, China and India. It examines why and how the Japanese investors rate different countries in respect of the important determinants for the location of investment. In the process it brings out the issues, strategies and prospects of Japanese FDI and its role in the changing global political economy. More specifically, the study endeavours to focus on the following issues:

1. To examine the massive flow of Japanese FDI, its trends and features in general and in Asian NIEs, ASEAN-4, China and India, in particular, over the period exhibiting its different phases.
2. To estimate and evaluate the variables which the Japanese MNEs have perceived as being critically important for the location of investment. In this process the study will bring out the factors causing low levels of Japanese FDI to some countries. The estimated average

ratings in terms of various criteria would implicitly throw light on the cross-country differences in attracting Japanese FDI. This would provide guidelines to the countries seeking to attract larger flows of Japanese FDI.
3. To assess the international orientation of Japanese firms and the factors involved in their internationalization. As such, the domestic-oriented companies will also come within the purview of analysis.
4. Econometrically to identify, estimate and analyse the main drivers of Japanese FDI to these countries: NIEs-4, ASEAN-4, China and India.
5. Draw conclusions helpful in FDI promotion policy.

## 1.7 Design and methodology

While the respective chapters will present the methodology relevant to the issues, here it is important to mention the overall design of the study. To investigate the issues stated above, the data collection included: namely, (i) Published data from the website compiled by the Ministry of Finance (MoF), Japan; the website of the Japan External Trade Organization (JETRO), and from JETRO's office in Delhi as mentioned in the acknowledgements; (ii) To supplement this, comprehensive data were collected from the primary sources through a Questionnaire Method addressing the investing companies; (iii) Personal interviews were held with the companies; and (iv) Interactions with the Chambers of Commerce and Industry of Japan at Tokyo, Yokohama, Nagoya, Hiroshima, and Osaka were made. In respect of other variables, we have relied and virtually exhausted all the available sources. These are listed in Table 5A.1.

The multi-method approach adopted in this study has a wider scope and is important because it suggests general policy instruments to attract Japanese FDI. The single-method econometric approach, however fine-tuned and sophisticated in methodology, cannot possibly lead to meaningful conclusions regarding not only the policy instruments or even for a clear identification of the parameters and the direction and magnitude of their manipulation.

The Japanese FDI flows – global, region-wise and country-wise – are analysed, examining a forty-year perspective from 1965 to 2006, unless dictated by the non-availability of data. The model estimates have been attempted using complete and consistent time series data in respect of all of these variables. The determinants of FDI flows have been estimated with the help of balanced panel data techniques – namely, the fixed and random effects models. We had sufficient degrees of freedom compared to many of the earlier studies relying on relatively short time series data which, consequently, suffered from too few degrees of freedom.

Most studies have based their results on secondary data. This is perhaps the first time that a primary survey has been conducted in which Japanese investors were asked directly how they perceive and assess the location advantages for investment in this region. The questionnaires were detailed. The responses to the questionnaires are analyzed in the relevant chapters. But it must be mentioned here that answers to most of the questions which were posed are based on the judgements of the investors themselves and are most important for providing informed views in respect of the critical variables, even though it does not provide statistics of the sort given in the *Statistical Abstracts* or similar publications.

There has been very little research identifying those variables which may offer an adequate explanation of the choice of location for Japanese FDI in the current global regime. In addition, the relative importance of the variables in the perspective of the MNEs considered as critical by them has not been studied. Most of the inferences have been drawn indirectly from secondary data. This study attempts to fill this gap. It also adds to the existing literature by directly collecting primary data from the investors to identify the determinants of its investment.

# 2
# Japanese FDI Outflows

## 2.1 Introduction

With the exception of the last decade or so, over the past half-century Japan has been the world's fastest-growing economy, outperforming all others, including Western Europe. The success during this golden period has been attributed to the high propensity to save, high per capita income and productivity, a huge reserve of technical skills, a characteristic catch-up effort bolstered in an unusual degree by government policy and a dedication to the achievement of specific goals.

The dramatic growth in Japanese FDI and the rise of MNEs were other important features of the golden period and constituted an important landmark in the development of the world economy. This emanated mainly from the accelerated pace of technical and managerial change and know-how and the emergence of integrated production networks. In many ways the rapid expansion of Japanese FDI was responsible for a turnaround in many developing countries, particularly in Asia. Japanese FDI, by virtue of its size and developmental character, has had important macro-level and micro-level consequences for the economies of host countries, as well as international trade flows. Among these benefits are improvements in the balance of payments, providing scarce foreign exchange resources, and the transfer of technology and skills – not available in the host economy – to enhance the competitiveness and profitability of local industries. Along the way, there have been shifts in the trend, scale, direction and timing of their FDI. There were 'waves' triggered by a combination of long-term factors that played out differently over the period for different regions, countries and industries.

These issues are explored in this chapter, which is organized as follows: first, it reflects upon the historical trends and developments in overall

Japanese FDI outflows over the period and presents its spatial region-wise dimension. This is followed by an examination of the trends in Japanese FDI flows in ten Asian countries – namely, NIEs-4, ASEAN-4, China and India. The industry-wise investment pattern is analysed briefly. The chapter ends with some concluding remarks and an assessment of the medium-term prospects for Japanese FDI to these countries.

## 2.2 Different waves in Japanese FDI

### 2.2.1 The first wave (1960s–70s)

In hindsight, the mid-1960s mark the 'first wave' when Japanese FDI increased by over five times from a meagre US$159 million in 1965 to $858 million in 1971, registering an average annual growth of 36.1 per cent – witnessing an annual average flow of US$521 million – over this period. The end of the fixed exchange rates regime in 1971 led to a strengthening of the yen *vis-à-vis* the dollar as well as against most other Asian currencies. This expanded Japan's global FDI in the decades since the 1970s. The level jumped to $2,338 million in 1972 – that is, by 172.5 per cent over the previous year and again from $2.8 billion in 1977 it increased to $4.6 billion – or by 64 per cent – in the subsequent year. Rising almost continuously it was close to US$5 billion by 1980, registering an average annual growth of 31.2 per cent between 1972 and 1980.

The protectionist atmosphere among developed countries and the threat of retaliation against Japanese exports, especially in the major western markets, created an international environment which played a crucial role in determining the size and direction of Japanese FDI by locating the production sites in the developing countries. There was an increasing protectionist attitude and trade conflicts generated by the bilateral trade imbalances with the USA and Europe and also by a reduction in the relative wage differentials between Japan and these nations. Japanese FDI expanded just as the Japanese firms expanded their international operations, strongly emphasizing their main firm-specific advantages – namely, ownership of knowledge and product innovation.

### 2.2.2 The second wave (1981–85)

The real boom in Japanese FDI outflows started in 1981 when it recorded a phenomenal growth from $4.7 billion in 1980 to $8.9 billion, marking the start of what may be called a 'second wave'. In this second phase of development, Japanese companies entered into the stage of globalization of business activities, which was made possible by a general rise in Japanese firms' managerial and technological capabilities. This was an important underlying factor behind the surge of Japanese FDI. Japan entered into an era of rapid economic growth, continuously improving international competitiveness by adopting domestic and international policy options to internationalize the economy (see also Urata 1993, 1998). This push was triggered by the major currency realignment resulting from the Plaza Accord in 1985, which brought about drastic changes in international competitiveness, particularly among the exporters of manufactured products.

During the mid-1980s, with the expansion of international finance and a sharp appreciation in the value of the yen, Japanese FDI underwent additional changes in composition. One, investments by financial and insurance companies rose sharply, as did those by trading houses and distribution intermediaries. Two, there was a surge in the establishment of finance and insurance operations by manufacturers and trading companies to provide better service to their foreign marketing organizations. By contrast, investment by manufacturing companies declined during 1985–86 mainly as the result of unstable exchange rates. In the early 1980s, more service-industry investments, finance and insurance were made in industrialized nations. Other reasons included the emergence of a high economic growth in the USA generating higher levels of demand, as well as tax incentives, and investment credits. The key elements in Japan's economic success at this time were the strong growth and productivity orientation of both government and business. According to Abegglen and Stalk (1985), the growth orientation of the *kaisha*, nurtured by strong domestic competition, made the Japanese corporations formidable international competitors.

### 2.2.3 The third wave (1986–89/90)

Growth accelerated further in the second half of the 1980s, due both to the booming economies at home and abroad, and the appreciation of the yen. Japan's FDI outflows during the period 1986–9 surpassed the country's total overseas investment for the entire post-war period up to 1986. By the late 1980s, Japan was investing more abroad than any other country in the world, with its FDI peaking at $67.5 billion (around 2.5 per cent of GDP) in 1989. This was the most spectacular phase – the 'globalization' period. There was a boom in Japanese FDI in the 'third wave' period 1986–90, marking a further rise in the internationalization of Japanese FDI. Japan became the dominant source of FDI, overtaking all developed countries in terms of volume. FDI increased rapidly in the 'wave' period of 1986–89, reaching a cumulative FDI outflow of $310.8 billion, reflecting Japan's newly-acquired economic power. The annual average outflow of Japanese FDI during the period 1986–89 was approximately $43 billion – reaching a peak of $ 67.5 billion in 1989 – compared to an average US figure of $25 billion. This was at its highest among the industrialized countries (see UNCTAD's *World Investment Reports*, 1998 to 2006 and JETRO's *White Papers*, 1995–2006). Much of the rise was due to a rapid increase of FDI to developed countries, from a figure of $2.6 billion in 1980 to $53 billion in 1989. During this period FDI to developing countries rose from $2.1 billion in 1980 to almost $14.7 billion in 1989.

It was also around this time that Japanese companies furthered the processes of 'globalization'. There was a strategy to establish the most effective production and sales bases and networks for serving the world market, while taking into account each country's resource endowments, macroeconomic stability and market conditions (market size, growth potential and demand for high value added goods: Tejima, 1994). The growth–productivity orientation of the Japanese economy altered the 'given' comparative advantage, or what Scott (1985) calls 'the dynamic (revised) theory of comparative advantage'. Effectively, this implied not subscribing to the static view of world advantage, but altering it to create other critical resources, such as technology, and fully exploiting the benefits of both the learning curve and the economies of scale of production in order to become internationally competitive. The strengthening of yen and a 'bubble economy' gave the companies ready access to low-cost capital in order to finance and stimulate their expansions to bases outside high-cost Japan.

### 2.2.4 A new phase – the downturns and revivals (since the 1990s)

The 1990s marked a new trend in the globalization of Japanese FDI. Japanese global FDI outflows fell rapidly from their 1989 peak as the economy fell into a near recession with the bursting of the asset-price bubble economy, the growth potential weakened witnessing diminishing returns and creating a deflationary situation. In the midst of this, the boom in Japanese FDI ended abruptly and a prolonged slump in demand began from the beginning of the 1990s. Japan's FDI outflows started an almost unbroken annual decline. There was a reversal in this trend during the period 1993–95, but the fall resumed and by 1997 it ranked fifth among the sources of FDI (after the USA, the UK, France and Germany) and accounted for a reduced 6 per cent of the vastly expanded world total FDI flow of $423.7 billion. Despite robust FDI growth in some years of the 1990s, the buoyant FDI flows became somewhat laggard. In 2004,

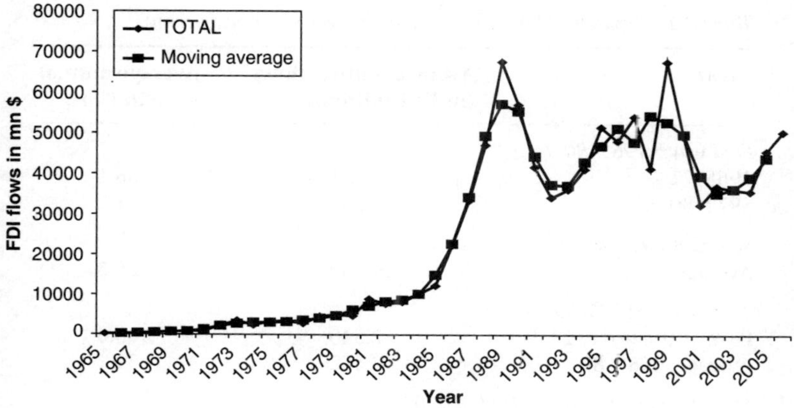


*Figure 2.1* Japanese FDI outflows (US$ million)

Japan ranked sixth after the USA, Luxemburg, France, the UK, and the Netherlands, accounting for 4.7 per cent of the total world FDI outflows of $612.2 billion (*World Investment Reports*, 1998 to 2005). The year 2005 witnessed marked changes in global outflows. The Netherlands emerged as the leading source of FDI with $119 billion, closely followed by France with $116 billion and the United Kingdom with $101 billion. Japan, although having a much lower outflow of $46 billion as compared to the above three, ranked fourth in the order (*World Investment Report 2006*).

Japanese FDI outflows for the forty-year time perspective from 1965 to 2006 are shown in Figure 2.1. As the year-wise flows pose problems of consistency, we have also presented three-yearly moving averages to smoothen the fluctuations.

Wave-wise comparison of the average annual Japanese FDI flows is presented in Table 2.1.

### 2.2.5 Summing up

In conclusion, the rise and fall in the scale and timing of Japanese FDI over the decades has been unprecedented. In the period of increases, in the second half of the 1980s the scale far exceeded the total FDI from all the previous years combined. At the peak, in 1989, Japan contributed 30 per cent of world flows and became the world's largest single foreign investor. The phase of decline – beginning in the early 1990s – was marked by a slower pace of global FDI flows, to when the bubble burst followed by the Asian financial crises. From the standpoint of growth rates, the 1980s was a period of steady growth – with the exception

*Table 2.1* Japanese FDI flows: global – wave-wise comparison

| Year | Average annual flows (in US$ million) | Average annual growth (%) |
|---|---|---|
| *First wave: 1965–80* | | |
| 1965–71 | 521 | 36.1 |
| 1972–80 | 3,562 | 31.2 |
| *Second wave: 1981–85* | | |
| Average | 9,430 | 25.5 |
| *Third wave: 1986–89* | | |
| Peak of the wave: 1989 | 67,540 | 43.6 |
| Average: 1986–89 | 42,562 | 54.2 |
| *Downturns and revivals: 1990–2006* | | |
| *Phase 1* | | |
| Downturn: 1990–92 | 44,211 | −20 |
| Revival: 1993–99 | 48,457 | 12.9 |
| *Phase 2* | | |
| Downturn: 2000–01 | 40,665 | −31 |
| Revival: 2002–06 | 40,825 | 9.8 |
| *Long-term average annual flows and growth rates (per cent)** | | |
| 1965–90 | 13,022 | 24.0 |
| 1991–2006 | 43,919 | 0.2 |
| 1965–2006 | 24,057 | 14.1 |

*Note*: *The Method for estimating growth rates is given in the technical note at the end.

of the year 1982, when Japan's contribution in total worldwide investment fell by 13.8 per cent. Otherwise, the period 1981–85 recorded an average growth of 25.5 per cent per annum and a phenomenal average growth of 54.2 per cent per annum – the highest ever during the period 1985–89. Growth over the 1990s, on the whole, was negative. It was negative during the period 1990–92, when it averaged −20 per cent per annum. There was again a negative growth of 6.6 per cent in 1996 and a still higher negative growth of 23.6 per cent in 1998. Investment picked up again in 1999 to US$ 67.5 billion, in line with the global FDI flows, but dramatically collapsed to US$49 billion in the year 2000 and further to US$32 billion in the year 2001, representing falls of 27.4 and 34.1 per cent respectively. There was an improvement in the year 2002, with FDI registering a growth of 14 per cent over the previous year, but this declined again in the years 2003 and 2004. Japanese global FDI outflows grew substantially in the years 2005 and 2006 (by 28 per cent and

11 per cent, respectively). According to the estimates, it stood at around $50.3 billion in 2006.

## 2.3 Developed and developing countries

### 2.3.1 Flow, share and growth rates

The dynamics and spatial distribution of Japanese FDI between developed and developing regions is characterized by several patterns and is punctuated by many dramatic turning points that exhibit a near-cyclical pattern. Coinciding with these movements have been substantial changes in the regional composition of FDI. Competitive pressures have been pushing the Japanese investor to seek markets in different regions and to strengthen their competitiveness in order to keep the economy dynamic and productive. The ownership-specific advantages of firms, the location-specific advantages of countries and the internalization advantages, using Dunning's well-known OLI terminology, had all combined to determine the extent and pattern of this expansion.

The cumulated outflows increased rapidly from US$83.65 billion at the end of 1985, to US$ 310.81 billion by the end of the 1990, registering an increase of 407.2 per cent in less than a decade. While this is in itself quite remarkable, what is more noticeable is that the total outflows to the developed countries over the same period increased by as much as 652.2 per cent. At the same time, investments in developing countries recorded a modest growth of 199.5 per cent. As a result, during the period 1981–85 to 1986–90 the shares of the developed countries increased from an annual average of 53.3 per cent to 74.8 per cent whereas the developing countries' share fell from 46.7 per cent to 25.2 per cent over the same period. It may be added that the developing countries' share was more than that of the developed countries throughout most of the 1970s, but the picture has been changing thereafter.

Table 2.2 presents a summary picture giving the five-yearly inter-period comparison relating to average annual flows, growth rates and share and also the long-term trends from 1965 to 2006.

The table highlights two important features: first, the average share of the developing countries' in the total Japanese FDI has been above 50 per cent during the 1970s; thereafter the developed region had a larger share. Secondly, the developing countries are now once more witnessing an upturn in Japanese FDI.

The changing profile of Japanese FDI between the developed and developing countries is clearly discernible from Figure 2.2(a&b).

*Table 2.2* Japanese FDI flows in developed and developing countries – an inter-period comparison: annual averages (flow figures are in US$ million)*

| Year | Flows | | | Growth rates (percentage) | | | Share (percentage) | |
|---|---|---|---|---|---|---|---|---|
| | Developing countries | Developed countries | Total | Developing countries | Developed countries | Total | Developing countries | Developed countries |
| 1965–70 | 208 | 257 | 465 | 26.9 | 59.9 | 43.4 | 44.7 | 55.3 |
| 1971–75 | 1,402 | 1,071 | 2473 | 38.5 | 22.7 | 31.1 | 56.7 | 43.3 |
| 1976–80 | 2,248 | 1,864 | 4,112 | 2.4 | 26.3 | 12.6 | 54.7 | 45.3 |
| 1981–85 | 4,400 | 5,031 | 9,431 | –1.4 | 20.1 | 9.4 | 46.7 | 53.3 |
| 1986–90 | 11,447 | 33,985 | 45,432 | 13.3 | 35.8 | 29.4 | 25.2 | 74.8 |
| 1991–95 | 12,951 | 27,887 | 40,838 | 14.0 | 2.9 | 6.3 | 31.7 | 68.3 |
| 1996–2000 | 15,696 | 36,256 | 51,952 | –9.4 | 8.2 | 2.7 | 30.2 | 69.8 |
| 2001–06 | 16,965 | 22,466 | 39,431 | 12.8 | 5.5 | 8.4 | 43.0 | 57.0 |
| *Long-term trends* | | | | | | | | |
| 1965–90 | 3,797 | 8,127 | 11,924 | 20.6 | 26.6 | 24.0 | 31.8 | 68.2 |
| 1991–2006 | 15,314 | 28,470 | 43,783 | 2.6 | –1.3 | 0.2 | 35.0 | 65.0 |
| 1965–2006 | 8,185 | 15,876 | 24,061 | 12.5 | 15.6 | 14.1 | 34.0 | 66.0 |

*Note*: *The figures relate to the annual averages attained in the respective periods.

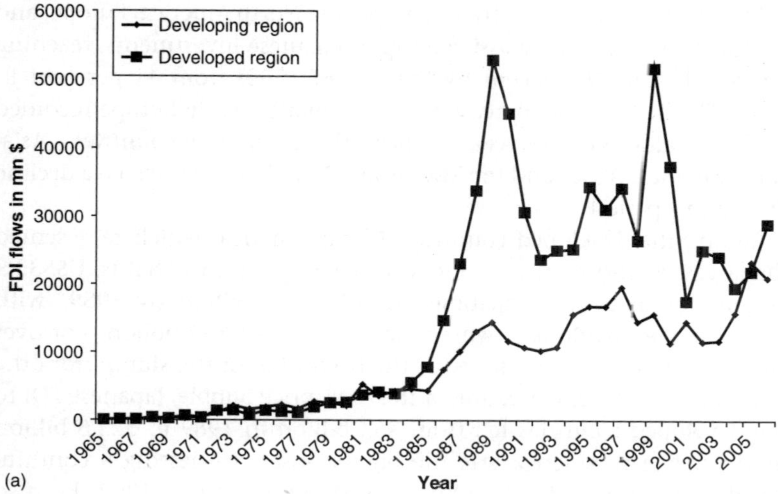


*Figure 2.2a* Japanese FDI flows in developed and developing countries

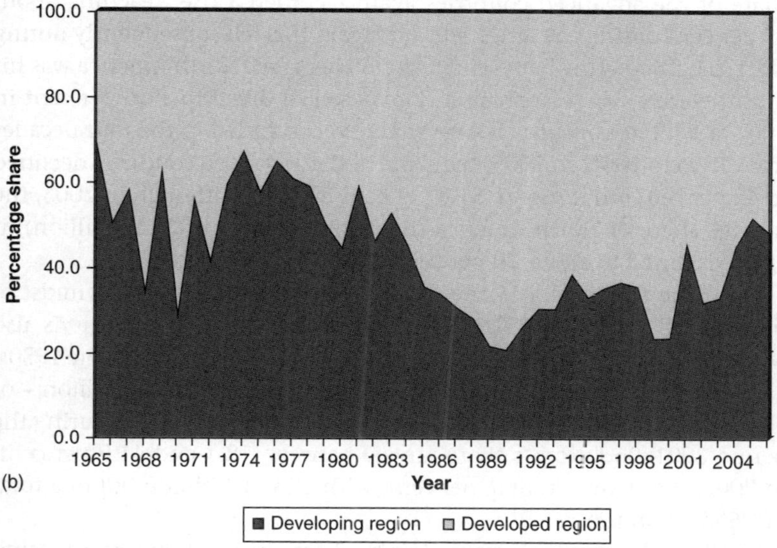


*Figure 2.2b* Share of developed and developing countries

### 2.3.2 Regional trends

The internationalization of Japanese investment over the period and its regional diversification has gone hand in hand. In the second half of the

1980s, the developed countries – comprising North America, Europe, and Australia – witnessed a massive jump in Japanese investments, reaching a peak of over 79 per cent by the end of 1980s from 41 per cent in 1981. The bulk of the increase went to America while Europe recorded a more modest increase. As a corollary, the developing countries – Asia, Latin America, Africa and the Middle and Near East – witnessed a decline during this period.

Among the developed countries, North America, which represented the largest export market, alone received 50 per cent – that is, US$33.9 billion out of a total Japanese FDI of $67.5 billion by 1989, with the developed world as a whole having received $53 billion – or over 78 per cent of the total. But with the beginning of the slump from the ensuing year after the bursting of the asset-price bubble, Japanese FDI to the developed countries fell from $53 billion in 1989 to $23.8 billion in 1992. North America was the biggest loser, witnessing a continuous decline from US$33.9 billion to US$14.6 billion by 1992. Even so the USA remained the largest recipient of Japanese FDI, accounting for 43 per cent of the total, with Europe receiving another 21 per cent. The share of the advanced countries again recorded a rise, reaching about 77 per cent during the late 1990s but again this fell subsequently during 2001–04, fluctuating between 55 and 68 per cent. North America was hit most severely when its share in Japanese FDI dived to 13.6 per cent in 2004 at $4.8 billion – the lowest share ever recorded in the four decades from 1965 to 2006. In 2005, the share of the advanced countries declined to 48 per cent but it rose to 51.8 per cent in 2006. Although in 2005, the relative share of North America rose to 28.9 per cent ($13.1 billion), it again declined to about 20 per cent ($10.2 billion) in 2006.

Thus, the role of North America is clearly discernible in the midst of rise and fall of Japanese FDI. The relative position of other regions also witnessed changes over time. Asia, which had a higher share in the 1970s, gave way to Europe in the late 1980s having received $24.5 billion – or almost 50 per cent of a total of $49 billion – in the year 2000. During the period 2001–06 Europe's share ranged between 18.1 and 41.9 per cent. In 2006, the share was 36.6 per cent, with US$18.4 billion out of a total of US$50.3 billion.

Of all the developing regions, Asia has been the most important recipient of Japanese FDI. Throughout most of the 1970s, the Asian share of Japanese FDI had even exceeded that of North America. For Japanese investors, the second most important region in the developing countries has been Latin America. Over the period 1982–8, its share exceeded that of Asia – it received $24.3 billion compared to $19.1 billion by Asia.

There was a steady decline in its share in the subsequent period, with only the occasional rise. With the exceptions of Asia and Latin America, Japanese FDI in other developing countries has been small-scale. In the case of the Middle East, for instance, aggregate FDI in the period 1965–2006 was about $6.5 billion while in the case of Africa, the cumulative FDI was $11.3 billion over the same period. This may be due to a lack of human resource development, capacity building and infrastructure development in these regions.

The share of Japanese FDI received by developing countries is again witnessing an upturn. In the year 2004, Asia received $9.4 billion and its share of total FDI was 26.4 per cent, compared to 13.6 per cent for North America. The decline of Japanese investment in the United States was in services, particularly in real estate, while the increase in FDI flows to Asia is in manufacturing.

Overall, during the 1960s and 1970s developing countries received more than half of Japanese FDI. The rise has been as sharp as the fall. The relative position of Asia has been changing over time. By the end of the 1980s, Europe had replaced Asia as the second most important destination for Japanese FDI. The relative positions shifted again in the mid-1990s, until the 1997 Asian crisis which caused Japanese firms to reduce their flows of investment into the region. Table 2.3 presents period-wise average annual flows in the developed and developing regions over the period 1965–2006.

The scale of growth and the preference of the Japanese investors for different regions should be made relatively clearer from Table 2.4, which gives the initial level and subsequent growth rates, and Table 2.5, which shows the percentage shares. Graphically, these are shown in Figures 2.3 and 2.4.

The study shows Europe in the developed and Asia in the developing region to be crucial for Japanese FDI outflows. Over 40 per cent of the Japanese FDI 'pulled' into the US during the second half of the 1980s and much of the 1990s is not likely to be repeated due to the changes in the economic fundamentals of these countries. The 'investment rush' in that period was the result of a combination of factors: the 'super-easy' monetary policy of Japan, the 'bubble'-induced situation and the motivation to invest in real estate in the US. The present-day macroeconomic realities and economic opportunities are different. Nevertheless, the shifting of geographic targets over time with changes in the international competitiveness is not new for Japanese investors if it is supportive of its global perspective. However, Japanese firms will need to institute a new wave of firm-specific advantages to bring a new tide in their global operations.

*Table 2.3* Region-wise average annual flows in different periods (US$ million), 1965–2006

| Year | Developed regions | | | | Developing regions | | | | | |
|---|---|---|---|---|---|---|---|---|---|---|
| | North America | Europe | Australia | Developed countries | Latin America | Asia | Mid & Near East | Africa | Oceania except Australia | Developing countries |
| 1965–70 | 119 | 103 | 34 | 257 | 58 | 100 | 25 | 14 | 12 | 208 |
| 1971–75 | 601 | 376 | 94 | 1,071 | 463 | 693 | 128 | 82 | 36 | 1,402 |
| 1976–80 | 1,176 | 390 | 297 | 1,864 | 657 | 1,122 | 257 | 189 | 22 | 2,248 |
| 1981–85 | 3,433 | 1,306 | 291 | 5,031 | 1,894 | 1,927 | 143 | 385 | 52 | 4,400 |
| 1986–90 | 21,844 | 9,652 | 2,488 | 33,985 | 4,969 | 5,611 | 92 | 491 | 283 | 11,447 |
| 1991–95 | 17,945 | 7,837 | 2,105 | 27,887 | 3,709 | 8,211 | 292 | 450 | 288 | 12,951 |
| 1996–2000 | 18,566 | 16,638 | 1,053 | 36,256 | 6,062 | 8,768 | 197 | 359 | 310 | 15,696 |
| 2001–06 | 8,976 | 12,510 | 980 | 22,466 | 6,221 | 10,240 | 144 | 234 | 127 | 16,965 |
| *Long-term trends* | | | | | | | | | | |
| 1965–90 | 5,230 | 2,279 | 618 | 8,127 | 1,549 | 1,822 | 125 | 224 | 78 | 3,798 |
| 1991–2006 | 14,775 | 12,340 | 1,354 | 28,469 | 5,386 | 9,146 | 207 | 341 | 235 | 15,315 |
| 1965–2006 | 8,867 | 6,111 | 898 | 15,876 | 3,010 | 4,612 | 156 | 268 | 138 | 8,184 |

*Table 2.4* Japanese FDI outflows – region-wise: level and growth rates

| Year | Growth-developed countries | | | | Growth-developing countries | | | | | |
|---|---|---|---|---|---|---|---|---|---|---|
| | North America | Europe | Australia | Developed countries | Latin America | Asia | Mid & Near East | Africa | Oceania except Australia | Developing countries |
| 1 | 2 | 3 | 4 | 5 | 6 | 7 | 8 | 9 | 10 | 11 |
| 1965 level (US$ million) | 44 | 5 | 0 | 49 | 62 | 35 | 11 | 2 | 0 | 110 |
| *Growth rates** | | | | | | | | | | |
| 1966–70 | 29.5 | 165.2 | 126.4 | 59.9 | 0.6 | 47.0 | 19.6 | 64.0 | 73.6 | 26.9 |
| 1971–75 | 35.6 | 12.3 | 24.8 | 22.7 | 33.1 | 44.3 | 23.2 | 63.3 | 6.1 | 38.5 |
| 1976–80 | 24.4 | 20.8 | 44.0 | 26.3 | 17.9 | 0.2 | −15.5 | −11.0 | −8.7 | 2.4 |
| 1981–85 | 19.2 | 29.2 | −6.4 | 20.1 | 22.3 | −14.2 | −7.0 | −24.5 | −5.5 | −1.4 |
| 1986–90 | 31.1 | 44.0 | 50.7 | 35.8 | −4.4 | 31.6 | −8.6 | 22.9 | 43.8 | 13.3 |
| 1991–95 | 6.4 | −3.0 | −4.4 | 2.9 | 10.0 | 20.7 | 1.7 | −9.3 | −29.2 | 14.0 |
| 1996–2000 | −10.2 | 38.3 | −12.0 | 8.2 | 5.6 | −16.7 | −47.8 | −30.3 | −18.8 | −9.4 |
| 2001–2006 | 8.2 | 2.6 | −5.4 | 5.5 | −13.4 | 26.7 | 72.6 | 3.0 | 48.1 | 12.8 |
| *Long-term trends* | | | | | | | | | | |
| 1965–90 | 27.5 | 29.1 | 23.6 | 26.6 | 22.8 | 21.0 | 5.2 | 22.4 | 19.7 | 20.6 |
| 1991–2006 | −6.0 | 4.9 | −7.8 | −1.3 | 2.9 | 2.6 | −12.3 | −9.5 | −8.2 | 2.6 |
| 1965–2006 | 14.5 | 18.7 | 11.3 | 15.6 | 12.9 | 13.5 | 1.3 | 7.8 | 9.5 | 12.5 |

*Note*: *The very high growth rates in some cases were due to extremely lower base is obvious.

*Table 2.5* Japanese FDI outflows – percentage shares of the regions

| Year | Developed regions | | | | Developing regions | | | | | |
|---|---|---|---|---|---|---|---|---|---|---|
| | North America | Europe | Australia | Developed countries | Latin America | Asia | Mid & Near East | Africa | Oceania except Australia | Developing countries |
| 1965–70 | 25.69 | 22.21 | 7.36 | 55.26 | 12.45 | 21.46 | 5.38 | 2.98 | 2.48 | 44.74 |
| 1971–75 | 24.30 | 15.19 | 3.81 | 43.30 | 18.72 | 28.04 | 5.19 | 3.30 | 1.45 | 56.70 |
| 1976–80 | 28.61 | 9.50 | 7.22 | 45.33 | 15.99 | 27.30 | 6.24 | 4.59 | 0.55 | 54.67 |
| 1981–85 | 36.41 | 13.85 | 3.09 | 53.34 | 20.08 | 20.43 | 1.51 | 4.08 | 0.55 | 46.66 |
| 1986–90 | 48.08 | 21.25 | 5.48 | 74.80 | 10.94 | 12.35 | 0.20 | 1.08 | 0.62 | 25.20 |
| 1991–95 | 43.94 | 19.19 | 5.15 | 68.29 | 9.08 | 20.11 | 0.71 | 1.10 | 0.71 | 31.71 |
| 1996–2000 | 35.74 | 32.03 | 2.03 | 69.79 | 11.67 | 16.88 | 0.38 | 0.69 | 0.51 | 30.21 |
| 2001–06 | 20.31 | 36.67 | 0.93 | 57.91 | 5.08 | 34.22 | 0.48 | 1.79 | 0.60 | 42.09 |
| *Long-term trends* | | | | | | | | | | |
| 1965–90 | 43.86 | 19.11 | 5.18 | 68.15 | 12.99 | 15.28 | 1.05 | 1.88 | 0.66 | 31.85 |
| 1991–2006 | 33.75 | 28.18 | 3.09 | 65.02 | 12.30 | 20.89 | 0.47 | 0.78 | 0.54 | 34.98 |
| 1965–2006 | 36.85 | 25.40 | 3.73 | 65.98 | 12.51 | 19.17 | 0.65 | 1.11 | 0.57 | 34.02 |

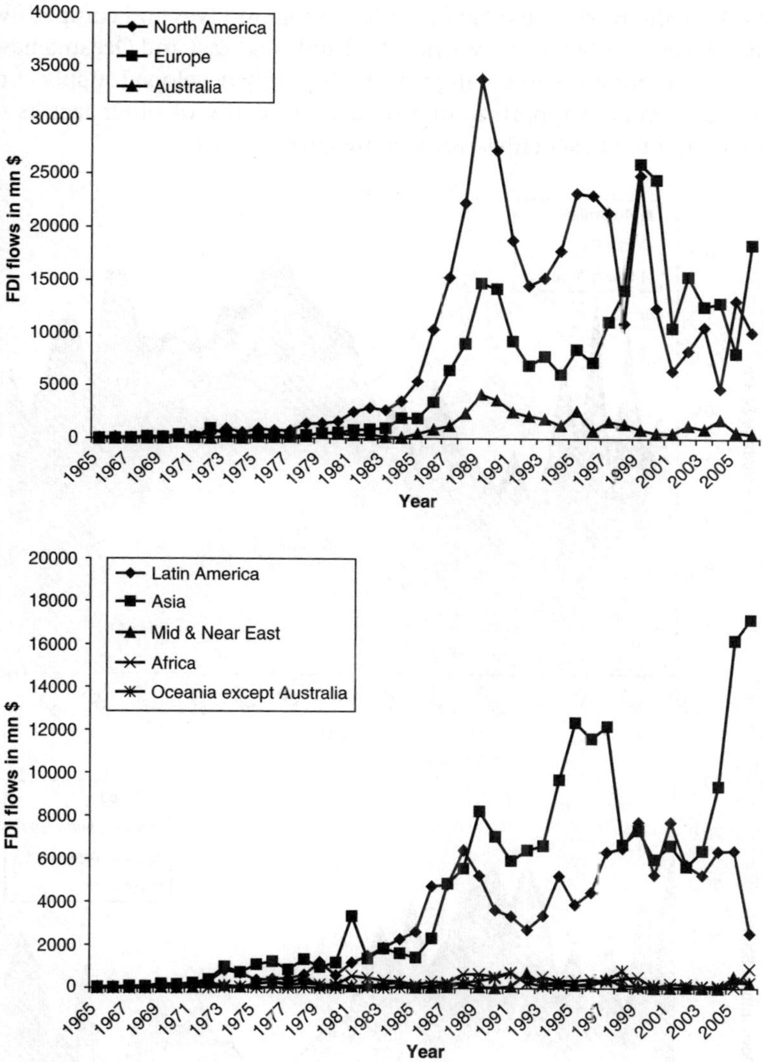


*Figure 2.3* Flows of Japanese FDI in different regions

Changes in the regional diversifications of Japanese FDI has, thus, been driven by various types of pull and push factors – often complex and also changing over time and differs between regions as well as between different value-adding activities. The asymmetry in Japanese FDI between countries within the regions may be ascribed partly to policy or FDI-facilitation-related factors or to varying motives and competitive advantages. Regions such as Africa, Mid and Near East and Oceania have a lot of 'catching-up' to do, improve their poorly developed supply conditions, develop supporting industries and quality of other factors of production to attract efficiency-seeking Japanese FDI.

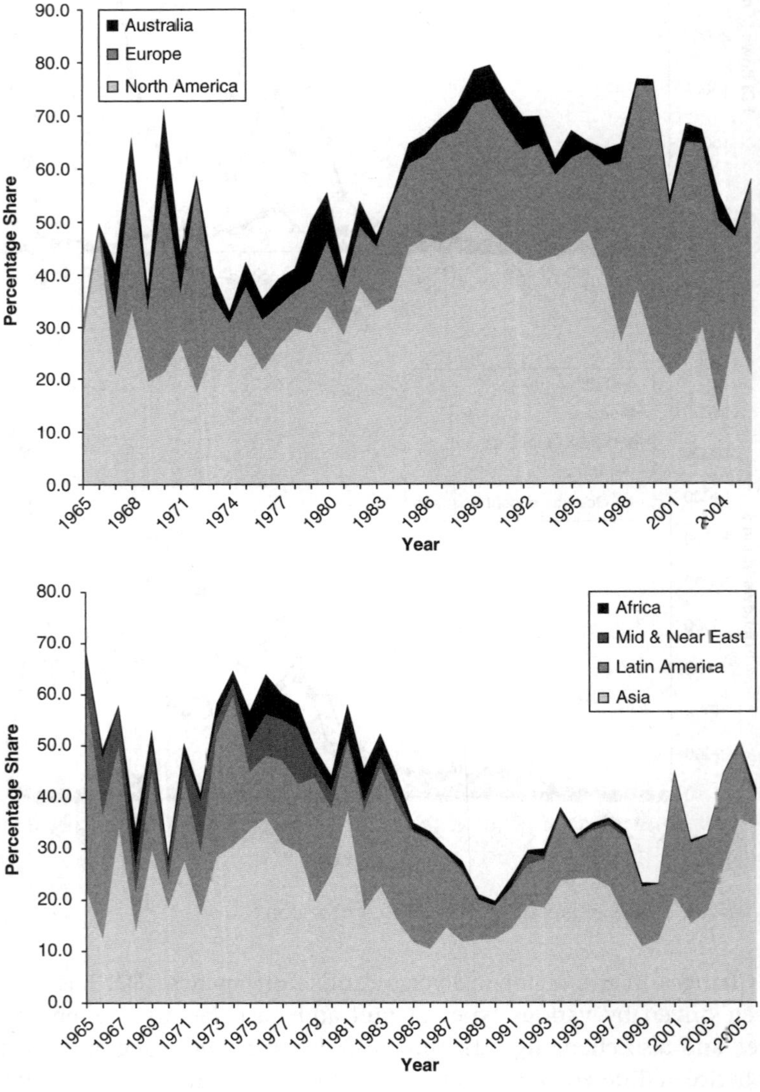


*Figure 2.4* Shares of the different regions

## 2.4 Japanese FDI flows in Asia (NIEs-4, ASEAN-4, China, and India)

### 2.4.1 The overview

Japanese 'globalization' has been repeatedly revitalized in Asia by extending the production and sales networks in the region. The local and export demand, as well as the factor characterization of the Asian 'four tigers' and the second generation industrializing powers, were well placed to attract Japanese FDI. Among the developing regions, East Asia led in attracting Japanese FDI which enabled these countries to achieve a sophisticated division of labour by bringing in capital, technology, skills, and other externalities. Japanese investors rapidly stepped up activities in these neighbouring countries when rising costs within Japan threatened their global competitiveness.

In fact, one of the most distinctive characteristics of Japanese FDI outflows to this region has been its successive phases of dynamism through developing linkages. From a meagre $32 million in 1965, the magnitude of Japanese FDI flow to these ten countries reached a level of $16.6 billion by 2006. In perspective, recording a rapid growth of 58.7 per cent in the 1960s and 56.8 per cent in the first part of the 1970s, it slowed down in the latter half but picked up rapidly, recording an average flow of over $8 billion by the mid-1990s and a peak of approximately $12 billion in 1995. There was a slower pace of expansion of Japanese FDI in the subsequent years and even a declining phase during the late 1990s and early 2000, but the year 2002 onwards shows a distinct upward trend – resurgence and now a robust growth. Cumulative investment in the period 1965–89 reached $40 billion and was around $190 billion during the period 1965–2006.

A forty-year perspective of the Japanese FDI growth profile in Asia may be seen in Figure 2.5. The year-to-year variations are affected or dictated by short-term factors, prevailing local conditions, currency and the economic crisis, and the international environment. Hence, in order to smoothen it, three-yearly moving averages are also given, along with the actual annual total flows.

Japan's global FDI *vis-à-vis* the share of Asia and that of the ten countries can be seen from Table 2.6.

### 2.4.2 The Asian NIEs

The Asian NIEs have been spearheading growth in the region. They were successful in securing the bulk of Japanese FDI, although its actual distribution has been significantly changing both within and throughout

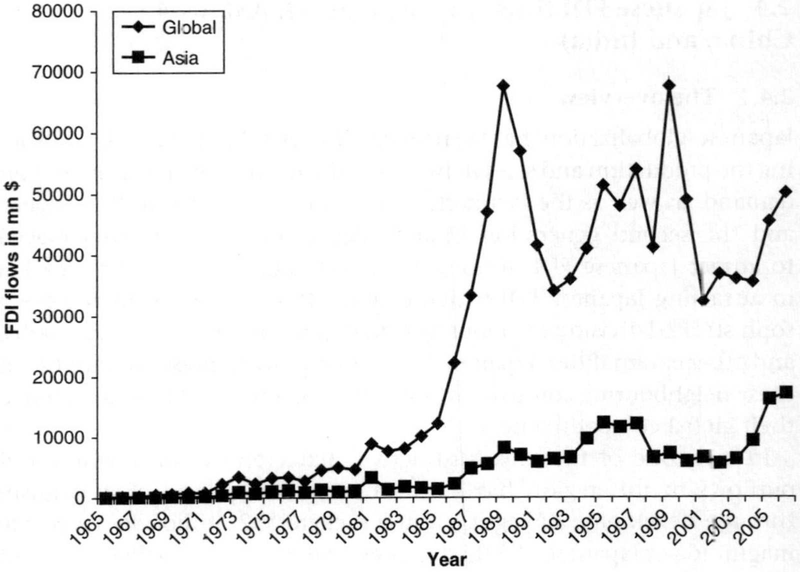


*Figure 2.5* Japanese FDI flows in Asia

*Table 2.6* Japanese FDI in Asia – annual averages

| Year | Global (US$ million) | Whole of Asia (US$ million) | Share of Asia in the global total (per cent) | FDI in ten countries (NIEs-4 + ASEAN-4 + India and China) (US$ million) | Share of ten countries in the global total (per cent) |
|---|---|---|---|---|---|
| 1965–70 | 465 | 100 | 21.7 | 84 | 19.1 |
| 1971–75 | 2,473 | 693 | 27.5 | 689 | 27.3 |
| 1976–80 | 4,111 | 1,122 | 28.1 | 1,118 | 28.0 |
| 1981–85 | 9,431 | 1,927 | 21.2 | 1,907 | 20.9 |
| 1986–90 | 45,431 | 5,611 | 12.3 | 5,568 | 12.2 |
| 1991–95 | 40,838 | 8,211 | 19.8 | 8,026 | 19.4 |
| 1996–2000 | 51,952 | 8,768 | 17.2 | 8,501 | 16.7 |
| 2001–06 | 39,424 | 10,240 | 25.0 | 10,052 | 24.5 |
| *Long-term trends* | | | | | |
| 1965–90 | 11,924 | 1,822 | 22.1 | 1,805 | 21.4 |
| 1991–2006 | 43,783 | 9,147 | 21.0 | 8,935 | 20.5 |
| 1965–2006 | 24,057 | 4,612 | 21.7 | 4,521 | 21.1 |

the period. In the wake of the Plaza Accord of 1985 and the subsequent appreciation of the yen, Japanese FDI to NIEs expanded rapidly in the 1970s and 1980s. This increase was matched by a well-calibrated FDI policy in the NIEs which was geared to the provision of an attractive investment environment, including liberalization policies, sound macroeconomic management and human resource development. These were able to capture considerable FDI inflows and to establish effective regional production and sales networks serving Japan and third country markets.

Notwithstanding the annual variation – moderate to sharp – in the total investment to these ten Asian countries during the 1980s (see Table 2.7), a major share has gone to NIEs, the actual percentage being 43.1 per cent during the period 1981–5, and 56.1 per cent during the period 1986–90. In other words, it expanded rapidly from an average annual flow of $0.82 billion during the period 1981–85 to an annual average of $3.13 billion – during the period 1986–90. This coincided with the eligibility of Asian NIEs to the General System of Preferences (GSP) being suspended. Trade frictions and rising labour costs reduced the profitability of the industries, leading to a decline in Japanese FDI to 12.4 per cent during 1991–95. The corresponding average annual flow also fell to $2.5 billion from an annual average of $3.1 billion during the period 1986–90. But this position changed subsequently and it rose again to over $2.9 billion in the period 1996–2000. During the period 2001–06, the average annual flows were $2.8 billion, while the average share was 28.1 per cent. Total Japanese FDI to the NIEs over the entire period 1965–2006 was approximately $67.7 billion while during the period 1991–2006, it amounted to about $44.4 billion.

An inter-period comparison of the flows, share and growth rates, is given in Table 2.7.

A forty-year perspective of Japanese FDI flows in the NIEs – country-wise – is portrayed in Figure 2.6.

Within the NIEs, Hong Kong ($25 billion) stands first, followed by Singapore ($20 billion), then Korea ($14 billion) and Taiwan ($9 billion) during the period 1965–2006. However, in terms of average per capita Japanese FDI Singapore comes first, with an average of $216 taking into account the entire period from 1981 to 2006, followed by Hong Kong, with $146. By contrast, the figure for Taiwan is $15.6 and the lowest figure is for South Korea with $10.2 during the same period.

*Table 2.7* Japanese FDI in the NIEs

| Year | Hong Kong | Singapore | Taiwan | Korea | NIEs total |
|---|---|---|---|---|---|
| **Average FDI flows in NIEs in US$ million** | | | | | |
| 1965–70 | 3 | 3 | 13 | 6 | 25 |
| 1971–75 | 70 | 48 | 23 | 111 | 252 |
| 1976–80 | 143 | 132 | 34 | 110 | 420 |
| 1981–85 | 367 | 266 | 78 | 109 | 821 |
| 1986–90 | 1,384 | 857 | 394 | 491 | 3,126 |
| 1991–95 | 1,036 | 833 | 344 | 316 | 2,529 |
| 1996–2000 | 950 | 1,018 | 399 | 592 | 2,958 |
| 2001–06 | 811 | 647 | 441 | 928 | 2,827 |
| *Long-term trends* | | | | | |
| 1965–90 | 388 | 248 | 104 | 160 | 901 |
| 1991–2006 | 926 | 820 | 398 | 632 | 2775 |
| 1965–2006 | 598 | 471 | 219 | 344 | 1632 |
| **Average percentage shares** | | | | | |
| 1965–70 | 3.95 | 3.56 | 15.22 | 6.52 | 29.25 |
| 1971–75 | 10.12 | 6.99 | 3.28 | 16.10 | 36.50 |
| 1976–80 | 12.82 | 11.84 | 3.08 | 9.82 | 37.56 |
| 1981–85 | 19.26 | 13.97 | 4.10 | 5.73 | 43.05 |
| 1986–90 | 24.85 | 15.39 | 7.08 | 8.82 | 56.14 |
| 1991–95 | 12.90 | 10.38 | 4.29 | 3.94 | 31.51 |
| 1996–2000 | 11.17 | 11.97 | 4.69 | 6.96 | 34.79 |
| 2001–06 | 8.05 | 6.41 | 4.39 | 9.24 | 28.13 |
| *Long-term trends* | | | | | |
| 1965–90 | 14.6 | 9.8 | 6.7 | 9.9 | 40.9 |
| 1991–2006 | 10.5 | 10.0 | 4.7 | 7.0 | 32.2 |
| 1965–2006 | 13.0 | 9.8 | 5.9 | 8.8 | 38.2 |
| **Annual growth rates (percentage)*** | | | | | |
| 1966–70 | 34.1 | 39.6 | 87.5 | 66.2 | 62.1 |
| 1971–75 | 27.1 | 30.7 | 29.4 | 19.3 | 22.5 |
| 1976–80 | 26.6 | 59.1 | 19.8 | −19.3 | 19.6 |
| 1981–85 | −16.6 | 7.3 | 18.1 | 13.3 | 0.8 |
| 1986–90 | 36.5 | 40.4 | 12.2 | −8.8 | 24.7 |
| 1991–95 | 9.0 | 19.4 | 1.9 | 18.2 | 12.4 |
| 1996–2000 | −5.6 | −20.9 | −4.8 | 23.9 | −5.4 |
| 2001–06 | 50.3 | −15.0 | 17.5 | 29.7 | 18.9 |
| *Long-term trends* | | | | | |
| 1965–90 | 32.7 | 31.4 | 19.9 | 21.0 | 26.0 |
| 1991–2006 | −2.3 | −3.8 | 2.0 | 10.9 | 1.2 |
| 1965–2006 | 15.3 | 15.8 | 12.6 | 12.6 | 13.8 |

*Note*: *The higher growth during the initial period was also due to the lower base.

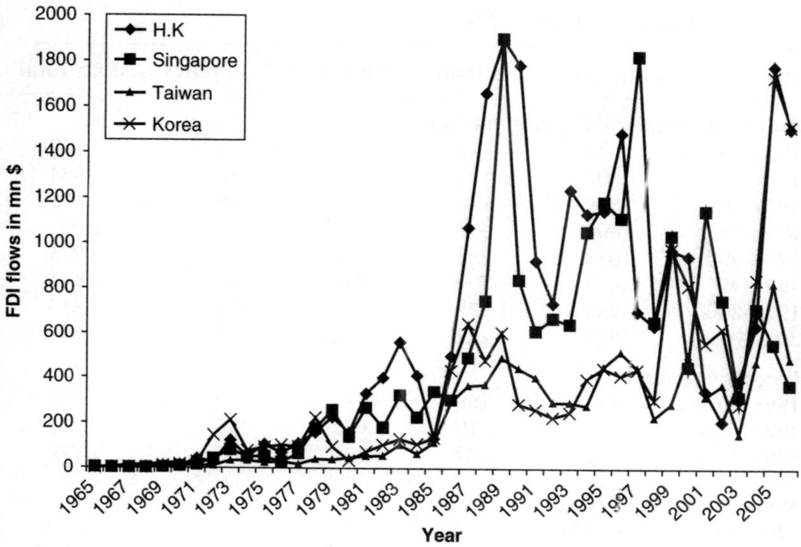


*Figure 2.6* Japanese FDI flows in NIEs

### 2.4.3 ASEAN-4

Japan is seen as the first-tier industrial power, with the NIEs as the second tier and the ASEAN countries of Thailand, Malaysia, Indonesia and Philippines as the third tier. Although these countries also shared in the Japanese investment boom witnessed during the second half of the 1980s, it was in the 1990s that the Japanese investors shifted their focus to this region to maintain their competitiveness. This is reflected in the cumulative investment to ASEAN-4 during 1991–2006 which was approximately $54 billion or 22 per cent more than to the NIEs during the same period. Flows within the ASEAN or for that matter to any country, however, should not be seen in isolation, but in comparison to the competing countries. There is some polarization, as we shall see later, between China and the ASEAN in the sense that increased flow to the former shows a decline to the latter region.

Within the ASEAN-4, the choice of Japanese investment destinations differs significantly. Indonesia, which was a major recipient throughout most of the 1980s and 1990s, has been losing ground because of economic uncertainties. On the whole, Thailand has been the most dynamic of the ASEAN-4 countries. It was the second most important

*Table 2.8* Japanese FDI in ASEAN-4

| Year | Indonesia | Thailand | Malaysia | Philippines | ASEAN total |
|---|---|---|---|---|---|
| **Annual average FDI flows in million US$** | | | | | |
| 1965–70 | 35 | 10 | 6 | 8 | 59 |
| 1971–75 | 307 | 24 | 50 | 53 | 434 |
| 1976–80 | 529 | 38 | 69 | 55 | 691 |
| 1981–85 | 800 | 73 | 95 | 56 | 1,024 |
| 1986–90 | 623 | 733 | 421 | 137 | 1,915 |
| 1991–95 | 1,409 | 800 | 740 | 391 | 3,341 |
| 1996–2000 | 1,485 | 1,289 | 529 | 513 | 3,815 |
| 2001–06 | 670 | 1,222 | 732 | 421 | 3,045 |
| *Long-term trends* | | | | | |
| 1965–90 | 443 | 169 | 124 | 60 | 795 |
| 1991–2006 | 1,157 | 1,110 | 671 | 440 | 3,378 |
| 1965–2006 | 715 | 527 | 332 | 205 | 1,779 |
| **Average annual shares** | | | | | |
| 1965–70 | 41.11 | 11.46 | 7.11 | 9.68 | 69.37 |
| 1971–75 | 44.56 | 3.42 | 7.28 | 7.72 | 62.98 |
| 1976–80 | 47.31 | 3.36 | 6.22 | 4.92 | 61.81 |
| 1981–85 | 41.95 | 3.02 | 4.98 | 2.92 | 53.67 |
| 1986–90 | 11.56 | 13.16 | 7.56 | 2.47 | 34.38 |
| 1991–95 | 17.56 | 9.97 | 9.22 | 4.87 | 41.62 |
| 1996–2000 | 17.46 | 15.16 | 6.22 | 6.04 | 44.88 |
| 2001–06 | 4.48 | 11.95 | 17.72 | 2.22 | 37.37 |
| *Long-term trends* | | | | | |
| 1965–90 | 35.8 | 7.4 | 7.1 | 4.9 | 55.2 |
| 1991–2006 | 13.5 | 12.4 | 7.3 | 5.3 | 38.6 |
| 1965–2006 | 27.3 | 9.3 | 7.2 | 5.1 | 48.9 |
| **Average annual growth rates (per cent)** | | | | | |
| 1966–70 | 38.1 | 36.3 | 11.8 | 57.4 | 37.1 |
| 1971–75 | 56.3 | 9.6 | 52.8 | 135.5 | 58.7 |
| 1976–80 | –19.5 | 13.0 | 14.2 | 58.8 | –9.8 |
| 1981–85 | –30.7 | 11.7 | 27.2 | –0.3 | –24.6 |
| 1986–90 | 36.6 | 83.9 | 56.3 | 83.1 | 57.3 |
| 1991–95 | 6.6 | 10.0 | –7.7 | 48.5 | 8.2 |
| 1996–2000 | 36.0 | –15.0 | –19.8 | –1.7 | –21.5 |
| 2001–06 | 7.5 | 29.3 | 60.3 | –8.5 | 23.5 |
| *Long-term trends* | | | | | |
| 1965–90 | 15.1 | 20.7 | 20.8 | 14.7 | 17.3 |
| 1991–2006 | –7.3 | 3.6 | –4.6 | 2.1 | –1.2 |
| 1965–2006 | 8.1 | 16.5 | 13.0 | 12.5 | 11.3 |

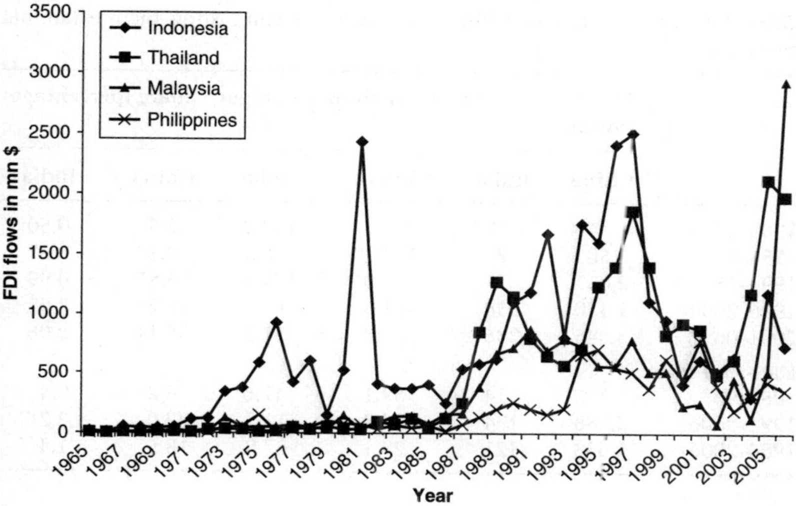


*Figure 2.7* Japanese FDI flows in ASEAN-4

among the ASEAN-4, and has overtaken Indonesia during a number of years. Malaysia, until almost the mid-1980s, was more impressive than Thailand but it was later left behind by Thailand. By contrast, even though the Philippines witnessed a rise during the late 1980s and 1990s, it remains the worst-performing of these four countries.

Individual country-wise Japanese FDI flows are given in Figure 2.7 while the average annual flows, shares and growth rates are presented in Table 2.8.

### 2.4.4 India and China

In the early years of the period under consideration, China and India did not figure on the Japanese investment map. However, Japanese FDI to India started much earlier in 1966 than to China where it came much later in 1979 subsequent to the reforms. But in the case of India, Japanese FDI has remained abysmally low, while China has moved faster and graduated to a higher level. Starting from a mere 2.55 per cent share in these ten Asian countries over the period 1980–85, it has risen progressively to 9.1 per cent in 1985–90, and 25.87 per cent in 1990–95. It did witness a decline to 17.29 per cent during the period 1996–2000, but the downturn had more to do with many of the policy changes resulting

*Table 2.9* Japanese FDI in China and India – a contrasting picture (annual averages)

| Year | FDI flows in US$ million | | Growth (percentage) | | Share (percentage) | |
|---|---|---|---|---|---|---|
| | China | India | China | India | China | India |
| 1980–85 | 46 | 9 | 738.1 | 159.2 | 2.55 | 0.50 |
| 1986–90 | 507 | 21 | 104.1 | 26.3 | 9.10 | 0.37 |
| 1991–95 | 2,077 | 79 | 67.0 | 171.3 | 25.87 | 0.99 |
| 1996–2000 | 1,470 | 258 | −21.6 | 17.5 | 17.29 | 3.03 |
| 2001–06 | 3,945 | 236 | 37.8 | 51.2 | 37.14 | 3.08 |
| *Long-term trends* | | | | | | |
| 1980–90 | 255 | 14 | 59.1 | 17.6 | 6.2 | 0.4 |
| 1991–2006 | 2,588 | 194 | 9.3 | 11.7 | 27.0 | 2.2 |
| 1980–2006 | 1,638 | 121 | 23.1 | 17.9 | 18.5 | 1.4 |

in Japan's retreat in many economic exchanges (Yamazawa and Ken-Ichi 2001). A fresh boom in Japanese FDI to China is signalled after 2000 – it jumped to 37.14 per cent during the period 2001–06 (Table 2.9).

India received about 17 times less Japanese FDI than China, i.e., $1.4 billion against $23.7 billion to China in the period 2001–06 which is less than 1 per cent of Japanese overseas investment, despite the fact that Japan has been showing serious interest in investing in India during this period. While there may be some similarities in both countries' approach to attract FDI – namely, the creation of export zones, regional component in the policy, some fiscal incentives – but a driving force in China's exceptional performance in attracting FDI has been due to the economic reforms that exhibit a gradual and logical continuum – a coherent flow of rigorous policies and FDI-promoting factors. China is viewed as being more business oriented; its decision-making is seen as faster and it is also seen as having a better investment climate. The opening up of China to the world economy, and in particular to trade and investment, the creation of Special Economic Zones in southern China and the promotion of FDI in joint ventures resulted in China becoming the largest recipient of FDI among developing countries.

Thus, China today is at a more advanced stage on the FDI growth path, attracting more than 39 per cent of the flows during the last two recorded years – 2005 and 2006. A number of studies provide insights to FDI growth, particularly to China explaining it in terms of market-seeking, resource-seeking and efficiency-seeking arguments even though

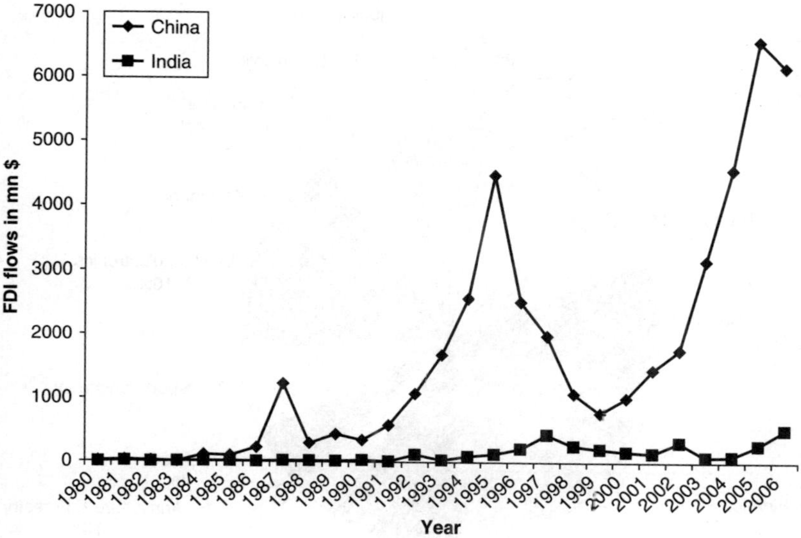


*Figure 2.8* Japanese FDI flows in China and India

the behaviour of different foreign investors has been different according to their origin (see Cheng and Zhao 1995; Cheng and Kwan 2000; Balasubramanyam *et al.* 1999; Agenor 2001).

Japanese FDI flows to China and India, shown in Figure 2.8, present an interesting picture.

## 2.5 Japanese investment in industry

### 2.5.1 The overall picture

Throughout the period under consideration, the changing pattern of Japanese FDI in industry is clearly evident. Factors explaining the inter-industry distribution of FDI reflect the competitive pressures, host country environment – that is, the size, market structure, level of competition, R&D level, nature of industry and the kind of linkages it has between the parent firms and the host country's domestic firms, its financial performance, output and investment strategies, advertisement intensity of the industry and, most importantly, the policy towards entry, ownership, and so on. FDI is expected to be prominent in those industries that are characterized by the ownership of intangible assets and high internalization and location incentives.

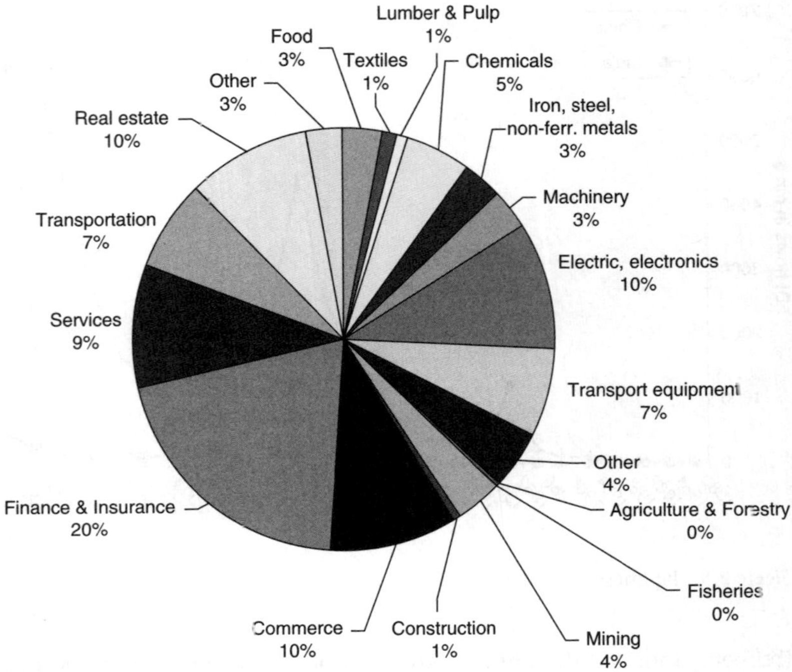


*Figure 2.9* Japanese FDI in industry, 1951–2006 (percentage share)

While Japanese FDI has grown in both manufacturing and non-manufacturing, investment in non-manufacturing constitutes a relatively prominent feature of the 1980s. The 1990s witnessed a rise in the overall ratio of investment in manufacturing and within this sector, it was investment in electronics, transport equipments, chemicals, and machinery which witnessed significant increases, accounting for more than half of the total investments while the primary sectors such as textiles and lumber & pulp recorded a sharp decline. In non-manufacturing, there has been a shift in investment from 'commerce' to 'finance & insurance' with the 'services' sector also recording an upward trend except for some marginal variations.

The overall picture of Japanese FDI in industry taking the period 1951–2006 brought out in Figure 2.9 shows the major driving sectors of Japanese FDI.

The broad trends and pattern of Japanese FDI in industry over the period may be seen from Table 2.10.

*Table 2.10* Japanese FDI outflows in industry, 1951–2006 (US$ million)

| | 1951–71 | 1972–80 | 1981–85 | 1986–90 | 1991–2006 | 1951–2006 |
|---|---|---|---|---|---|---|
| Food | 69 | 516 | 505 | 2,995 | 27,151 | 31,236 |
| Textiles | 254 | 1,384 | 445 | 1,915 | 7,005 | 11,003 |
| Lumber & pulp | 260 | 498 | 362 | 1,847 | 5,878 | 8,845 |
| Chemicals | 69 | 2,860 | 1,356 | 6,958 | 40,584 | 51,827 |
| Iron, steel, non-ferrous metals | 187 | 2,433 | 2,571 | 5,119 | 19,279 | 29,589 |
| Machinery | 91 | 804 | 1,077 | 5,961 | 23,349 | 31,282 |
| Electric, electronics | 104 | 1,477 | 2,166 | 16,613 | 77,183 | 97,543 |
| Transport equipment | 99 | 879 | 2,395 | 7,507 | 57,557 | 68,437 |
| Other | 85 | 808 | 947 | 8,297 | 33,822 | 43,959 |
| **Manufacturing** | **1,218** | **11,359** | **11,824** | **57,212** | **291,809** | **373,422** |
| Agriculture & forestry | 65 | 543 | 171 | 578 | 1,441 | 2,798 |
| Fisheries | 38 | 265 | 141 | 296 | 1,012 | 1,752 |
| Mining | 995 | 6,078 | 4,683 | 4,783 | 19,283 | 35,822 |
| Construction | 38 | 357 | 401 | 1,592 | 4,208 | 6,596 |
| Commerce | 530 | 4,879 | 7,269 | 18,638 | 67,445 | 98,761 |
| Finance & insurance | 373 | 2,056 | 8,433 | 54,459 | 140,002 | 205,323 |
| Services | 280 | 1,114 | 3,293 | 29,980 | 61,277 | 95,944 |
| Transportation | 0 | 0 | 5,900 | 11,538 | 51,849 | 69,287 |
| Real estate | 0 | 0 | 2,533 | 43,316 | 52,343 | 98,192 |
| Other | 899 | 5,414 | 2,500 | 4,764 | 13,336 | 26,913 |
| **Non-manufacturing** | **3,218** | **20,706** | **35,324** | **169,944** | **402,076** | **631,268** |
| Total | 4,436 | 32,064 | 47,148 | 227,156 | 700,374 | 1,011,178 |
| *Percentage Share* | | | | | | |
| Food | 1.6 | 1.6 | 1.1 | 1.3 | 3.9 | 3.1 |
| Textiles | 5.7 | 4.3 | 0.9 | 0.8 | 1.0 | 1.1 |
| Lumber & pulp | 5.9 | 1.6 | 0.8 | 0.8 | 0.8 | 0.9 |
| Chemicals | 1.6 | 8.9 | 2.9 | 3.1 | 5.8 | 5.1 |
| Iron, steel, non-ferrous metals | 4.2 | 7.6 | 5.5 | 2.3 | 2.8 | 2.9 |
| Machinery | 2.1 | 2.5 | 2.3 | 2.6 | 3.3 | 3.1 |
| Electric, electronics | 2.3 | 4.6 | 4.6 | 7.3 | 11.0 | 9.6 |
| Transport equipment | 2.2 | 2.7 | 5.1 | 3.3 | 8.2 | 6.8 |
| Other | 1.9 | 2.5 | 2.0 | 3.7 | 4.8 | 4.3 |
| **Manufacturing** | **27.5** | **35.4** | **25.1** | **25.2** | **41.7** | **36.9** |
| Agriculture & forestry | 1.5 | 1.7 | 0.4 | 0.3 | 0.2 | 0.3 |
| Fisheries | 0.9 | 0.8 | 0.3 | 0.1 | 0.1 | 0.2 |
| Mining | 22.4 | 19.0 | 9.9 | 2.1 | 2.8 | 3.5 |
| Construction | 0.9 | 1.1 | 0.9 | 0.7 | 0.6 | 0.7 |
| Commerce | 11.9 | 15.2 | 15.4 | 8.2 | 9.6 | 9.8 |

(*Continued*)

*Table 2.10* (*Continued*)

| | 1951–71 | 1972–80 | 1981–85 | 1986–90 | 1991–2006 | 1951–2006 |
|---|---|---|---|---|---|---|
| Finance & insurance | 8.4 | 6.4 | 17.9 | 24.0 | 20.0 | 20.3 |
| Services | 6.3 | 3.5 | 7.0 | 13.2 | 8.7 | 9.5 |
| Transportation | 0.0 | 0.0 | 12.5 | 5.1 | 7.4 | 6.9 |
| Real estate | 0.0 | 0.0 | 5.4 | 19.1 | 7.5 | 9.7 |
| Other | 20.3 | 16.9 | 5.3 | 2.1 | 1.9 | 2.7 |
| **Non-manufacturing** | **72.5** | **64.6** | **74.9** | **74.8** | **57.4** | **62.4** |
| Total | 100.0 | 100.0 | 100.0 | 100.0 | 100.0 | 100.0 |

### 2.5.2 Region-wise trends

The region-wise investment flows in industry have been quite diverse – a noticeable feature being its changing inter-industry pattern, both over time and between regions – a result of the changing interaction of the ownership advantages of FDI and the internalization of the location advantages in the host country. Given the ownership advantages, the differences in the region-wise industry pattern are mostly industry- and host country-specific.

A distinctive feature of the investment trend over time has been the rise in manufacturing investment – the highest being in Asia, and then

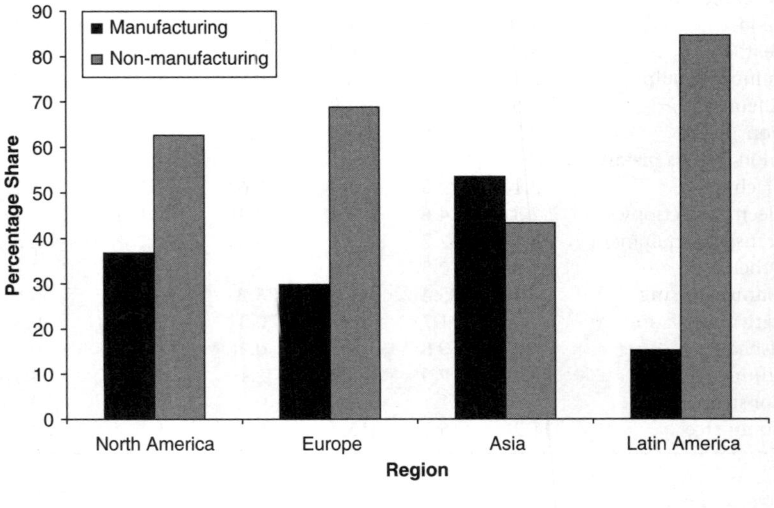


*Figure 2.10* Share of manufacturing and non-manufacturing investment in the total

*Table 2.11* Japanese FDI in manufacturing and non-manufacturing (percentages)

| | 1951–80 | 1981–85 | 1986–90 | 1991–2004 | 1951–2004 |
|---|---|---|---|---|---|
| 1. North America | | | | | |
| Manufacturing | 24.8 | 30.7 | 29.9 | 41.4 | 36.8 |
| Non-manufacturing | 69.5 | 67.7 | 69.5 | 58.4 | 62.6 |
| 2. Europe | | | | | |
| Manufacturing | 18.7 | 19 | 21.6 | 32.7 | 29.8 |
| Non-manufacturing | 78.4 | 75.9 | 75.1 | 65.6 | 68.8 |
| 3. Asia | | | | | |
| Manufacturing | 46.5 | 30.6 | 39.6 | 59.6 | 53.6 |
| Non-manufacturing | 52.3 | 68 | 58.9 | 36.9 | 43.4 |
| 4. Latin America | | | | | |
| Manufacturing | 45.0 | 18.8 | 6.9 | 15.2 | 15.2 |
| Non-manufacturing | 54.3 | 88.1 | 93.1 | 84.7 | 84.6 |
| 5. Oceania | | | | | |
| Manufacturing | 31.4 | 15.5 | 9.1 | 23.7 | 19.0 |
| Non-manufacturing | 68.1 | 84.2 | 90.0 | 75.9 | 80.4 |
| 6. Africa | | | | | |
| Manufacturing | 4.1 | 4.4 | 0.0 | 21.2 | 11.1 |
| Non-manufacturing | 95.8 | 95.6 | 100.0 | 78.8 | 88.9 |
| 7. Middle East | | | | | |
| Manufacturing | 46.7 | 27.5 | 2.3 | 32.8 | 27.9 |
| Non-manufacturing | 7.2 | 37.8 | 59.0 | 37.7 | 35.1 |
| *Overall* | | | | | |
| Manufacturing | 34.5 | 25.1 | 25.2 | 38.3 | 34.2 |
| Non-manufacturing | 61.1 | 72.8 | 73.1 | 61.2 | 64.7 |

*Notes*: 1. Manufacturing and non-manufacturing share does not add up to 100. The remaining is accounted for by investment in 'branches'.
2. Region-wise investment figures for manufacturing and non-manufacturing are available only up to the year 2004.

in Europe and the USA. In the case of Latin America, non-manufacturing attracted greater investment flows. In Oceania, investment declined in the 1980s and experienced only a marginal increase in the 1990s. In Africa and the Middle East, it was both marginal and erratic. This may be the result of economic, financial and institutional reasons and weak inter-firm linkages. Overall, FDI in manufacturing accounts for about 60 per cent in Asia, followed by North America with over 41 per cent and for Europe about 33 per cent (Figure 2.10). The overall average in manufacturing stands at 35.3 per cent.

Japanese FDI outflows in different regions in manufacturing and non-manufacturing may be seen from Table 2.11.

*Table 2.12* Japanese FDI in top sectors, 1951–2004

| Region | Sectors | Percentage |
|---|---|---|
| 1. North America | Manufacturing | 36.8 |
| | With in non-manufacturing: | 62.6 |
| | Real estate | 17.7 |
| | Services | 16.6 |
| | Finance & insurance | 12.2 |
| | Commerce | 10.8 |
| 2. Europe | Manufacturing | 29.8 |
| | With in non-manufacturing: | 68.8 |
| | Finance & insurance | 34.9 |
| | Commerce | 11.5 |
| | Transportation | 7.4 |
| | Real Estate | 6.5 |
| 3. Asia | Manufacturing | 53.6 |
| | With in non-manufacturing: | 43.4 |
| | Finance & insurance | 8.9 |
| | Commerce | 8.7 |
| | Services | 8.3 |
| | Mining | 6.7 |
| 4. Latin America | Manufacturing | 15.2 |
| | With in non-manufacturing: | 84.6 |
| | Finance & insurance | 43.5 |
| | Transportation | 25.8 |
| | Commerce | 4.9 |
| | Mining | 2.4 |
| 5. Oceania | Manufacturing | 19.0 |
| | With in non-manufacturing: | 80.4 |
| | Real estate | 31.4 |
| | Mining | 17.9 |
| | Services | 12.2 |
| | Commerce | 8.0 |

(*Continued*)

With the exception of Asia, non-manufacturing had a major share in the total with a concentration in commerce, finance & insurance, services, transportation and real estate accounting for a significant portion of Japanese FDI.

Sectors receiving a relatively higher percentage share of Japanese FDI in non-manufacturing for different regions over the entire period 1951–2004 are given in Table 2.12.

*Table 2.12* (*Continued*)

| **Region** | **Sectors** | **Percentage** |
|---|---|---|
| 6. Middle East | Manufacturing | 35.1 |
| | With in non-manufacturing: | 27.9 |
| | Mining | 18.0 |
| | Finance & insurance | 3.6 |
| | Commerce | 3.4 |
| | Services | 0.6 |
| 7. Africa | Manufacturing | 11.1 |
| | With in non-manufacturing: | 88.9 |
| | Transportation | 62.2 |
| | Services | 7.6 |
| | Mining | 4.8 |
| Overall | Manufacturing | 34.2 |
| | With in non-manufacturing: | 64.7 |
| | Finance & insurance | 20.9 |
| | Real estate | 10.7 |
| | Services | 10.3 |
| | Commerce | 9.6 |

*Note*: Region-wise investments in industry are available only up to the year 2004.

### 2.5.3 Investment in industry in Asia

Asia remained the most important destination of manufacturing FDI, well ahead of other regions. Japanese investors found it easier to transfer their management system and production technologies in the manufacturing sector because of the extensive networking with overseas associates in East Asia.

The sector-wise composition changed significantly in the latter half of the 1980s, the most remarkable development of which was the sharp expansion of FDI in electrical machinery (including electronics). Until the mid-1980s, electronics had had a relatively small share compared to the other sectors. The growth performance of the industry, the host country FDI policy towards the industry and the Japanese firms' comparative advantages stimulated FDI flows in this sector. The recent technological revolution allows such firms selectively to separate the parts and locate their production in different countries according to their comparative costs or to divert its existing, but more often

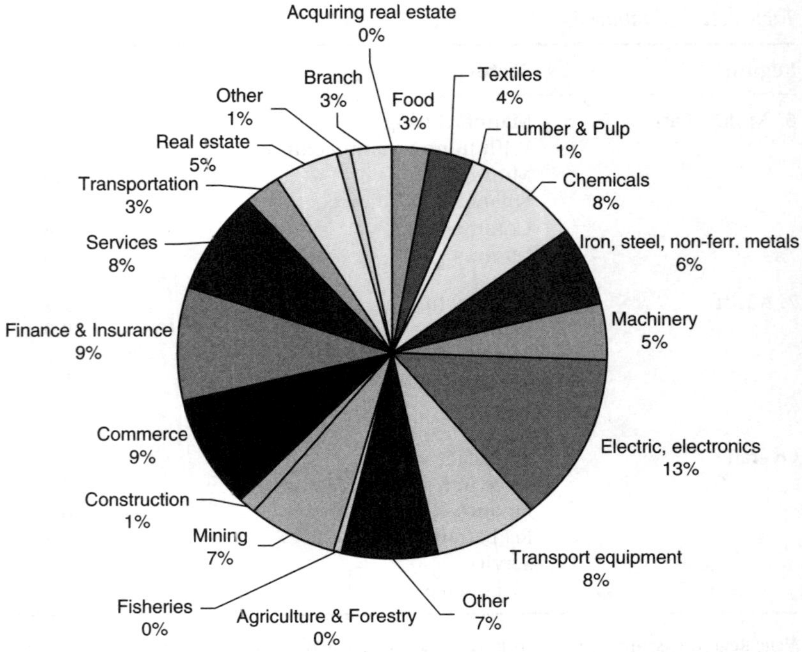


*Figure 2.11* Japanese FDI in industry in Asia, 1951–2004 (percentage shares)

future production from a given location to another country in order to become more cost competitive by raising the cost-efficiency of its product.

In the non-manufacturing sector, Japanese FDI contributes a major share to finance & insurance, commerce and services where it grew significantly. This is presented in Figure 2.11 while the period-wise picture is given in Table 2.13.

The changing profile of investment in industry in Asia over the period is outlined in Table 2.13.

The incidence of FDI is high, particularly in sectors like electronics, where the intangible assets have provided investors with a significant competitive edge. Macroeconomic developments and other country-specific advantages have also been among the crucial factors in Japanese FDI in industry in Asia.

*Table 2.13* Period-wise percentage share of Japanese investment in industry in Asia

| | 1951–80 | 1981–85 | 1986–90 | 1991–2004 | 1951–2004 |
|---|---|---|---|---|---|
| Food | 1.5 | 1.1 | 3.3 | 2.8 | 2.7 |
| Textiles | 9.4 | 2.7 | 2.4 | 3.4 | 3.6 |
| Lumber & pulp | 1.4 | 0.5 | 1.2 | 1.0 | 1.0 |
| Chemicals | 7.4 | 6.0 | 4.7 | 8.5 | 7.6 |
| Iron, steel, non-ferrous metals | 10.5 | 7.0 | 4.0 | 6.3 | 6.2 |
| Machinery | 2.8 | 3.2 | 3.8 | 5.0 | 4.5 |
| Electric, electronics | 5.5 | 3.0 | 12.0 | 15 0 | 13.2 |
| Transport equipment | 2.7 | 4.4 | 3.6 | 9.5 | 7.8 |
| Other | 5.3 | 2.6 | 4.7 | 8.1 | 7.0 |
| **Manufacturing** | **46.5** | **30.6** | **39.6** | **59.6** | **53.6** |
| Agriculture & forestry | 2.2 | 0.3 | 0.3 | 0.2 | 0.4 |
| Fisheries | 0.7 | 0.3 | 0.3 | 0.5 | 0.5 |
| Mining | 30.8 | 33.3 | 4.1 | 3.0 | 6.7 |
| Construction | 0.8 | 1.6 | 1.8 | 1.4 | 1.5 |
| Commerce | 4 | 6.8 | 9.4 | 9.1 | 8.7 |
| Finance & insurance | 2.8 | 5.5 | 12.7 | 8.8 | 8.9 |
| Services | 6.4 | 12.7 | 13.5 | 6.8 | 8.3 |
| Transportation | 0.0 | 2.7 | 3.1 | 2.9 | 2.7 |
| Real estate | 0.4 | 3.2 | 9.4 | 4.2 | 4.8 |
| Other | 4.6 | 1.7 | 3.9 | 0.1 | 1.1 |
| **Non-manufacturing** | **52.7** | **68.0** | **58.9** | **36.9** | **43.5** |
| Branch | 0.9 | 1.4 | 1.9 | 3.5 | 2.9 |
| Total | 100.0 | 100.0 | 100.0 | 100.0 | 100.0 |

## 2.6 A summary profile

Internationalization of Japanese FDI and the dramatic scale of its growth – reaching about one-quarter of total global outflows in the 1980s – constitute an important landmark in the development of the world economy and a turnaround in the case of many of the developing countries. One striking feature of this is its near-cyclical pattern with twists and turns. It was triggered by a combination of 'push' and 'pull' factors operating in Japan and in the major recipients of FDI. The 'push' factors included the rising cost pressures driving out production activities to cheaper cites located across the borders while the 'pull' factors being the attractive determinants. The strengthening yen, and the 'bubble economy', gave firms ready access to low-cost capital in order to finance expansion abroad, and also stimulated manufacturing firms to rapidly expand their production operations outside high-cost Japan.

Secondly, the dynamic aspect in the internationalization pattern of Japanese FDI has been an orientation and a return to developing countries where they had a competitive advantage – *albeit* partly due to *late development factors*. For instance, the internationalization of Japanese firms in the 1960s and 1970s represented an export of Japan's 'double structure' of labour-intensive trading industries which went abroad and capital-intensive modern heavy industry which stayed primarily at home (Ozawa 1990).

Thirdly, the overwhelming portion of Japanese FDI continues to go to developed countries – now mostly to Europe – although in recent years the overall share has been declining. It is observed that, on the whole, while in the rising phase, the developed countries attracted more Japanese investment, in the declining phase of Japanese FDI outflows; the developed countries were more adversely affected than the developing countries. The developed countries are considered to be a desirable destination by most Japanese investors as these countries represent the largest export markets, effective production and sales bases and networks for serving the world market conditions (market size, growth potential, demand for high value added goods and so on). The interest in developing countries has been confined to production for export and making use of the trade treaties that developing countries have with developed ones, which enabled Japan to export to these countries competitively.

Fourthly, the changing geography of Japanese FDI outflows reflects the dynamic interaction of the new parameters of international location – economic, technical, and organizational and policy factors. The shifts in the geographical pattern of Japanese FDI indicate significant changes – both worldwide as well as within Asia. Until the early 1980s, with few exceptions, developing countries drew more than half of Japanese FDI. However, subsequently, developed countries witnessed a jump, reaching a peak of over 79 per cent in 1990. And North America was the largest recipient of Japanese FDI until almost the year 2000. Thereafter, Europe has taken the lead – the average share of Europe during the period 2000–04 was 35.5 per cent, compared to 21.6 per cent for North America. Japanese FDI flows have been very meagre in the low-income countries of Africa and the Middle East. This may be principally because investors lack any motive to invest there – that is, whether or not the motive is resource-seeking, market-seeking, efficiency-seeking or strategic asset-seeking.

Fifthly, Asia is important in terms of both the internalization and the revitalization of Japanese FDI. As Japan was exploring new efficiency-making production bases, the East Asian economies moved much faster as they put in place an attractive investment environment, comprising improved macroeconomic fundamentals, infrastructure and systems of incentives. In comparison with the pattern in other regions, the manufacturing sector in Asia has been attracting a major share of Japanese FDI. This was mainly driven by the sharply expanding investment in the electrical industry, followed by transport equipment and the chemical industry which has been one of its distinctive characteristics in this region. Internalization advantages arising out of skill intensity, high R&D, and market promotion activities seem to have been greater in the case of these sectors.

### 2.6.1 Perspectives and challenges

1. The study reveals that Europe in the developed region and Asia in the developing region hold the future of Japanese FDI outflows.
2. In Asia, the waves of Japanese FDI activity over the decades signal the different phases of economic dynamism and linkages. The *first phase* – until almost the latter half of the 1980s – saw the flows rise sharply to NIEs while in the *second phase* beginning in the early 1990s, which also marks the start of the downturn in Japanese FDI outflows, the focus shifted to ASEAN countries. In the *third phase*, since 2001, a major portion of the FDI to East Asia is now flowing to China which has attracted substantially more FDI than the ASEAN-4 countries taken as a whole. A comparative picture of the Japanese FDI flows in China and ASEAN-4 given in Figure 2.12 shows clearly how, from a meagre start, China has overtaken ASEAN-4.

   Five-yearly average annual Japanese FDI flows from 1980 to 2006 are given in Table 2.14.
3. Economic attractions appear to be becoming stronger in China, compared to the ASEAN-4. After China's accession to the WTO, the Japanese MNCs have rapidly expanded their production sites in China. Now it has become the top destination of Japanese FDI outflows attracting $4.6 billion out of the total of $9.4 billion to Asia in 2004 – that is, 49 per cent of the level attained in that year. In 2005 and 2006, China attracted as much as $6.8 billion and $6.7 billion out of $16 billion and $16.6 billion respectively flowing to this region. For the ASEAN region, there are rising challenges from China. Even though ASEAN is working steadily towards greater integration, Japan can play a critical role in further upgrading these economies.
4. The quality of the basic economic determinants of FDI remains at the heart of the wide gap in inter-country, inter-temporal variation in Japanese FDI outflows between and within NIEs, ASEAN-4, China and India.[1] In perspective, this is vindicated by the fact that among the Asian NIEs, Hong Kong and Singapore have had the lion's share

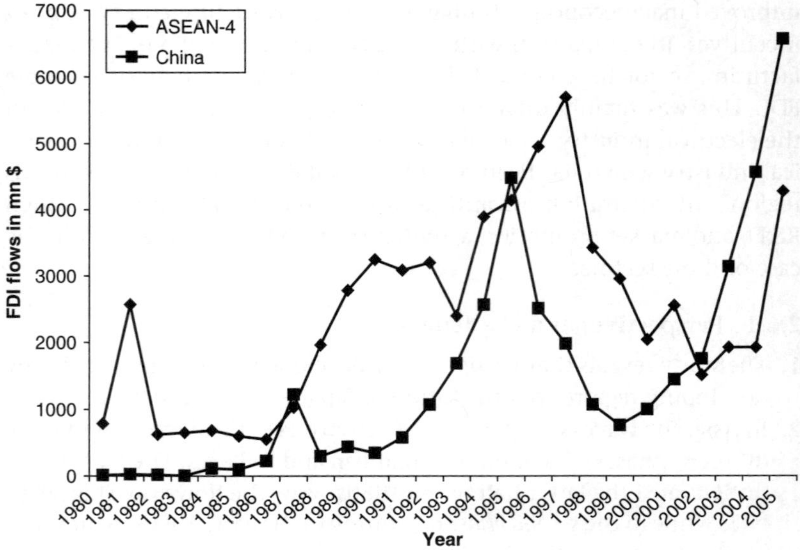


*Figure 2.12* Japanese FDI in China and ASEAN-4

*Table 2.14* Average annual Japanese FDI flows in China and ASEAN-4 (US$ million)

| Year | China | ASEAN-4 |
|---|---|---|
| 1980–85 | 46 | 1,023 |
| 1986–90 | 507 | 1,915 |
| 1991–95 | 2,077 | 3,341 |
| 1996–2000 | 1,470 | 3,815 |
| 2001–06 | 3,945 | 3,045 |

of the region's FDI flows since the early 1970s. Prior to that, Korea and Taiwan had major shares. Among the ASEAN-4, Thailand's performance in attracting FDI was the most dramatic, with its share in the regional flows growing from about 8 per cent to over 28 per cent over the period while Malaysia and the Philippines were lower down the scale. The most affected country was Indonesia, which received the maximum share of almost 50 per cent of the total in the 1960s, falling to about 4 per cent by 2006. Thus, China and the countries of East Asia lie at a more advanced stage on the Japanese FDI path. India is well behind the others in enticing Japanese FDI.[2]

# 3 Japanese Investors' Perceptions of Location Advantages

## 3.1 Introduction

Asia's industrializing economies – the NIEs and the ASEAN-4 – have been one of the most rapidly liberalizing host regions for Japanese FDI from the developing countries. China has now emerged and is one of the front-runners in this process. India is also set to join this league. And although India and China have received the world's attention for being the 'last significant untapped markets left in the 21st century', yet India, as we saw in the last chapter, ranks lowest in the ladder in attracting Japanese FDI. It appears to be trapped in a self-fulfilling low level unable to attract Japanese FDI, which remains at less than 1 per cent of overseas Japanese foreign investment. Therefore, we had to look for an answer which might offer an adequate explanation of Japanese investors' perceptions of location advantages and devise an appropriate methodology.

Before doing so, some broad observations are called for. China's total FDI – which includes that from Japan – averaged about US$47 billion per annum in the period from 1998 to 2004. Compared to this, India's average was a mere $3 billion a year – that is, 6.4 per cent of China during the same period. Taking the recent three years from 2003 to 2005, the average annual investment in the case of China comes to US$62.2 billion while that of India comes to an average of a mere US$5.6 billion, despite claiming FDI-friendly improvement. In fact, China attained a level of $72.4 billion in 2005, excluding Hong Kong, as against US$6.6 billion by India in that year (see UNCTAD's *World Investment Reports*, from 1998 to 2006).

In the impressive growth of FDI flows to China, Japan has played an important role, as is also the case for NIEs and ASEAN-4. China has now become a leading country in attracting Japanese FDI in Asia. This is borne out by the fact that in the year 2004, it received almost 50 per cent of total Japanese FDI in Asia. During the period 2001–06 the share stood at 24.3 per cent, compared to 1.2 per cent to India during the same period (JETRO's *White Papers* and the website).

The relative share of Japanese investment in India's total FDI has not only been minimal, but has also been subject to a high degree of fluctuation. For instance, the share of Japanese FDI in the total, which stood at above 8 per cent during the early 1980s, fell in the second half of the 1980s to less than 4 per cent. Japanese companies showed a good response during the initial years of India's economic reforms – that is, 1991 and 1992. But the response seems to have cooled later and the percentage share fell and has remained as low as in the 3–5 per cent range from 1980 to 2005 (*Foreign Collaborations*, Ministry of Science & Technology, Government of India).

India has not been successful as China and other major FDI-seeking East Asian countries in attracting Japanese FDI, even though it has regularly been receiving Japanese aid (ODA) since the 1950s. By 1986, Japan had become India's largest donor. In fact, India received its highest level of economic support at a particularly critical moment, when it faced a payments crisis in 1991. Secondly, of all of the developing economies, India is one of the few countries in which Japan showed a keen interest to invest even before investing in China, but this did not meet with much success. Thirdly, the 'triad pattern' of investment, displaying a high correlation between ODA, trade and FDI, did not apply to India despite the desire of Japanese investors to do so. Despite having close historical and economic ties, Japanese firms have not been motivated to re-locate facilities and establish production bases in India as was done in the case of China and East Asia as they could not foresee any comparative advantage in this. The relocation of Japanese production bases within East Asia has also been driven by the changing comparative advantages of host countries – that is, the NIEs, ASEAN countries, and China in a manner predicted by the 'Flying Geese' theory (see Ozawa 1990; Urata 1998).

The data available are not sufficient to bring out a close analysis of the significant variables for apparent Japanese reluctance with respect to India. In addition, the available data on factors that influence the location are too scarce. A number of factors that influence the decision on FDI flows, such as control systems, exchange regulation, an adequate policy framework, the reaction of the investors to bureaucratic control, the strength of trade unionism and labour laws supportive of the unions and the investors' assessment of the efficiency of the management capability in the host country, are not amenable to quantification. This leads to the use of surrogates, which may not adequately reflect the intended explanatory variable. Thus, given the limited type of data available and the level of significance we could not confidently say that any association that may be found to be statistically significant between measurable independent variables would be meaningfully usable, to ensure that their manipulation by government will result in corresponding increases in Japanese FDI flows. Additionally, it has also often been pointed out that although the Indian policy environment is comparable to that of the East Asian economies is still unable to attract the same level of FDI as these countries.

## 3.2 Methodology

It is important to investigate why Japan – a global investor – has been lukewarm in its choice of India as a destination for FDI, despite the fact that India also has a liberalized FDI regime which is almost comparable to that of China and the ASEAN countries and is also the largest recipient of Japanese development assistance (ODA). In order to do this it was necessary to compare the perception of Japanese MNEs investing in India, China and the countries of East Asia and also to examine the experience of the investors investing in other foreign countries but not in India and the reasons for not making India a destination for FDI. This required data on different parameters to analyse the presence of Japanese MNEs in these countries on a comparable basis. However, the data set covering important policy and structural aspects is hard to come by. In addition, there is little available data on the factors influencing the location of Japanese FDI. We decided to approach the investors directly.[1] Questionnaires were prepared to collect first-hand primary information directly from the investors. Needless to add, there is a clear advantage in using information originating directly from the MNEs of the source country.

### 3.2.1 The questionnaires

Country-specific advantages are comparative in nature. MNEs decide on location-specific advantages between comparable countries. For example, a rating of the location advantages of India is not comparable with those of the USA and Western Europe, but it is comparable to China and East Asia. This was kept in mind while devising the questionnaires.

Two sets of questionnaires were prepared and circulated to prominent Japanese MNEs to get their feedback on the experience gained by them from investment in India, China and East Asia, and from investors investing in countries other than India. This method would better explain the exact reasons for Japanese investors' apathy to investment in India and the environmental, institutional and policy milieu required to entice them. In devising a suitable methodology, the aim is to achieve an accelerated growth of Japanese FDI for India, as is the case with China and East Asia. It is clear from this that such an analysis requires much more than the tinkering with parameters that has characterized many of the earlier studies that have relied on the use of secondary data.

A relatively small set of multinational enterprises (MNEs) account for most of the world's investment. In the global context, the largest 500 MNEs account for over 90 per cent of the world's stock of FDI (Rugman and Verbeke 2004). Vast majorities operate within their home leg. And for Japanese MNEs, China, South and East Asia constitute the home leg countries. We were fortunate to obtain a full response from the Japanese MNEs operating in this region. In this respect, the Chambers of Commerce and Industry of Japan, Nagoya, Osaka, Hiroshima and Yokohama, with whom a series of detailed discussions were held, were extremely helpful. Based on the discussions, the MNEs were addressed.

To obtain comprehensive and elaborate answers, detailed questionnaires were designed for two groups of Japanese MNEs, as shown below:

(i) Firms investing in India, China and East Asian countries; and
(ii) Firms having investments in China and East Asia, but not in India.

A separate questionnaire was also devised for domestic-oriented companies in order to elicit their views on international orientation. Since these are not connected to the issues raised here, they are considered in the next chapter.

The questions ranged from simple queries to more basic issues such as their business objectives, the goals achieved, their preference for doing business in the countries of East Asia, China and India, the strengths and weaknesses of doing business in these countries, control systems, the status of the infrastructure, the management style, their interest in making further investment in India, and so on.[2] The MNEs represented diverse areas of activity – from high-tech electronics, automotive, chemical industries, capital goods machinery to consumer-durables and non-durables. These include a range of companies, from super giant companies to relatively medium-sized ones. Thus, the distribution of these MNEs is not skewed but fairly even.

### 3.2.2 Identification and the rating of variables

Variables were identified after detailed discussions with the chambers of commerce and industry and the investors. These related to:

(i) Business preferences
(ii) Infrastructure
(iii) Management practices
(iv) Controls and restrictions
(v) Administrative complexities
(vi) Market size and labour.

In the questionnaires, two grading methods were applied. *First,* the Japanese MNEs were asked to give their grading for certain performances with regard to investment in India *vis-à-vis* China and East Asia on a five-point scale ranging from: (–) 2: very bad; (–) 1: bad; (0): indifferent; (+) 1: good; and (+) 2: very good. A zero rating would mean that with respect to the given variables there are few differences between India and other Asian countries, (–) 2 would indicate an adverse comment on India compared to the other Asian countries, and (+) 2 a very positive comment.

Secondly, for certain variables, such as the desire to invest, the use of management techniques, networking etc., a binary yes/no method was applied. All of these MNEs have subsidiaries and/or joint ventures in the concerned countries, in addition to their activities in Japan.

### 3.2.3 Weighting diagram

Companies with a larger scale of operation are likely to be more valuable than those that are smaller. Therefore, an attempt has been made to estimate the average values from the ratings given by the firms to the criteria chosen for the present study and on which we have gathered information through our survey. As the first elementary analysis, each firm was given equal weight regardless of size. However, while the simple average gives a reasonable idea of how Japanese investors as a whole feel about the FDI in a country compared to the others, it does not give adequate weight to the size or the standing of the firm giving the ratings.

The *Japan Company Handbooks* furnish the financial and operational details of a large number of companies in Japan. Of the information given in the *Handbooks* (2004), we examined three variables – namely, total assets; total capital stock; and total number of employees for each firm. Using these variables as weights it was possible to estimate the weighted average ratings corresponding to each, which could give the size of the firm a proper representation in ascertaining the strength of the reasons advanced by the firms regarding investment.

Thus, four alternative systems of averaging – i.e., simple average and three weighted averages using three different systems of weighting, viz., total assets, total capital stock and total number of employees as weights – have been used. But, wherever the weighted averages based on these three variables were giving almost similar results, we presented a single weighted average based on 'total assets' as weights alongside the un-weighted one. But wherever there was a difference, we have presented the results of all the four alternative systems of weighting to get a comparative picture.

Furthermore, since the data are qualitative in nature, an attempt has also been made to undertake a limited application of the ordered logit model in order to identify the significant variables affecting the investment decision of the Japanese MNEs.

## 3.3 Investors' perception of India, China and East Asia: motives and preferences

### 3.3.1 Business motivations

Studies on the motives of MNEs in general and of Japanese investments in particular, in developed and developing countries were surveyed from the literature (namely, Barrell and Pain 1999; Bayoumi and Lipworth 1998; Benjamin and Ilan 1996; Buckley and Casson 1991; Caves 1996; Dunning 1992; Grosse and Trevino 1996; Rugman 2002; Cleeve 2000; Sazanami 1992; Tuman and Craig 1999; Mody *et al.* 1999).

The investors have multiple goals in mind and approach different countries with different combinations of goals in view. The MNEs were asked to identify their objectives for investment in these countries. The main reasons offered were: (a) Market, (b) Export to Japan, (c) Export to third country, (d) Relatively cheaper labour, (e) Presence of other Japanese firms, (f) Presence of R&D institutions.

Results varied widely. The results had shown that in all 26 combinations of objectives have taken place – theoretically, as many as 63 combinations can occur (see the endnote to chapter 3: 'business objectives'). In the case of both India and China, the 'market' variable got highest occurrence followed by 'market with relatively cheap labour'. In the case of China, exports to 'third country' and 'to Japan' came next. This was followed by the 'presence of other Japanese firms'. The lowest was 'presence of R&D institutions'. In the case of East Asia, however, export to Japan and to third countries constituted the main goals. Most Japanese companies have invested in the region as part of their global expansion plans to enter a large market and to serve as a base for export.[3] Japanese FDI in India has been essentially market-seeking in nature (see Table 3A.1 at the end of this book).

In respect of the achievement of goals, there was a wide variation in the responses of investors. The stated objectives seem to have been realized in different degrees from the countries. In the case of India, goals were realized but mostly only partially, especially where the stated objectives were other than the market. This is borne out from the replies given by the investors. Several factors seem to have contributed to making the country unattractive to foreign investors.[4]

### 3.3.2 Business preference under equal conditions

The general perception of India and China as being promising market and prospective investment destinations is reflected in the evaluation of India by Japanese firms from time to time. According to a survey by the former Export–Import Bank of Japan (now known as the Japan Bank for International Cooperation – JBIC) in 1998, India ranked third among the prospective destinations for their long-term (ten years) target planning, behind only China and the USA. In another survey in 2003, the Japan Bank of International Cooperation (JBIC) asked the investors about their business plans over the medium term. In a ranking of the most promising for business development, the top three positions were occupied by China, followed by Thailand and the USA. These were followed by Vietnam and India. The ranking of India slipped down, but nonetheless it was there. However, despite high evaluations of India as a promising investment destination, FDI from Japan to India has shown little increase in contrast to the significant increases for China and the ASEAN countries.[5]

*Business preference: results*

According to our study, the business preference for India *vis-à-vis* China and East Asia revealed that, other things being equal, 33 per cent of the firms feel that there would be no difference between these countries, while another 40 per cent feel that it would be either good or very good to invest in India. Only 27 per cent feel it is either bad or very bad to invest in India compared to China and East Asia. This finding is reinforced when weighted averages are used, as may be seen from Table 3.1.

The overall un-weighted average rating turns out to be positive (+0.13), *albeit* only marginally so. By and large, the un-weighted average shows some indifference between India *vis-à-vis* China and East Asia. However, if weights indicating the size of the firms are used, the tendency is for a greater preference for India for the entire three alternative weighting

*Table 3.1* Business preference for India *vis-à-vis* China and East Asia: overall parametric values of mean and standard deviation

| | **Un-weighted** | **Weighted** | | |
|---|---|---|---|---|
| | | **Total assets** | **Capital stock** | **Employment** |
| Mean | 0.13 | 0.41 | 0.26 | 0.33 |
| S.D. | 1.12 | 1.28 | 1.26 | 1.35 |
| Range | (–) 0.99 to 1.25 | (–) 0.87 to +1.69 | (–) 1.00 to 1.52 | (–) 1.02 to 1.68 |

*Note*: *Here by range is meant mean ± s.d.

patterns. It shows that, given the other things, Japanese firms would have a greater preference to invest in India as against China, though this was not translated into reality.

## 3.4 Constraints

### 3.4.1 Infrastructure

Infrastructure – physical, social and of governance – is one of the most powerful instruments of economic and social change that the world has ever seen and decisively requires a sharp policy focus. The development of world-class infrastructure is a pivotal factor for globalization and a major vehicle of growth. Its characterization is often depicted on binary oppositions such as strong/weak, efficient/inefficient, good/bad – as something needed or lacking in terms of international standards. Many critical infrastructures such as electricity – improving, strengthening and promoting its efficacy – involves the use of 'networking' permitting an 'unbundling' of activities – such as generation, transmission, and distribution functions, establishment of the regulatory system and so forth. There is also the question of promotion of efficient and responsive service delivery and improving the quality. In short, infrastructure encompasses diverse sectors in an equally wide range of setting. Here, however, we consider a few of the cross-cutting issues in the context of attracting FDI.

*Position of physical infrastructure*

The data published on physical infrastructure in respect of these Asian countries, and presented in Table 3.2, throws some light on their relative position.

Infrastructure and development are known to be parallel processes as its dynamic stimulation and linkages to the economy are multiple and complex because it affects production and consumption directly, and

*Table 3.2* The position of physical infrastructure

| Country | Paved roads (%) | Per capita electric consumption | | | Telephone (per 000 people) | | Access to improved water source |
|---|---|---|---|---|---|---|---|
| | 2000–04 | 2000 | 2002 | 2004 | 2001 | 2005 | 2005 @ |
| India | 47.4 | 355 | 380 | 457 | 38 | 45 (82) | 1,152 |
| China | 81.0 | 827 | 987 | 1,585 | 137 | 269 (302) | 2,156 |
| Hong Kong | 100.0 | – | 5,612 | 5,699 | – | 546 (1,252) | – |
| Korea | 86.8 | 5,607 | 6,171 | 7,391 | 486 | 492 (794) | 1,344 |
| Singapore | 100.0 | 6948 | 7,039 | 8,170 | – | 425 (1,010) | – |
| Philippines | – | 477 | 459 | 597 | 41 | 41 (419) | 5,767 |
| Thailand | 98.5 | 1,448 | 1,626 | 1,865 | 99 | 110 (430) | 3,269 |
| Malaysia | 81.3 | 2,628 | 2,832 | 3,166 | – | 172 (771) | 22,882 |
| Indonesia | 58.0 | 384 | 411 | 478 | 35 | 58 (213) | 12,867 |
| Low income | – | – | 312 | 375 | 30 | 37 (77) | 3,149 |
| Middle income | 50.5 | – | 1,422 | 1,840 | 152 | 211 (379) | 8,677 |
| High income | 100.0 | – | 8,693 | 9,609 | 593 | 503 (835) | 9,640 |
| World | – | – | 2,225 | 2,606 | 172 | 180 (342) | 6,794 |

*Notes*: 1. Figures within brackets indicate mobile subscribers per 1,000 people.
2. @ Refers to renewable internal freshwater resources in terms of per capita cu.m.
3. –: Not available.
*Source*: *World Development Indicators*, 2002 to 2007; *Human Development Report*, 2003 to 2006.

generates developmental and spillover effects. Illustratively, in Japan the technological innovations in the infrastructure sector dramatically improved its economic performance. During the 1960s and 1970s at the beginning of the period of rapid economic growth, emergency priority was given to achieving much higher levels of transport power. This caused widespread changes in transportation. The plan to build the Shinkansen making use of state-of-the-art automation technology was part of this plan.

The *World Development Report* (1994) divides this into physical and social-institutional infrastructure – the former includes services such as electricity, transport, roads, water system, communication, and so on, while the latter includes education, health facilities and other forms of infrastructure. The *Report* has given startlingly high returns of infrastructure. This is obvious because it is a driving force in generating surplus, for cost reduction, for intensive exploitation of factors of production and potential resources, in improving the distribution system, in integrating the market forces. This is rated as a driving force in the location choice of FDI.

### *FDI and infrastructure*

There appears to be a high degree of correlation between FDI and infrastructure. The empirical evidence shows that FDI is attracted to countries that possess acceptable levels of infrastructure facilities. Wheeler and Mody (1992) analysed the determinants in the case of US MNEs in manufacturing and electronics and found that tax and other short-run incentives have only a limited impact on location choice, but countries with good infrastructure development and with specialized input suppliers attracted FDI. In their analysis, Root and Ahmed (1979) also found infrastructure to be an important determinant for LDCs.

Belderbos *et al.* (2001) confirms that for Japanese MNEs' FDI vertical linkages, the size of the local component industry and infrastructure facilities is important. Likewise, Loree and Guisinger (1995) for US MNEs, Cheng and Kwan (2000) for China, and Kokko and Zejan (1996) for a study based on Vietnam stressed that weak infrastructure was an impediment to investment. Some of the studies have emphasized certain specific infrastructure facilities like railways (Chen 1996), transport infrastructure (Coughlin *et al.* 1991), and the facility to network (Chen and Chen 1998) for FDI.

### *Results of the study*

India's infrastructure sector, characterized by a growing demand and looming shortages, gets the worst rating when compared to China

*Table 3.3* Rating of infrastructure: India compared to NIEs, ASEAN-4 and China (un-weighted and weighted mean & standard deviation*)

| | **Physical infrastructure*** | | | |
|---|---|---|---|---|
| | **Telecom** | **Electricity** | **Transport** | **Water** |
| *Un-weighted* | | | | |
| Mean | (–) 1.2 | (–) 1.43 | (–) 1.23 | (–) 1.13 |
| SD | 0.65 | 0.61 | 0.61 | 0.62 |
| *Weighted* | | | | |
| Mean | (–) 1.46 | (–) 1.74 | (–) 1.32 | (–) 1.21 |
| SD | 0.53 | 0.44 | 0.53 | 0.47 |

*Note*: *Responses relate to all corporate MNEs having investments in all the countries under study.
Irrespective of the nature and size of industry, all have given a rating between (–) 2 and (–1) for poor basic physical infrastructure in India compared to other countries.

and East Asia and is perceived to be the most inadequate – that is, in the fields of electricity, transport, water and telecommunications. The un-weighted average is uniformly negative for all of the components of infrastructure; with electricity receiving a maximum negative average of (–) 1.43, followed by transport (–) 1.23, telecom (–) 1.2, and water (–) 1.13 in the five grades ranging from (–) 2 to (+) 2.

The weighted averages further aggravate the negative ratings, being most marked in the case of electricity (–) 1.74. In the case of other areas of physical infrastructures also, it is more than (–) 1. Electricity and transport, which are the pivotal factors of development, receive the worst rating, followed by telecommunications and water. The results are given in Table 3.3.

The negative rating by investors is an expression of the reluctance to invest by those who are already in India and have the experience of other Asian countries. Infrastructure constraints are also hampering the process of ongoing reforms.

A very poor infrastructure network is posing many daunting problems in India which received the worst rating by the investors compared to the other countries under study. Problems with India's infrastructure sector are legendary. It is a poor infrastructure, be it in terms of electricity, water or public transport. In fact, the entire gamut of infrastructure is a classic test case known for unsatisfactory service to its customers, whether firms or households, which disrupts all aspects of life. Even though far short of demand, yet politics dominates and even determines its shape and course of events. For instance, the political economy of providing free electricity to rich farmers or under-pricing it, organizing free loan festivals is just one illustration. In most cases, the beneficiaries are influential and powerful and can influence the voters for political purposes. It is not merely a problem of resources, but it has become a highly political tool in the hands of politicians. There being no accountability, governments frequently keep prices below costs with a view to lure the voters to come to power. This mechanism has inherent contradictions, which creates adverse lock-ins and complicates the eventual introduction or efficient functioning of markets.

### 3.4.2 Public administration – governance

Public administration constitutes the most vital part of governance and also covers most of its dimensions (see Kaufmann *et al.* 1999, 2004). In fact, both 'public administration' and 'governance' are embedded and constitute the most vital part of governance infrastructure. Good public administration synonymous with good governance is country-specific and grounded solidly in the economic, political, social and administrative capacity and other realities of the country. It is recognized that a country's quality of governance is highly correlated with both its institutional quality and its level of development. A strong positive relationship exists between the quality of public administration and the efficient functioning of the economy. Among other benefits, it helps to reduce transaction costs; to reduce risks by clearly defining and enforcing the contracts; to safeguard the interests of the investors; and to circumscribe arbitrary interventions by interest groups and politicians.

*FDI and governance*

A responsive, transparent and accountable 'public administration' provides significant explanatory power for attracting FDI. Its dimensions include an effective, impartial and transparent administration, which is at the same time credible, honest and stable enough to secure investors' confidence. It embodies several elements – rules of behaviour, way and means of enforcing these rules, procedures for the mediation of conflicts, sanctions in the case of breach of the rules and organizations supporting market transactions, the effectiveness of the rule of law and control of corruption. There may be many policy declarations on paper to lure foreign investors, or many governments make big statements and even issue white papers, but the investors will be reluctant to invest in the county if they are not sure of the enforcement.

One of the biggest problems with governance is that of pervasive corruption, including political corruption. Widespread corruption entails heavy economic and social costs affecting economic and social outcomes. The pernicious role of corruption on FDI is important since it produces bottlenecks, raises costs, and heightens the level of uncertainty. It can also create distortions, because a corrupt economy does not provide open and equal market access to all competitors – it provides some companies with preferential access to profitable markets. In addition, it leads to poor enforcement of law, weakens the regulatory system, adds to political uncertainty, and makes the government less effective – all of which determine the quality of governance in any country. This situation stems from a mirage of rules simplification of which will reduce corruption and greatly influence economic performance and thereby create conditions to attract FDI.

In a study that analysed data on FDI from 12 source countries to 45 host countries in the early 1990s, Wei (2000) revealed that corruption has a significant and negative effect on FDI. Husted (1999) states that most of the correlation between government size and corruption appears to be accounted for by the power distance variable. Habib and Zurawicki (2002) provide support for the negative impact of corruption on FDI. Drabek and Payne (1999), while testing how FDI was affected by non-transparency, by a combination of corruption, unstable economic policies, and poor property rights protection and poor governance showed a negative impact of high levels of non-transparency on FDI.

*Results of the study*

It is difficult to measure the quality of governance in quantitative terms, so it was also graded on a 5-point scale from (+) 2 to (–) 2. India gets a negative rating by the investors compared to East Asia and China, as may be seen from Table 3.4.

The ratings remain negative compared to other Asian countries, whatever the measure of weight. This also very well explains Japanese reluctance as this rating is an authentic expression of Japanese investors in India who also have experience in other Asian countries. India's governance structure and institutional matrix is not only complex; but it is made more cumbersome by the different political interests of all hues.

In India over the period there is an increasing disenchantment with the quality of governance as with all other institutions of public administration. These are seen to be lacking in accountability, transparency and responsiveness. Laws have increased over the period and have become cumbersome and increasingly complex to understand while leaving a

*Table 3.4* Rating of the public administration by investors: India compared to China and East Asia

| | Un-weighted | Weighted | | |
|---|---|---|---|---|
| | | Assets | Capital stock | Employment |
| Mean | (–) 0.77 | (–) 0.53 | (–) 0.78 | (–) 0.70 |
| S.D. | 0.67 | 1.12 | 1.02 | 1.05 |
| Range | (–) 1.44 to (–) 0.10 | (–) 1.65 to (–) 0.59 | (–) 1.80 to (–) 0.24 | (–) 1.75 to (–) 0.35 |

*Note*: * Here by range is meant mean ± s.d.

lot to the discretionary powers. Flaws in the public administration are also due to a decline in bureaucratic quality, pervasive corruption and political interference. This is often compounded by a nexus between the criminals, policy makers and executive giving rise to institutionalization of competitive corruption and reflection on the extent of failure of governance.

In a survey of foreign company executives, Hong Kong-based Political & Economic Risk Consultancy Ltd. (PERC) has found that corruption had the greatest impact on India. It was dubbed the second most corrupt after Indonesia in Asia, while Singapore was ranked as the least corrupt (*Times of India*, 13 March 2003).

The *Human Development Report for South Asia*, 1999 (published by the Ul Huq Center in Islamabad) states that if India's corruption level fell to the level found in Scandinavian countries, India's FDI would grow by 12 per cent and its GDP by 1.5 per cent. It is mostly directed to lure the voters through some short-term populist policy measures.

'The Berlin Transparency International also brings out the corruption perceptions of the countries. In the year 2003 the corruption perception rank had placed China at 66 while India was ranked at 83 out of 133 countries listed in the index. The NIEs were least corrupt – Singapore was at 5th while Hong Kong and Taiwan were at the 15th and 30th positions respectively, but Korea was placed at 52. All the ASEAN-4, however, did not score well in this matrix with the exception of Malaysia, which was ranked 37. Thailand and Philippines were way down the list, at 75 and 97 respectively. The most corrupt was Indonesia at 122. However, the 2006 ranking shows marginal improvement in the corruption profile of most of these countries excepting Philippines and Indonesia which have shown further deterioration – the former has moved to 126 and the latter to 134 out of the 163 countries listed in the index. India ranked at 74 while China at 71, suggesting very little fundamental difference between India's and China's corruption profile. These countries are not in the right zone for attracting FDI from a long-term perspective. Corruption robs countries of their potential and is a daunting obstacle to development if combative measures are not taken. A country could get away with it in the short-term but faces serious long-term consequences.

In their study, Kaufmann *et al.* (1999, 2004) have taken six dimensions of governance: (i) government effectiveness, (ii) regulatory quality, (iii) rule of law, (iv) control of corruption, (v) voice and accountability, and (vi) political stability and the absence of violence. China received a better ranking than India in terms of political stability and government effectiveness while India was ranked marginally better for rule of law. In the matter of graft also, India was rated as more corrupt than China. These measures, in particular the first four, are highly correlated making it difficult to econometrically test for their relative importance. Independently taken, they have explanatory significance. However, the dimensions of governance which the authors suggest do not reveal stark differences. They are too generalized and need to be analysed cautiously. But the fact remains that shoddy governance, among other factors, is retarding India's prospects as a business destination compared to China and East Asia.

### 3.4.3 Japanese Management Technique (JMT)

The Japanese MNEs prefer to transfer home-centred management practices and systems – popularly known as Japanese Management Technique (JMT) – in their transplants in foreign locations as these are viewed to be the key to competitive advantage. JMT is very attractive to countries if it is successfully implemented and sustained over time. JMT is based not just on operational logistics or operational effectiveness, product differentiation, and market focus, but also on corporate governance such as company alliances and *keiretsu* relations built on tangible and intangible assets; decentralized management hierarchies and affable organizational structure. The introduction of JMT, including total quality control (TQC), just-in-time (JIT) and cellular manufacturing, is not merely a set of technical solutions, but a process which also involves social innovations. It is not a static concept and does not remain still; rather, it has been evolving over time to more subtle practices. It is not like one-shot algorithm but a continuous process of improvement involving social innovations. For instance, the long-run smooth and efficient inter-firm linkages with the 'club of suppliers' allow the companies to co-specialize in the development and production of complex products and facilitate technological diffusion. The existence of conglomerates called *keiretsu or* corporate alliances sheds further light on how the affiliates share certain intangible assets and exploit economies of scope (Kimura 1989). Linkages among the firms' activities in technology, production and marketing offer the firms opportunities to exploit economies of scope while minimizing the disadvantages of internal diversification. This enables members to integrate market and technology information (Kodama 1995). These practices then become integrated in the governance structure and provide for coordination and incentives, thereby allowing the companies to achieve a lower transaction cost and to maximize transaction value (Dyer & Ouchi 1993). The differential behaviour leads to vital differences in their conduct and performance.

The Japanese practices are upgraded and reinforced by ideological factors such as 'decision by consensus' system and workers' participation impending radical choices and creativity in the formation of governance structures that cultivate the development of contextual knowledge leading to the efficient and effective production of complex products, which are also a prerequisite of a successful governance strategy. These are company-ownership assets that are hard to imitate. But it is also true that a number of well-known Japanese management practices adopted during the 1970s and 1980s, such as JIT and the TQC, had later become standard practices used by non-Japanese companies. Most often quoted are Japanese automobile companies. 'By transforming traditional mass production techniques and adopting continuous improvement, cross-functional teamwork, just-in-time delivery and automation where appropriate, Japanese manufacturers were able to produce cars at lower cost, in a shorter time, using less space and fewer workers.' Operational logistics such as the system of teamwork, job rotation, and worker participation to cut costs, improve quality, assimilate new technology and develop new products have become standard industrial practices.

JMT involves first, a smooth and efficient inter-firm linkages in which all of the firms in the production chain collaborate from the outset; second it requires managerial commitment and capability at all the levels of the hierarchies; and third a qualitative human-ware technology that takes full advantage of the motivation, responsibility, creativity of the workers and places an emphasis on the acquisition of more knowledge and newer skills to enhance the learning capacity of the organization. This human-ware technology developed by Japan has demonstrated its effectiveness in raising the quality, and productivity apart from cutting costs in industries.

Japanese investors' propensity to transfer JMT across borders has been analysed exhaustively. The transplants abroad typically require the adoption of investment criteria, management information systems and productivity benchmarks which are almost identical to those used in Japan. The Japanese firms face a 'dilemma' problem when applying the system to settings in foreign countries – namely, the problem of adapting to the local managerial and regulatory environment, and the difficulties or even trade-offs that exist in the application-adaptation aspect of the transplanted production system. Differences in technology and value systems are assumed to play a major role in determining the extent to which the management practices are adopted. The most serious problem faced by the Japanese management system in the multinational setting is the challenge to effectively integrate local nationals into the mainstream of management in the foreign subsidiaries. Some have tended to emphasize the relatively short experience of Japanese companies abroad – that is, life-cycle factors – as the reason while some consider home country-factors as the primary cause for the limited success.

As the social contexts in host countries generally differ from that prevailing in Japan, the technique is being transferred, often selectively and with various adaptations in the transplants in different countries, to create a distinctive national 'hybrid' management regime – also termed the 'third culture' (Graen and Wakabayashi, 1994). While technical practices are transferred from Japan, social practices are modified or recreated through management participation, human resource development and training and the introduction of new organizational methods. However, various applications and adaptations generate different patterns of 'hybrids' blending Japanese elements and local influences within the subsidiary plants.

The systematic application of JMT seems to offer substantial efficiency benefits to investment, worker motivation, innovation and coordination (see Kawabe and Kimbara 1991; Koike 1994; Porter *et al.* 2000; Williamson 1989; Delery and Doty 1996; Lazear 1998; Gibbons and Waldman 1999; Dickens *et al.* 1986; Harriss 1995, for automobiles in Indonesia; D'Costa 1995, for automobiles in India; Kaplinsky 1994, 1995, for Latin America, India and Zimbabwe; Bos and Cole 1994 for Brazilian electronic sector; and Humphrey 1995). Japanese multinationals have also pioneered the introduction of JMT practices in western economies (Doeringer, Lorenz and Terkla 2003 for the USA, the UK and France; Kenney and Florida, 1993; Doeringer *et al.* 1998; Kujawa 1983 for the USA; Munday 1990; Elger and Smith 1998; Wakabayashi *et al.* 1991).

Japanese multinationals operating in western countries provide the most extensive evidence on the extent to which Japanese-style management is transferred. Among the western countries – in particular, among the USA, the UK and France – it is the USA that has the highest adoption of JMT – being almost entirely accounted for by the exceptionally high adoption rate of quality circles and self-managing teams – followed by France and then the UK (Doeringer *et al.* 2003). Kujawa and associates investigated the outcomes of Japanese management practices at ten US plants of Japanese manufacturers and argued that it has improved its quality and production efficiency. Kujawa's major finding was that at the larger plants, JMT was used more extensively and concluded that the implementation decision would ultimately depend on the judgement and initiative of the local management.

*Results of the present study – degree of adoption*

In our sample most of the investors also feel it is relevant to use JMT in their subsidiaries abroad, but few were able to introduce the system successfully. The degree of adoption, as well as the nature of impediments that investors face, differs from country to country (Table 3.5).

Only 30 per cent of the Japanese transplants in India could partially adopt their management practices, even though more than 60 per cent consider it to be relevant to adopt. Furthermore, even those who adopted this could rarely adopt the complete management system that is found to be in operation in their large enterprises in Japan.

In China and East Asia, where the 'miracle' of economic growth was primarily FDI-led, the success percentage is much higher. Japanese manufacturing firms implemented the transfer of their management systems with production technologies to these economies. These countries are characterized by a fundamentally sequential-staged development from Japan.

*Table 3.5* Degree of adoption of JMT in India, China and East Asia

| **Degree of adoption (percentage)** | | | **Whether JMT is relevant to the transplants abroad? (percentage)** |
|---|---|---|---|
| **India** | **China** | **East Asia** | |
| 30 = Yes<br>60 = No<br>10 = No response | 50 = Yes<br>33 = No<br>17 = No response | 60 = Yes<br>30 = No<br>10 = No response | 63 = Yes<br>30 = No<br>7 = No response |

A Japanese Multinational Enterprise Study Group (JMNESG) also investigated how Japanese transplants have been transferring production systems to local settings in different Asian countries and found that the Japanese system, on the whole, got a higher application score there compared to other countries.

*Impediments*

The operating conditions and the institutional environment are significantly different in these countries to be amenable to the systematic implementation of JMT in its breadth of diffusion and depth of adoption. A number of system-level obstacles come in the way of its adoption. These include: lack of intense human resource management systems, face-to-face information sharing, negotiation, and coordination based on dense human network and quality of human resources. These are compounded by the difficulty of maintaining efficient inter-firm linkages and lack of managerial commitment at different levels of the hierarchies to the adoption of JMT (see also Kaplinsky 1994, 1995). Furthermore, there are relatively complex and tough bureaucratic procedures determining job classification and the structure of internal job ladders and labour force. There is lack of managerial commitment; poor infrastructure and the lack of strict adherence to total quality control (TQC) and the just-in-time (JIT) procedures. It is not like a one-shot algorithm but is a continuous process of improvement involving social innovations.

Investors' observations regarding the constraints to the adoption of JMT in their subsidiaries in these countries are significant. Table 3.6 presents the major impediments faced by the Japanese investors in India, China and East Asia.

Japanese transplants in India, except partially in isolated cases, could not adopt the complete system of management practices found in their large enterprises in Japan. Those adopting JMT in India fall into the category of 'moderately successful follower' to 'weakly successful follower' using Kaplinsky's terminology. They are not adopting it as an integrated package but as 'stand alone', making use of isolated aspects where possible. Among the industries, the automobile sector is relatively more successful, followed by machinery and electronics.

The focal point of JMT is the human factor. Its core components are: quality circles, job rotation, self-managing teams and employees having responsibility for quality. But most companies consider Indian labour to be slow, not quality conscious, careless and lacking in the team spirit and information-sharing so vital for the application of the JMT. Then

*Table 3.6* Impediments to the adoption of JMT in India, China and East Asia as reported by the investors

| Countries | | |
|---|---|---|
| **India** | **China** | **East Asia** |
| 1. Large gap between management concepts of India and Japan and even in the introduction of modern management systems | 1. Difficult to maintain the quality of the product | 1. Do not maintain business secrets |
| 2. Corporate culture differences, e.g., Japanese corporate culture develops suppliers while India selects suppliers | 2. Directed to produce according to the government's desire | 2. Job hopping |
| 3. Difference in views on the sense of punctuality and about job-work by the labor | 3. Imitate the product with out license | 3. Not good in information sharing |
| 4. Lack of team spirit | 4. Job hopping | |
| 5. Gap in the perception between labor & management | 5. Not good in sharing information | |
| 6. Labour slow and not quality conscious | 6. Problem of raw material | |
| 7. Differences in perception and don't want to learn from foreign countries | 7. Non-execution of credit and debt contracts | |
| 8. Restrictive and unclear labour laws | 8. Foreign currency regulations | |
| 9. Problems of strike, labour union and asserting their rights by using labour laws, difficult to lay-off | | |
| 10. Infrastructure problems | | |
| 11. Different environment and social practices; unable to understand the values and concept | | |
| 12. Unsuitable business environment, problem of graft, caste problem | | |
| 13. Difficulty in getting the high quality raw materials | | |
| 14. Unreasonable bureaucracy | | |

*Note*: These are exactly the points advanced by the investors.

they are work-specific and difficult to lay-off. The Indian worker is alien to the key elements of JMT. The Japanese management, however, prefers multi-skilled, soft and job-rotating type of labour.

In the case of China and East Asia, the labour problems are of a different nature. They relate principally to the problem of maintaining business information, job-hopping and information-sharing drawbacks.

The responses of Japanese MNEs to the adoption of JMT in their transplants in India, China and East Asia clearly underline the quality of the workforce as central to the success of the technique.

### 3.4.4 Controls and restrictions

The control systems refer to controls on the import of capital goods, components, materials and finished goods, controls on the repatriation of profits, investment, manufacturing of goods and exchange controls. These can either directly or indirectly affect FDI through their effect on market imperfections. Mody *et al.* (1999) found that the inability to repatriate earnings was a strong disincentive for Japanese investment. Studies show that openness and a liberalized investment regime attract FDI (see Caves 1996; Lecraw 1984; Koechlin 1992). UNCTC (1992) documented the general relaxation of LDC host controls on FDI, finding a positive effect of more favourable terms on foreign investment. A study by the IMF (2000) corroborates this finding. Control systems increase the transaction costs and stand in the way of FDI. Cleeve (2000) found transaction costs to be important in influencing FDI while wage differences were not. Veugelers (1991) found controls and administrative complexities not important for investment in the developed countries but significant for investments in LDCs.

*Investors' rating*

In the matter of control systems, India is again not the preferred option. As many as 48 per cent of the sample firms characterized India's control system as being either bad or very bad for investment. Only 20 per cent felt it was just good while 32 per cent perceived no difference compared to the countries of Southeast Asia.

It is seen that the adverse reaction under the simple average is further corroborated by using size as weights, which shows that, regardless of size, all firms have an equally adverse reaction to the Indian control system on the ground, notwithstanding its policy pronouncements on paper. Estimation of the overall average ratings, both un-weighted and weighted, are presented in Table 3.7. The results further reinforce the negative perceptions regarding the Indian control systems.

*Barriers to entry*

Another aspect of the control system refers to entry barriers or limits to ownership. There are legal barriers and vary to a large degree between India, China, and the ASEAN countries. Japanese FDI flows are the recorded achievements of ASEAN and China having removed most of

*Table 3.7* Average ratings of the control system in India compared to the countries of East Asia and China

| | Un-weighted | Weighted | | |
|---|---|---|---|---|
| | | Assets | Capital stock | Employment |
| Mean | (–) 0.4 | (–) 0.38 | (–) 0.58 | (–) 0.60 |
| S.D. | 0.94 | 1.62 | 1.07 | 1.04 |
| Range | (–) 1.34 to 0.54 | (–) 2.00 to 1.24 | (–) 1.65 to 0.49 | (–) 1.64 to 0.44 |

*Note*: *Here by range is meant mean ± s.d.

the barriers. In India, imposing a ban on FDI in the fast-growing retail sector, real estate sectors, disinvestment of public sector undertakings and allowing a limited entry into a number of industrial, financial and service activities – for instance, in the small-scale sector FDI is limited to a mere 24 per cent while in the insurance sector it is 26 per cent. The same is the case with the banking sector. India is still nowhere near setting up institutions that are essential for an efficient market economy and competing in the global economy. The contemporary comparative experience also does not seem to clearly favor such a policy stance.

The other types of regulatory burdens faced by the investors in these countries also pose as barriers to entry. These are mainly: First, a number of procedures, time and cost over runs are involved both in starting a business and dealing with licenses; secondly, registering the property, enforcing the contracts and closing a business pose daunting problems; and thirdly, there are rigidities in employment and hiring and firing. On the whole NIEs present a better picture, with Singapore at the top, followed by ASEAN, excepting Indonesia. More importantly, India and China, the two Asian giants also reveal stark differences – the latter, even though less liberal and not politically open, has less regulatory burdens, rigidities and gives better impetus to investors in doing business compared to India.

### 3.4.5 Administrative and other complexities

The control system discussed above is compounded by the administrative and other complexities. These refer to lengthy procedures, bureaucratic delays, lack of transparency and accountability in the policy framework which again vary both in nature and extent between these countries. Animated lengthy debates over the need to curb the FDI also send wrong signals to investors desiring to invest in a country. This is indicative of lack of perspective, and poor governance and shows the kind of reforms required by the countries. Illustratively, even though a country may try to lower the entry costs, FDI may be discouraged because of the costs due to employment protection legislation, hiring and firing restrictions, lay-off payments and other potential exit costs when leaving a host country. The location decisions of the MNEs are vitally affected by these factors (Flamm 1984; Gorg and Strobl 2003; Alvarez and Gorg 2005).

The World Bank's study (*Doing Business in 2006*) has made some assessment of the countries for doing business taking into account the ease in starting a business, receiving credit, enforcing contracts and ease of exit among others. The ten Asian countries under study present a diverse picture. On the whole, NIEs are found in a better position with Singapore at the top both in terms of the ease in doing business and time to start a business followed by Hong Kong. The other two NIEs – Korea and Taiwan – are coming after Thailand and Malaysia. However, China is above the Philippines and Indonesia. The numbers of procedures are minimum in Hong Kong with five and Korea at 12. In ASEAN-4, the number of procedures range from eight in Thailand to 12 in Indonesia. India fares abysmally to start a business and in doing a business. It is a tough place for doing business, ranking tenth – that is, last – while to start a business it ranks ninth among the ten countries – Indonesia being another such case. India does not compare favourably with other countries. The World Bank's survey lends support to our results in Table 3.7 which gives the average ratings of the control system in India.

*Multiple control and command centres*

Countries having multiple control and command centres are mostly difficult places for investors. For instance, one of the principal reasons for India being among the tough countries for doing business is the existence of multiple control and command centres with a limited role for the market. India ranks poor in dealing with licenses, and in the hiring and firing of workers, in closing a business and so forth. For closing a business it takes an average of ten years compared with 2.4 years in China and the number of procedures for enforcing a contract comes to 40 against 25 in China. There are substantially more state level and secondary clearance requirements than most countries in the region (*Investment Guide*, 1999). Lack of coordination between the centre and the states and non-standard regulations governing the interstate commerce are among several other irritants in the system. Political complexities and combative politics in the Indian democratic system are also creating risks and uncertainties in the minds of investors. Furthermore, there is increasing unease about the quality of public administration, legal systems, bureaucratic inefficiency, and parallel government as the nexus between the public administration, political leaders and criminal elements directly impacts on the integrity, efficiency and neutrality of public administration.

## 3.5 Companies investing outside but not in India

Another questionnaire was addressed to a group of prominent Japanese MNEs investing abroad, including in China and East Asia, but not in India. Their assessment with regard to the business environment in India, based on which the companies decided against venturing into India, is of importance in providing useful guidelines and the policy imperatives to attract the investors.

Several reasons were identified and differently graded from (–) 2 to (+) 2 but almost all gave (–) 2 or (–) 1, that is, either very bad or bad, that made many Japanese MNEs opt against investing in India as compared to China and East Asia. The identification of the variables, which cause the maximum damage to Japanese investment sentiments towards India, the average ratings – simple and weighted – are quite revealing as may be seen from Table 3.8.

The grading was uniformly negative on all points. The biggest negative un-weighted average rating of (–) 1.78 goes to poor 'quality of factor inputs and business supplier services' falling below their expectations, followed by poor 'administrative and institutional infrastructure' (–) 1.0, with none of the companies giving positive ratings to either of these. It may be recalled that the survey results for firms with investment in India have also shown extremely poor ratings for the entire gamut of infrastructure, which further confirms the findings of these companies. The other high negative ratings of (–) 0.87 and (–) 0.93 are recorded by the statements 'base for exports' and 'proximity of local supplies', respectively.

These firms would like to invest when the use of the host country as an export base is profitable, but could not do so in view of the constraints. The weighted average repeats the pattern of the un-weighted average except in the cases of 'market' and 'labour force'. It is seen that introducing the weighting patterns does, in some cases, alter the ratings – but for the worse. For instance, 'administrative infrastructure' becomes worse and gets the lowest average rating of (–) 1.49. The unsuitability of India as a country with poor infrastructure is confirmed under all the weighting patterns, showing this to be invariable with regard to size of the firm.

The variables are highly correlated with business environment as may be seen from Table 3.8. Even though there is a potential problem created by inter-correlations among the variables underscoring the difficulty in

*Table 3.8* Un-weighted and weighted means and S.D. (Standard Deviation) relating to the perceived bottlenecks

| | Un-weighted | Weighted |
|---|---|---|
| 1 | 2 | 4 |
| 1. Business environment | | |
| Mean | (–) 0.80 | (–) 0.28 |
| S.D. | 1.00 | 0.98 |
| 2. Market size | | |
| Mean | (–) 0.21 | (+) 0.39 |
| S.D. | 1.47 | 1.41 |
| 3. Base for exports | | |
| Mean | (–) 0.87 | (–) 0.97 |
| S.D. | 0.81 | 0.17 |
| 4. Physical infrastructure | | |
| Mean | (–) 0.78 | (–) 0.67 |
| S.D. | 0.79 | 0.78 |
| 5. Administrative and institutional infrastructure | | |
| Mean | (–) 1.0 | (–) 1.49 |
| S.D. | 0.69 | 0.84 |
| 6. Quality of factor inputs and other services | | |
| Mean | (–) 1.78 | (–) 0.58 |
| S.D. | 0.68 | 0.83 |
| 7. Incentive system | | |
| Mean | (–) 0.21 | (–) 0.18 |
| S.D. | 0.67 | 0.61 |
| 8. Business contacts | | |
| Mean | (–) 0.69 | (–) 0.97 |
| S.D. | 0.77 | 0.24 |
| 9. Production efficiency | | |
| Mean | (–) 0.41 | (–) 0.49 |
| S.D. | 0.85 | 0.72 |
| 10. Proximity of local supplies | | |
| Mean | (–) 0.93 | (–) 0.80 |
| S.D. | 0.59 | 0.50 |
| 11. R&D | | |
| Mean | (–) 0.25 | (–) 0.11 |
| S.D. | 0.72 | 0.35 |
| 12. Labour | | |
| Mean | (–) 0.05 | (+) 1.27 |
| S.D. | 1.00 | 0.97 |

*Table 3.9* Correlation matrix: business environment variables

| | a | b | c | d | e | f | g | h | i | j | k | l |
|---|---|---|---|---|---|---|---|---|---|---|---|---|
| a | 1.00 | 0.95 | 0.97 | 0.98 | 0.98 | 0.94 | 0.97 | 0.98 | 0.96 | 0.89 | 0.93 | 0.97 |
| b | | | 0.94 | 0.94 | 0.94 | 0.89 | 0.91 | 0.94 | 0.97 | 0.91 | 0.90 | 0.94 |
| c | | | | 0.99 | 0.98 | 0.98 | 0.97 | 0.97 | 0.97 | 0.99 | 0.95 | 0.97 |
| d | | | | | 0.98 | 0.98 | 0.99 | 0.96 | 0.96 | 0.99 | 0.95 | 0.98 |
| e | | | | | | 0.96 | 0.97 | 0.96 | 0.99 | 0.99 | 0.98 | 0.98 |
| f | | | | | | | 0.98 | 0.95 | 0.94 | 0.96 | 0.94 | 0.97 |
| g | | | | | | | | 0.93 | 0.95 | 0.97 | 0.93 | 0.98 |
| h | | | | | | | | | 0.96 | 0.97 | 0.96 | 0.97 |
| i | | | | | | | | | | 0.96 | 0.97 | 0.96 |
| j | | | | | | | | | | | 0.97 | 0.96 |
| k | | | | | | | | | | | | 0.95 |
| l | | | | | | | | | | | | 1.00 |

*Notes*: 1. a: Business environment, b: Market size, c: Base for exports, d: Physical infrastructure, e: Production efficiency, f: Proximity of local suppliers, g: Administrative infrastructure, h: Incentive system, i: Labour force, j: Quality of service, k: R&D, l: Business contacts.
2. The variables are not continuous. They were in five grades ranging from (–) 2 to (+) 2. Response to every variable was similar. It is, therefore, not surprising that most of the correlations are above 0.9.

statistically identifying the influence of specific variables, the focus is on finding the relationship of the responses given by the MNEs to some selected business environment variables (Table 3.9).

## 3.6 Results of the logit model

To further examine and identify the significant variables affecting the Japanese investors, a limited application of the binary logit model has been attempted. The model is given at the end of this book. Here we present only the main points.

### 3.6.1 Dependent variable

Decision to invest in India compared to China. The MNEs were asked the question, 'Are you interested in investing in India compared to China and East Asia?' The obvious assumption is that this is a conscious decision on the part of the investors. Value one was given to a 'yes' answer and zero to a 'no' answer. This is a binary variable taking the value zero or one.

*Table 3.10* Main results of the logit model
Dependent variable: Decision to invest in India compared to China and ASEAN

| **Independent variables** | **Excluding labour** | **Including labour** |
|---|---|---|
| Constant | 2.194 | 2.311 |
| | (1.446) | (1.492) |
| Infrastructure | 3.288* | 4.006* |
| | (1.146) | (1.332) |
| JMT | 2.422* | 2.671** |
| | (1.033) | (1.145) |
| Control system | −1.247*** | −1.600*** |
| | (0.737) | (0.875) |
| Administrative complexities | −1.022 | −0.966 |
| | (0.836) | (0.885) |
| Labour | | 1.623 |
| | | (1.138) |

*Note*: Figures in parenthesis denote the standard errors of the coefficients.
* Significant at 1 per cent.
** Significant at 5 per cent.
*** Significant at 10 per cent.

### 3.6.2 Independent variables

The Japanese MNEs were asked to mark their opinion of the Indian business environment as compared to China and the East Asian countries on a five-point scale: −2, −1, 0, +1, and +2. A zero score would indicate that in the opinion of the firm, the Indian situation is not very different from that of China and other East Asian countries; a positive score would indicate that the Indian situation is better or preferred, while a negative score would indicate that the Indian situation is considered to be worse than that in other Asian countries.

The variables included in the model estimation are: Infrastructure, Control system, Administrative complexities, Japanese Management Techniques. In the literature, labour costs are considered an important advantage for attracting FDI (Chen 1996 for China; Wheeler and Mody 1992 for investment by the US MNEs; Aitken *et al.* 1996 for Mexico, Venezuela and the USA). However, in our study investors did not consider this variable to be significantly different for India compared to China. Hence, in the regression equation we have examined the results both with and without labour.

Infrastructure and Japanese management techniques have turned out to be the most important determinants for attracting Japanese FDI to India. The coefficient of INFST is significantly positive at $p < 0.004$, while that of JMT is significantly positive at $p < 0.019$. The results also give credence to the negative impact of 'controls' on FDI (using a one tail test). The variable is significantly negative at $p < 0.09$.

There was no evidence of any autocorrelation between these variables. Labour has not emerged as statistically significant as it is considered to be cheap and abundant in both India and China. In fact, labour productivity has been rated as being higher in China than in India. Likewise, 'Administrative complexities' is not statistically significant. This could be because both the Indian and Chinese systems are wrought with complexities, perhaps in different ways, and which scores better may have been difficult for the investors to choose. In addition, China and India have different kinds of systems and institutions and therefore it might have been difficult for the investors to decide. For instance, China is yet to create institutions relating to commercial dispute settlements, monitoring patents and intellectual property rights and a judicial system as required by the WTO regime. Its banking system is said to be riddled with bad loans. Chinese prices are low because of forced loans. One year the state-owned enterprises might be criticized for not making money, the next year they would be making a 100 per cent profit. India, on the other hand, has the institutions in place, but they do not function efficiently. On balance, therefore, it would have been difficult for the firms to decide which offers the better environment in which to invest.

The responses to other variables, like 'partnership' and 'networking', were too small to be included in the model. In the case of both India and China, 'market size' has been rated as big and hence neither derives a location advantage over the other. The same finding applies to 'labour', which has been given the same rating. The responses of all MNEs were similar in both cases.

## 3.7 Concluding remarks

The results of the survey are quite revealing. They bring out the Japanese MNEs' perception of a favourable climate for investment. It also brings out the reasons for their reluctance to invest in India in relation to China and East Asia. The results of the survey, in particular, highlight the deficiency in India's foreign investment policies compared to China and East Asia, something of which there had previously been an insufficient awareness. The following points deserve specific mention:

1. In making location decisions, the Japanese MNEs are not likely to compare the Asian countries with the developed countries as they are

not comparable. Nevertheless, having taken the decision to locate in Asia, the MNE would evaluate alternative locations within that region. In doing so, the MNE will not be guided by the common location advantages that these Asian countries share – such as the availability of skilled workforce at low wages – but would focus on other advantages/disadvantages that could differ between these countries.

2. Contrary to popular notion and the findings of many studies, this cross-country analysis shows that the competitive advantages of a country in terms of market and availability of labor at low cost, even though important, are not of great significance in influencing the FDI flows into a country. The countries that have attracted the largest FDI inflows are those that have not only a large and growing domestic market, growth potential but well-developed infrastructure facilities and a policy framework with proactive measures adopted to promote and facilitate the location of FDI. The cross country examination of the Japanese investors' responses from our survey and personal interviews prominently brought out that most of the firms – about 70 per cent – had a preference for India but could not invest. An examination of the average ratings and other responses has led to an identification of the critical factors which cause maximum damage to Japanese investment in India as compared to China and the East Asian countries.
3. Japanese MNEs were asked to evaluate six location advantages in these countries: viz., infrastructure, the adoption of Japanese Management Technique (JMT), controls and restrictions, administrative complexities, market size, and labour cost. It was hypothesized that a better score would be positively related to their decision to invest.
   - India's infrastructure gets the most adverse rating by investors compared to East Asia and China – almost close to (–) 2 in the five grades ranging from (+) 2 to (–) 2. The weighted average grades have generally become worse in all of the cases where they were negative in the simple comparison. India is deficient in all the areas of infrastructure and requires substantial improvements.
   - The same applies to its public administration. India's is perceived as being poor, deficient, and suffering from lack of accountability – as well as imposing inordinate delays. In addition, those Japanese investors who are investing elsewhere, but not in India have all cited weak infrastructure and the poor quality of governance among others as the basic reasons for their decision not to invest in India.

- In the sample we had asked all of the firms whether or not JMT was relevant for their investment decision. The results show JMT to be an important determinant. The Japanese MNEs appear to prefer to invest in countries where the adoption of their management techniques is easier. This was suspected by earlier studies but this study, to the best of our knowledge, is the first to provide strong evidence in its favour. The results show the percentage of adoption significantly differs between India, China and East Asia – the minimum score being in India.
- Our next question was obviously what difficulties they faced in the introduction of JMT in India, China and the East Asian countries. With regard to India, most of the firms complained about the lack of team spirit, the gap between labour and management, the lack of quality consciousness, and trade-based labour laws and unions that have made the introduction of job rotation and multiple skills – two important constituents of JMT – difficult. In India, most of the constraints relate to an inability to understand JMT and the poor knowledge base of the labour force and lack of inter-firm linkages. But the human resource development – or, rather, the lack of it – acts as the greatest obstacle to the implementation of JMT most. In the case of China they faced a different set of problems. Their main difficulty was the interference of the government and, in particular, the government's direction to produce according to its desire. The main problem with the East Asian countries was job-hopping and the consequent difficulties in maintaining business secrets. Successful adoptions of JMT – like just-in-time delivery and total quality control – requires simultaneous transfer of technology or what Kaplinsky (1995) refers to as 'simultaneous engineering' and participation in the component manufacturing enterprises.
- The majority of the sample firms characterized India's control system as either bad or very bad. Most regulations, whether relating to approvals or permissions or understanding the legal system, tax laws, foreign exchange regulations, import duty, and other formalities, are so complex in India that they could not be understood by these companies. In addition, sudden and continuous changes in policies have also made it difficult for the companies to prepare their business plans. Control bottlenecks are further compounded by the administrative difficulties and entry barriers.

4. The responses were also subjected to an econometric analysis using a binary logit model. Although the number of observations were limited, yet the results were interesting. Infrastructure and adoption

of Japanese management techniques emerged most significant. Controls and restrictions had a negative impact on FDI. Administrative complexities have not turned out to be significant. The insignificance of the variable in the statistical analysis could be due to the presence of high levels of complexities and corruption in both India and China and the consequent inability of the Japanese MNEs to evaluate the Indian scene in comparison to China and other Asian countries. Labour is considered to be cheap and abundant being given a similar rating, as was the case with market size. The response of almost all of the MNEs was identical in this regard. Finally, it may also be added that when the size parameters are presented according to the increasing order of ranking, by and large, the rating seems not to be influenced by the size of the firm.

5. It is difficult to statistically measure the policy aspects. So we took recourse to a different method – that is, addressing companies investing in the other countries while bypassing India. The average ratings given by Japanese investors investing in those countries but not in India on 12 different aspects of Indian policy regarding reasons for not investing in India are uniformly negative. Here again, infrastructure in all its forms and administrative complexities are the basic reasons. Difficulties in understanding the regulations, tax laws and other procedures and formalities, relatively higher rates of individual and corporate taxes, tariffs, lack of policy coordination and policy announcements not being reflected in the operational procedures and in the attitude of government personnel responsible for implementation of policy are the main factors in the FDI decision not to invest in India.

The MNEs mostly seek pluralistic objectives and engage in FDI that combines the characteristics of multiple goals. In India, with the exception of the large size of the market – something that is shared with China – all of the factors are working in the opposite direction. India will have to act in an expeditious fashion to introduce specific domestic policy reforms, create a culture to make the business environment compatible at least with the middle-income group countries, if not at the international level of the high-income countries.

In order to remove internal constraints, India will have to introduce several changes. The major instruments which cut across and create an enabling environment are an improvement in the quality of governance, promoting competition, improving the infrastructure, simplifying transactions, strengthening accountability, developing network arrangements, improving the realities on the ground, and augmenting skills, productivity, technological capabilities, and other variables which play a dominant role in efficiency-seeking FDI. In addition, India and China are attracting increasing global attention and it is now time to open up not only their financial and services sectors, but also the retail and the real estate to foreign competition to improve their productivity and competitiveness.

# 4
# Japanese Domestic Companies' Perception for Investment Abroad

## 4.1 Introduction

Japan has created an internal dynamics of inter-firm collaboration in which domestic companies constitute an integral part. Japanese production alliances through networking in this sector are providing an important vehicle for technology transfer, enhancing investment flows and providing access to larger markets. Networking and inter-firm linkages have increased knowledge diffusion and skills which are of great importance to enhance the dynamism and competitiveness of the domestic companies to internationalize. With greater regional integration and networking, the Japanese domestic-oriented companies seek to internationalize their production.

In the present chapter we focus on the international orientation of Japanese companies and investigate the factors involved in their internationalization. In this context we analyse the perception of Japanese domestic-oriented firms, and consider what is felt to be important for their international orientation. In order to do this, we have, first, taken recourse to the Japanese electronic industry and examined the important variables relating to its international orientation. Data for the industry were taken from the *Japan Company Handbook, 2004*, covering 214 companies. Secondly, a questionnaire about investing abroad was prepared and circulated among Japanese domestic-oriented companies. As potential investors, their observations are particularly important. Finally, our analysis benefited from receiving the views of the Chambers of Commerce and Industry in Japan which also supplemented the data base. The Nagoya Chamber of Commerce and Industry, in particular, had furnished detailed replies relating to domestic-oriented companies' perception for international orientation. However, before doing so, it would be pertinent to offer a brief discussion of some relevant theoretical issues.

## 4.2 Internalization and internationalization process models

There is no predictive theory of FDI. There is, in a broad sense, an alternative conceptualization to explain the dynamics of overseas involvement. This is in terms of the internalization and internationalization process models of international expansion. The internalization school focuses on market imperfections that involve business/usage specificity, whereas the internationalization school starts from imperfections arising from location specificity. Internationalization of the firms is a process in which the firms gradually increase their international involvement in foreign markets. On the other hand, the internalization model of foreign expansion suggests that firms will establish foreign affiliates in the case of strong ownership advantages, location advantages and internalization advantages. International operation is conditional to ownership of certain intangible assets which gives the owning firm an advantage over local firms. In fact, sales subsidiary, export, and licensing of technology (including hybrid modes) are treated as alternative means of possible internationalization strategies.

It is a well-known proposition that an international operation is conditional on the ownership of certain intangible assets which give the owning firm an advantage over local firms. In the 1960s and 1970s MNE theory strongly emphasized product innovation as the key firm-specific ownership advantage with which a company could expand abroad. A firm wishing to operate abroad must possess firm-specific ownership advantages adequate to more than offset the handicaps faced in an alien atmosphere and to cover the risks (Hymer 1976; Caves 1974, 1996). These advantages emanate from the ownership of proprietary assets, which include, among others, brand goodwill, technology, managerial and marketing skills, access to cheaper sources of capital and raw materials. Initially (in the first phase of the product cycle, *à la* Vernon), these advantages are exploited abroad through export from the home base. In subsequent stages, production is moved closer to the export markets through FDI, because of the emergence of location advantages, which make it more profitable than exports. These advantages arise from factors, such as tariffs and quantitative restrictions, communication and transport costs, and inter-country differences in input/factor prices and productivity. The ownership of intangible assets and the presence of location advantages, although necessary, are not sufficient conditions for FDI. These advantages are complemented by some incentives for the internalization of the markets of intangible assets and hence undertake intra-firm transfer. Firms overcome these through internalizing the transactions by undertaking FDI. The internalization advantages arise because of market failure, information asymmetry and infirmities involved in its transfer.

Since Hymer made a first systematic attempt to explain the internationalization of firms, the theory has evolved, through the work of Vernon (1966), Caves (1974, 1996), Dunning (1993), Rugman (1980), Teece (1977, 1986), Williamson (1979, 1985, 1989) and Hennart (1986). FDI takes place when firms combine their ownership-specific advantages with the location-specific advantages of host countries through internalization – that is, through intra-firm rather than arm's-length transactions. In the initial stages of the product cycle, it is appropriated through exports and through foreign production (Vernon 1966). Foreign production can be accomplished through renting out (licensing) the intangible asset or through FDI, that is setting up an affiliate (which may take the form of an overseas branch, subsidiary, or a joint venture) and thus internalize the transfer of the intangible asset. The choice is mainly determined by the relative transaction cost involved in the market transfer (Buckley and Casson 1976; Williamson 1975, 1981; Rugman 1980). The higher the transaction costs, the greater the incentive to internalize or resort to FDI. Therefore, FDI is expected to be prominent in those industries in which intangible assets with high internalization and locational incentives are important. The licensing mode of production is expected to be preferred in industries where intangible assets with high locational incentives exist, but low internalization incentives are present. The ownership of intangible assets is, thus, central in explaining the process of internalization of firms.

For a long time, however, researchers have examined the order of selection of foreign markets. Since Cyert and March (1963), the behavioural model has attempted to identify the markets; firms enter first and determine how they organize within the new market. A decision to enter a foreign market is a function of knowledge and experience, and the selection of a similar market reduces uncertainty (Aharoni 1966). In the 1970s, Scandinavian authors categorized the 'psychic distance' to assert that companies enter markets perceived to be psychologically closer before considering the remote ones (Johanson and Wiedersheim-Paul 1975; Johanson and Vahlne 1977). Among the important aspects which have been emphasized are: (i) a lower level of uncertainty in psychically close countries (Johanson and Vahlne 1990), and (ii) psychic closeness facilitating learning about the targeted host countries.

Over the period, more studies (for instance, Davidson 1980; Nordstrom and Vahlne 1992) have corroborated the hypothesis that firms expand first to the psychically close countries and then to psychically remote ones. However, Ghemawat (2001) has suggested four dimensions of distance, namely: cultural, administrative, geographic and economic that influence companies considering geographical expansion.

In contrast, the internationalization model of the Scandinavian school argues that firms will incrementally build foreign operations, starting with low resource commitments in culturally proximate countries, and then expanding the scale and geographical scope of these commitments. The internationalization of the firms is, thus, seen as a process in which the firms gradually increase their involvement in the individual foreign country and successively establish operations in new countries after they have gained international experience through trade and/or licensing. Here experimental learning is critical, and path dependencies can be observed in the growth of the MNEs, especially with regard to knowledge of the markets (Barkema *et al.* 1996; Johanson and Vahlne 1977, 1990). The internationalization process model posits that the international orientation occurs in stages, commencing with irregular export activity via an independent agent, a sales subsidiary, or, eventually, full production in foreign markets (Johanson and Wiedersheim-Paul 1975; Johanson and Vahlne 1990). Progression through the stages is driven by experiential knowledge accumulation. Each stage calls for more commitment to international markets and enables firms to gain in knowledge, skill and confidence. Because the knowledge relates to the existing mode of operation, firms tend to move gradually, adopting new modes which make most use of past experience. Some studies have treated this as one stage in the multi-stage process of the internationalization of firms. Johanson and Vahlne, based on their studies in international business of Swedish firms at the University of Uppsala show that they often develop their international business in small steps. They hold that internationalization is a product of a series of incremental decisions – gradual acquisition, integration, and the use of knowledge about foreign markets and operation, successively increasing commitment to foreign markets – that is, export to a country, the establishment of export channels, to start a selling subsidiary, and so forth. These common characteristics are important to subsequent internationalization. The basic assumptions are that the lack of such knowledge acts as an important obstacle to the development of international operations and that the necessary knowledge can be acquired mainly through operations abroad.

Gradual internationalization is not an exclusively Swedish phenomenon. With regard to the overseas direct investment of US producers, Gruber, Mehta and Vernon (1967) have stated 'they are the final step in a process which begins with the involvement of such producers in export trade'. Knickerbocker (1973) also refers to this process and explicitly distinguishes agents and sales subsidiaries as separate steps in the process. Lipsey and Weiss (1969, 1972) have referred to a 'market cycle' model with similar characteristics.

The internationalization process is, thus, seen as a sequence of the incremental nature of successive learning through stages of increasing commitment to foreign markets, which, according to Johanson and Vahlne (1990), will proceed along incremental stages whether or not strategic decisions are made in this direction. Firms in many countries have skipped the initial 'domestic only', or primary stage and very quickly introduced a policy of FDI. 'Born global' behaviour has been observed in many countries. Caves (1996) has presented an excellent discussion of such standard explanations of MNEs and FDI.

This model also has another strand which asserts that the location pattern of FDI is determined by 'psychic distance', defined as the cost of acquiring and internalizing relevant information about business conditions in other countries, the perception of risk and uncertainty involved in foreign operations, and the resources required to gain access to foreign networks (Johanson and Vahlne 1977). The model asserts that the costs involved in overcoming psychic distance decline over time as a function of the experience gained by the firm in each market. Firms are expected to enter familiar, probably neighbouring markets first because of their historical familiarity and then to fan out into progressively more remote territory.

The sequence of foreign expansion described in many studies of internationalization implies that companies perform best in those foreign markets that bear the greatest similarities to their domestic markets (Johanson and Vahlne 1977). However, despite some of the assertions of a negative relationship between psychic distance and organizational performance, the empirical findings are rather inconclusive. Research has not been able to conclusively establish a negative relationship between psychic distance and organizational performance. Moreover, some support for a psychic distance paradox, where the perception of differences between the home and foreign markets actually enhances performance, has also been found.

The internationalization process school, explaining modal choice on the basis of a firm's knowledge gained through experience in the international market, retains considerable influence based on empirical studies. The model is based on behavioural theories, with assumptions about the lack of information and the importance of perceived risk and uncertainty. This process is not seen as a sequence of deliberately planned steps founded on rational analysis. Instead, it is the successive learning through stages of increasing commitment to foreign markets and will proceed along whether strategic decisions are made in this direction or not.

Historical evidence confirms the incremental approach that companies have taken to become foreign investors. Technology and the creation of other firm-specific knowledge also play a central role in the evolution of national firms into international or multinational enterprises. MNEs may also arise when an enterprise finds itself with opportunities to start or link up with an establishment in another country endowed to support this. National qualities influence the prevalence of MNEs directly. For instance, real resource endowments or cultural affinity provide an efficient environment for the development of potential MNEs.

The model is limited in its applicability to the early stages of internationalization and is also deterministic in nature (Melin 1992; Anderson 1993; Calof and Beamish 1995). In addition, there are exceptions to this incremental process (Johanson and Vahlne 1990; Anderson 1993). First, large firms can take bigger internationalization steps. Secondly, when market conditions are stable, knowledge can be gained in ways other than through experience. Thirdly, experience in similar markets may allow a firm to generalize this experience. These exceptions may allow the firms to jump stages.

There is no conclusive evidence that firms grow through the process of staged involvement – through exporting, licensing and franchising – what Teece (1986) called 'transitioning' – nor is there sound empirical evidence on whether or not MNEs grow by sequentially passing through the stages of overseas involvement at all. In the actual world, it may fall between these two forms.

The study of FDI has generally tended to focus on two reasons for locating in a particular country. Firms are motivated by the search for the lower costs of supplying a market. Secondly, firms may want to gain improved access to that country's or some other country's market. Buckley and Casson (1981) specify the optimal timing of FDI for a single firm by reference to costs, demands and market growth. There are three possible hierarchical entry mode choices: full equity control through greenfield investment; full equity control through acquisition/merger and JVs. that are either greenfield investment or acquisition. The theory of entry mode choice is rarely specified in empirical work, although most of the empirical literature focuses on market entry choices and not forms of involvement.

Japanese firms have ownership advantages in terms of the ownership of intangible assets like technology, managerial practices and brand names. So the location-specific advantages of the countries in attracting FDI, the influence of these on the FDI flows and the ownership arrangements preferred by the investors to capture the advantages of internationalization is imperative.

## 4.3 Principal determinants of international orientation

In order to examine the international orientation of the Japanese firms, using firm-level data covering 214 firms from the Japanese electronic and electrical goods industry, an attempt has been made to study the international orientation of Japanese firms. The most important variables which are empirically estimated typically include one representing firm size and factor endowments as well as technology indicators.

### 4.3.1 Size of firm

Firms with a higher level of international experience enter a new international market earlier than firms with a lower level of international experience. One of the most important characteristics enabling a firm to achieve international orientation, especially in imperfect markets, is large size. Historically, firm size has been related to market power in both domestic and international contexts (Hymer 1976; Knickerbocker 1973). The conventional argument for firm size is premised on how large firms exercise their power. It is argued that larger firms compete in a broader spectrum of products and markets using economies of both scale and scope. They are able to make pre-emptive moves that limit or prevent later entrants from gaining access to suppliers, markets, customers and other scarce assets. Larger firms have more resources to invest in innovations, to pursue aggressive expansions, are able to incur the costs, bear the risks, and achieve a better performance. Other advantages include access to privileged learning channels, and risk reduction through wider portfolios, and from a stronger bargaining power to gain concessions and incentives from host country government. There is also additional empirical support that pioneering entrants into new markets are able to enter on a large scale and invest heavily in building a strong market position, while late entrants are predominantly smaller firms. Within this perspective, it is hypothesized that larger-sized firms are more likely to make an earlier entry into a foreign market than smaller-sized firms.

Larger firms with market power can achieve scale economies and product-differentiated output. They may also have advantages in terms of superior information, greater risk-bearing capacity, lower unit costs, brand names and price-setting power. Despite its intuitive appeal, there are a number of studies that do not support some of these hypothesized effects of firm size prompting researchers to conclude that, in itself, firm size is not a precursor to market entry, but that the *effects* of size are what are consequential. In related formulations, researchers have expanded the effects of size in terms of overall ownership advantage (Dunning 1988). Ownership advantage is defined generally as 'any income generating assets which makes it possible for firms to engage in foreign production'. Within such formulations, the timing of market entry becomes conditional. Rivoli and Salorio (1996) point out, for example, that firms cannot afford to delay the entry if the ownership advantages possessed are less unique and non-monopolistic (Casson 1987). Because firm size is not a unique form of ownership advantage (Casson 1987), there are conditions when a firm might actually delay market entry (Rivoli and Salorio 1996).

The possible reconciliation of conventional arguments about firm size and contemporary treatments of ownership advantage might come with the size of the targeted market entry. Specifically, we argue that firms will quickly capitalize on their size, particularly when facing large markets, such as India or China. This is because larger firms will be able to leverage their resources when demand is high – a condition that smaller firms might not be able to capitalize on as effectively. While uncertainty conditions posited by Rivoli and Salorio (1996) prevail, larger-sized firms are in a better position to adopt standardized marketing strategies in particularly large markets, as in the case of Sony, Toyota, and other similar corporations. It is being hypothesized that for a potentially large host country market, larger firm size will encourage earlier entry.

### 4.3.2 Scope economies

The impact of economies of scope on entry timing comes from two sources. First, a broader scope of products and services means a wide portfolio of offerings to choose from; this implies a better chance of providing the right product and service to the newly-opened market. In this case, firms with a broader strategic scope are better prepared to handle the uncertainty about the types of product that are needed in the new market. Secondly, a broader scope of products enables the firm to develop a synergy across different product sectors. This synergy gives rise to both efficiency and quality in product development, product line extension, production, distribution and market support. Taken together, firms with a broader product scope have a higher likelihood of entering the market early. Firms with a broader scope of products and services enter a new international market earlier than those with a narrower scope.

Further, the timing and mode of entry are inextricably related. The entry-decision of the firm will be affected by its competitor's behaviour. In particular, entry by competitors will accelerate the entry of a firm into an international market and the greater the market growth in a specific product sector in a new international market, the earlier a firm will enter that market. In addition, the lower the level of risk in a new international market, the earlier a firm will enter that market. Modes of entry can be viewed as being equity-based, (that is, equity joint ventures and wholly-owned subsidiaries) or as non-equity-based, that is, exporting; licensing; non-equity alliances.

## 4.4 Model results

A simple model which captures the major determinants of international orientation of Japanese firms taking an illustrative case of electronics industry is given in the technical annex at the end. The results are presented in Table 4.1.

*Table 4.1* Model results: dependent variable – overseas sales ratio (OSR)

| **Independent Variables** | **Binary logit** | | **Normal tobit** | |
|---|---|---|---|---|
| | **Coefficient** | **Std. Error** | **Coefficient** | **Std. Error** |
| C: Constant | −13.480* | 2.288 | −114.254* | 18.301 |
| KL: Capital–labour ratio | 0.0097** | 0.005 | 0.147* | 0.038 |
| L: Sales | 1.264* | 0.216 | 11.439* | 1.681 |
| RD: Research and development | 10.856*** | 6.459 | 40.520 | 83.447 |
| FOR: Foreign ownership | 0.009 | 0.016 | 0.233 | 0.185 |

*Note*: * Significant at 1 per cent; ** Significant at 5 per cent; *** Significant at 10 per cent.

The results show that Japanese MNEs with higher levels of capital structure tended to have higher levels of overseas sales ratio (OSR). The principal variables that turn out to be the significant determinants in the international orientation of the companies are:

- Capital intensity – technologically intensive
- Large volume of sales – scale economies
- High R&D.

High OSR is significantly dependent on the above three variables. The domestic-oriented companies are less capital-intensive, have low sales turnover, and spend little on R&D.

## 4.5 Japanese domestic companies' perception for international orientation

In order to carry out further analysis of the Japanese investors' perception of investment abroad, a questionnaire was prepared and circulated, principally to Japanese domestic-oriented companies based on the advice tendered by various chambers of commerce & industry in Japan to elicit their perception regarding foreign investment. They were, *inter alia*, asked to give their reasons for not investing outside Japan and their responses, along with the underlying reasons, are given in Table 4.2.

*Table 4.2* Reasons for not investing outside Japan (number of firms is given in percentages)

| **Market familiarization** a | **Scale of production (size)** b | **Management problem** c | **Financing problem** d | **Technological problem** e |
|---|---|---|---|---|
| 45 | 20 | 20 | 10 | 5 |

Among the reasons cited for not investing outside Japan, 'market familiarization' appears to be dominant. Although domestic companies want to establish market presence in foreign countries through investment, their ability is constrained by their lack of multinational experience. To some degree these observations corroborate the sequential process of foreign expansion as described in many studies of internationalization. This implies that companies will perform best in foreign markets where they are familiar or which are most similar to their domestic market. They would incrementally build their foreign operation, starting with low resource commitments in culturally proximate countries, and then expand these commitments and geographic scope. Here experimental learning is critical, and path dependencies can be observed with regard to knowledge of the markets.

### 4.5.1 Business goals for overseas investment

With regard to the business objectives to be fulfilled by the country in which an investment is made, the following picture emerged from the responses (Table 4.3).

*Table 4.3* Business objectives from the countries (percentages)

| Principal reasons | | | Peripheral reasons | | | |
|---|---|---|---|---|---|---|
| Market | Production base for export to third countries | Export to Japan | Low wages | Trained labour force | Other Japanese firms | Presence of R&D |
| a | b | c | d | e | f | g |
| 25 | 25 | 15 | 10 | 10 | 10 | 5 |

### 4.5.2 Cross-country perception

Buckley and Casson (1981) specify the timing of FDI for a single firm, taking costs, demands and market growth into account. The relationship between production costs, market access and strategic behaviour in determining FDI is examined by Horstmann and Markusen (1987); Markusen (1995); and Markusen and Venables (1998).

Japanese domestic investors appear to show a preference towards market proximity. This might be explained by the general structure of the Japanese production process. While large European and US companies typically internalize a substantial share of the intermediate production, Japanese manufacturers rely heavily on a wide supplier network. Thus, ties with the domestic suppliers are maintained, requiring the companies to stay relatively close to the home base. In their globalization strategy during the 1980s, it may be recalled that Japanese companies emphasized proximity to the sales market. With respect to the industrial countries also, this proximity argument was of particular importance in response to increasing trade frictions. To circumvent export constraints and potential future barriers, Japanese manufacturers had decided to move production directly into the destination through FDI to avoid potential loss of market.

Japanese domestic companies emphasized proximity as an important factor in their perception affecting their location choices of the firms concerned. For instance, many companies feel that carrying out business in India is no different from carrying out business in China and East Asia, yet they have preferred either China or East Asia if they get the choice to invest outside Japan. Understanding and trust come from multi-layered relationships and can create low-cost enforcement opportunities and lower transaction costs. The study of FDI has generally tended to focus on two reasons for locating in a particular country. First, firms are motivated by the search for lower costs of supplying a market. Secondly, firms may want to gain improved access to that country or to some other country's market.

Statistical results from several studies also strongly buttress the argument that foreign investors are inclined to favour such locations that could minimize information costs and offer a variety of agglomeration economies (He Canfei 2002). For example, even though the Internet is having some effect on the location of economic activity, most economic activities continue to take place within geographically-limited neighbourhoods as these have many built-in advantages that are difficult to overcome. Cultural and relational dimensions, or the wide array of institutionalized human network-building processes, cannot be replaced by internet. Proximity is an important source of competitiveness (also see Kogut 1983; Kim 1995). FDI literature has placed little emphasis on the potential role of proximity and neighbourhood nor has it given an adequate explanation of this proposition – rather, it has explained the findings in terms of investment behaviour. The regression models have offered a description, but not an explanation for this. Some studies have hypothesized that factors such as local neighbourhood may also play an important role in the perceived FDI flows. The local scope of experimentation implies that near neighbourhood investment is preferred (see Levinthal and March, 1993). Interestingly, even the USA, in the early twentieth century, began investing abroad, predominantly in its local neighbourhood (Twomey, 2001). The neighbourhood approach is closer to the incremental nature of successive learning through stages of increasing commitment to foreign markets, which, according to Johanson and Vahlne (1990), will proceed along the presented stages whether strategic decisions are made in this direction or not.

### 4.5.3 Cross-country barriers perceived by the companies

Business environment and networking constitute the most important factors perceived by the domestic companies for international operation. This is vindicated by their responses as given in Table 4.4(a & b).

*Table 4.4a* Perception of domestic companies for investment abroad (frequency distribution)

| Scale (Rating) | Business environment – distribution of firms according to perceived barriers (percentage) | | Distribution of firms according to the importance of networking as a factor for international orientation (percentage) | |
|---|---|---|---|---|
| | Regulation | Infrastructure | Through establishing information network | Through having informal network |
| −2 | 18 | 36 | 0 | 0 |
| −1 | 18 | 45 | 8 | 16 |
| 0 | 45 | 9 | 33 | 33 |
| +1 | 9 | 9 | 50 | 42 |
| +2 | 9 | 0 | 8 | 8 |

*Table 4.4b* India *vis-à-vis* China and East Asia – mean and S.D. (standard deviation) of the rating

| | Mean | Standard deviation | Range |
|---|---|---|---|
| Business environment | | | |
| 1 Regulation | (−) 0.27 | 1.13 | (−) 1.40 to +0.86 |
| 2 Infrastructure | (−) 1.09 | 0.84 | (−) 1.93 to −0.25 |
| Lack of network | | | |
| 1 Develop information network | (+) 0.58 | 0.76 | (−) 0.18 to +1.34 |
| 2 Strengthen informal network | (+) 0.42 | 0.83 | (−) 1.25 to +0.41 |

*Note*: *By range is meant mean ± s.d.

Compared to China and East Asia, India gets an overall poor rating mainly on account of its poor 'business environment' even though the item, 'preference for doing business' India gets a positive rating *vis-à-vis* China and East Asia. To improve 'proximity', the domestic-oriented companies would like to have strong network arrangements – both formal and informal. Proximity to the market, including intangible cultural and relational dimensions, affects the wide array of institutionalized human network-building which play a role that is more important than the conventional concept of comparative advantage. Thus, even after the very substantial transportation and communication improvements that have taken place during the twentieth century, geographically limited 'neighbourhoods' is an important factor.

In regard to 'business environment' it is seen that India gets a poor rating of (–) 1.1 for 'infrastructure' and a rating of (–) 0.3 for 'regulation' to foreign investment *vis-à-vis* East Asia. Most of them feel that the level of infrastructure in India is inadequate. Secondly, measures to improve the investment climate in the context of specific policy areas such as regulation, taxation, and labour market is desirable. The domestic companies specifically suggested:

- Improvement in the network arrangement – both formal and informal. This would help to develop cooperative international liaisons; integrate new technologies; and foster social networking between the investors and the host country; and
- Host countries should provide global standardization to build competitiveness.

## 4.6 Concluding remarks

Size and technology have been important players in the international orientation of Japanese companies. Using micro-level data, the study shows that two variables have been the most significant determinants in shaping the international orientation of Japanese companies. The domestic-oriented companies are less capital-intensive, had lower sales turnover, and spent little on R&D.

As regards the survey, the results reveal that the domestic-oriented companies on the strength of accumulated knowledge would like to establish market presence in those foreign countries which are especially familiar ones, even if their ability to do so is constrained by a lack of multinational experience. The survey also shows that firms would normally test a foreign market by exports, to begin with and later switch over to production through licensing, or sales subsidiary and eventually full production through direct investment. This is the process of gradual internationalization. Proximity is important and can be narrowed through a networking arrangement; by promoting a business environment through adequate 'soft' infrastructure and investment-friendly ties which constitute the most important factors to become global and attract investment.

In addition to familiarization, demand conditions and market growth are equally important for their international expansion. Given the opportunity, and other things being equal, the domestic companies, taking a 'start-small' approach, would prefer China and East Asia, in view of the market and proximity where they will face significantly lower transaction costs with the added advantage of knowing local consumer preferences. Otherwise, as argued by Teece *et al.*, a foreign firm faces significantly higher costs than its local competitor due to differences in language, culture, nature and level of economic development between the host and home countries. The lower set-up costs constitute important motivating points.[1]

In addition, domestic companies are more sensitive to Japanese agglomeration than the larger ones. In foreign locations they tend to establish plants closer to the large MNEs that source components and materials from them. Therefore, to some extent their decision to locate is influenced by the decision of the MNEs from the home country.

Domestic companies, evolving through experience, networking and linkages, have become important channels through which the existing MNEs are passing on their intangible and tangible assets which constitute the stepping stone towards strengthening their competitiveness, giving them a foothold in international production and embedding in host economies. However, they prefer markets that are perceived to be psychologically closer in their most immediate neighbourhood before considering the remote ones and beginning with export activity before expanding to full production in foreign markets.[2]

The current technological revolution has shortened the length of the product life cycle and for many products, size advantages do not exist. Linkages and networking have augmented the capabilities of domestic firms and made them globally knowledge-sharing for technical collaboration in industries that are knowledge-based which includes: electronics, telecommunications, petrochemicals, automobiles, engineering plastics, shipbuilding, non-conventional energy sources, industrial robotics, superconductors, office-automation equipment, pollution-control equipment and information technology. The rapidly changing nature of technology, technological diversities and knowledge-sharing with changing paradigms are also providing domestic companies with opportunities for innovative technological applications. In the case of many Chinese and East Asian countries, Japanese firms are forging transactional relationships with host country firms. It has not only transferred know-how, but has also induced local production and strengthened their interdependence in creating liaisons among themselves. This cooperative alliance has facilitated the diffusion and increased the speed of change – economic as well as technological; it has also created a new stage in the expansion of the globalization process considered essential and beneficial for the countries' development. With intense competition for FDI, and a proactive approach geared to the development of domestic firms, the next wave of Japanese FDI is likely to come from domestic companies, seeking faster catch-up for international operation.

# 5 Determinants of Japanese FDI Flows

## 5.1 Introduction

Japanese FDI outflows are distributed globally in a very uneven manner with a handful of countries receiving the bulk – and the Asian countries are no exception (chapter 2). Even though the pattern of FDI distribution has changed over the decades, with some countries gaining at the expense of others, the pattern of distribution continues to be concentrated. However, its impressive growth in the East Asian countries and China has generated a lot of debate about the major determinants of these flows and the country-specific location advantages that these economies enjoy in providing motivation and opportunities for the activities of Japanese MNEs. Even though these countries are geographically close, and having almost similar development trajectories and the regional integration is encouraging the expansion of their market network yet their economic characterization in attracting Japanese FDI greatly differs from one another, leading to wide differences in the scale of Japanese FDI flows both within and between NIEs, ASEAN, China and India throughout this period.

Cross-country differences in country-specific location advantages may be at the core of this finding. The economic fundamentals of the host countries and their FDI policies influence the ability of Japanese MNEs to internalize their operations for as far as the regional bias is concerned, it applies equally to all of these countries and so do the investor's ownership advantages. In addition, different location selection criteria apply to projects of different motivation – that is, whether for the export platform or for the domestic market. Broadly speaking, the configuration of OLI advantages (Dunning 1981b, 1993) and the stages of competitive development of the host countries (Porter 1990) and host government policies (Brewer 1993) provide motivations that influence the ability of MNEs to internalize their operations. However, the complex nature of the location advantage concept has substantially broadened its analytical scope over the last few decades because of its in-depth focus on the actual behaviour of MNEs and the dynamics of the current international environment.

Importantly, in the current global environment, the efficiency-seeking investments are likely to dominate over host country market-seeking investments. MNEs could be motivated to go where knowledge is to be found and where partnerships with knowledge-intensive enterprises can be formed. While traditional factor endowments play a less important role in influencing FDI, the 'created' competences and capabilities, the availability and quality of supporting industries, the characteristics of the local competition, the nature of consumer demand and the macro and micro policies of governments play a more important role. The new competitive context has raised new challenges for both governments and MNEs. Ownership advantages are changing and MNEs are seeking to enhance their own competitiveness in an international context the vital part of which is to improve competitiveness through higher value-added activities in line with logistics and market demands.

It is also pertinent to mention that the Japanese FDI is recent in origin and is seen as having a greater 'vantage effect' than that of the US or Europe. This aspect has led to a highlighting of the importance of Japan as a source country of FDI (see Kojima 1978, 1982, 1985; Dunning 1988, 1994, 1995; Doyle, Saunders and Wong 1992; Yamamura 1994; Schroath, Hu and Chen 1993; Encarnation 1999; and Ravenhill 1999). The evolving nature of Japanese FDI and its determinants need to be tested periodically.

The 'waves' in Japanese FDI outflows examined in the previous chapter showed wide inter-temporal and inter-country differences in its scale both within and between the NIEs, ASEAN-4, China and India.

Some relevant economic characteristics of these countries are given in Table 5.1.

Over the decades Japanese FDI activity is consistent with different phases of the dynamism of the host country. This can be better captured by the Japanese FDI to GDP ratio. Illustratively, taking the period 1981–2005 into consideration, on average, Singapore received Japanese FDI equal to 1.64 per cent of its GDP, followed by Hong Kong , with 1.12 per cent. By contrast, India was able to attract only 0.028 per cent of its GDP – the lowest of all. This is shown in Figure 5.1.

*Table 5.1* Selected economic characteristics – overall annual averages, 1981–2005

| Group | Country | Average per capita Japanese FDI ($) | Average ratio of Japanese FDI to GDP | Average per capita income ($) | Average ratio of GDCF to GDP | Average ratio of Japanese trade to GDP |
|---|---|---|---|---|---|---|
| **NIEs** | | | | | | |
| | Hong Kong | 146 | 1.1 | 16457 | 29.0 | 24.7 |
| | Singapore | 216 | 1.6 | 16026 | 34.5 | 38.7 |
| | Taiwan | 15.6 | 0.18 | 9183 | 22.68 | 15.47 |
| | Korea | 10.24 | 0.18 | 7527 | 25.21 | 11.39 |
| **ASEAN-4** | | | | | | |
| | Indonesia | 5.31 | 0.73 | 769 | 26.71 | 12.17 |
| | Thailand | 13.24 | 0.70 | 1732 | 30.05 | 15.49 |
| | Malaysia | 20.81 | 0.70 | 3119 | 31.43 | 25.79 |
| | Philippines | 4.26 | 0.47 | 837 | 20.45 | 11.33 |
| **China** | | 1.2 | 0.18 | 609 | 38.8 | 6.3 |
| **India** | | 0.12 | 0.03 | 357 | 25.69 | 1.08 |

*Note*: Year-wise trends relating to important economic characteristics are given in Table 5A.3 at the end of the book.

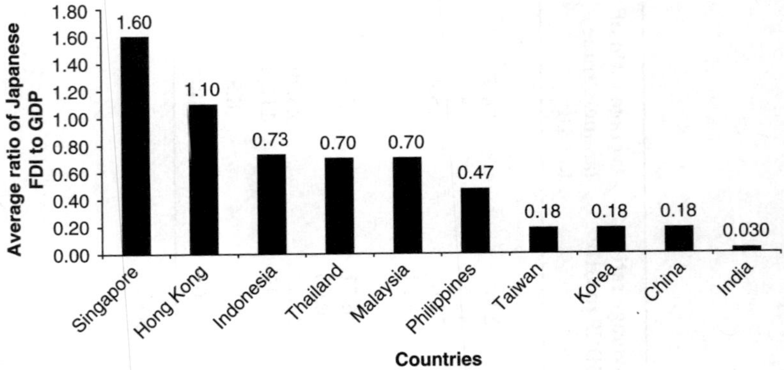


*Figure 5.1* Average Japanese FDI to GDP ratio, 1981–2005

## 5.2 Main goals

Japanese FDI flows to the ten countries have responded to a variety of motivations over the period and the 'pull' factors have differed according to the host country. Against this backdrop, the two goals of the study are: *First,* to investigate the driving factors of Japanese FDI outflows to the country-groups. It is important to conduct a comprehensive test of the determinants, keeping in view the characteristics of the host countries and the evolving nature of Japanese FDI. *Secondly,* to determine the differentiating variables, if any, between the country-groups which may be influencing the distribution of Japanese FDI flows amongst them.

To investigate this we have developed a general model using a set of economic variables. Restricted models have also been developed, based upon the statistical significance of the variables and the basic economic reasoning implicit in these groups. This is important because, despite many similarities, these countries are a heterogeneous group of economies representing somewhat diverse investment regimes, economic trends, ownership structures, and belong to different levels of technology and form varying levels of linkages with Japan. There are also general asymmetries in their macroeconomic fundamentals, as also in the FDI activities of the NIEs and the ASEAN countries, China and India. To the best of our knowledge, no such attempt has been made previously to examine the determinants of Japanese FDI to these country-groups.

## 5.3 Determinants of FDI and literature survey

### 5.3.1 The determinants

Variables considered by us and those used in other studies are given in Table 5.2.

The definitions of the variables and the sources of data are reported in Table 5A.1.

### 5.3.2 Literature survey

*1. Market size*

A survey of the literature on the determinants of FDI, including that by Dunning (1973), Kobrin (1976), Root and Ahmed (1979), Levis (1979), Agarwal (1980) and Contractor (1990), had all found evidence that market size influencined the levels of FDI. In their study covering 42 countries Wheeler and Mody (1992) emphasized, in addition to other factors, the significance of market size in attracting US FDI. Wells and Wint (1991) and Grosse and Trevino (1996) found GDP per capita to be a significant explanatory variable for FDI, reflecting a high level of potential consumption in the host country. An UNCTAD study also found that the rate of change in GNP has a significant effect on FDI inflows.

If we consider the country-groups under study, the market variable has been investigated in some studies. For example, Wang and Swain (1995), Wei (1995), Liu *et al.* (1997), Dees (1998), Zhang (2000), Hong and Chen (2001) and Wei and Liu (2001) investigated the determinants of FDI at the national level in the case of China. But they relate to one country and rely on relatively short period time series data and consequently suffer from the problem of too few degrees of freedom. Chen, Chang and Zhang (1995) as well as Sun (1998) have also fitted regression equations to establish that the FDI inflow was a significant factor in the growth of China's GDP. Lardy (1995), Chen (1996), Henley *et al.* (1999) and Zhang (2001) identified market size, and preferential policies, among others, as primary factors for China.

Two important characteristics – that is, average per capita GDP, and average per capita Japanese FDI given in Figures 5.2 and 5.3 in the ten countries under study present an interesting picture of inter-country variation.

*2. Infrastructure*

Empirical evidence shows that FDI is attracted towards countries with acceptable levels of infrastructure. Belderbos *et al.* (2001) confirms the size of the local component industry and infrastructure facilities as being

*Table 5.2* Determining variables

| Determinants | Variables used in the literature | Empirical studies | Variables used in this study | Expected sign |
|---|---|---|---|---|
| 1. Market size-current and potential | 1. Log GDP<br>2. Per capita income<br>3. GDP growth rate<br>4. Per capita growth rate | A large number are cited in the text, viz., Lardy (1995), Chen (1996), Henley *et al.* (1999); Zhang (2001) | Log GDP | + |
| 2. Gross Domestic Capital formation | Domestic investment | Sun *et al.* (2002); Bosworth and Colins (1999) | Gross domestic capital formation to GDP ratio (GDCF/GDP) | + |
| 3. Trade with Japan | Trade–FDI relationship | Kojima (1973, 1975, 1978, 1985, 1986); Urata (1993, 1998); Sakakibara and Yamakawa (2003 a&b) | Trade with Japan to GDP (FTJGDP) ratio | + |
| 4. Real Effective Exchange rate | Real effective exchange rate | Klein and Rosengren (1994), Dewenter (1995), Goldberg and Klein (1997), Bayoumi and Lipworth (1998), Sazanami *et al.* (2003) | Real effective exchange rate | – |
| 5. Yen appreciation | Rate of change in yen to $ | A large body of literature following the Plaza Accord on yen appreciation exists. (Also see Ito 2000) | Rate of change in yen to $ | + |
| 6. Infrastructure | Investment in infrastructure | Bende-Nabende *et al.* (2000), Cheng and Kwan (2000), Belderbos *et al.* (2001) Loree and Guisinger (1995) | Investment in infrastructure | + |
| 7. Economic stability | Budget surplus/ deficit to GDP ratio | Trevino, *et al.* (2002) | Budget surplus/deficit to GDP ratio | + |
| 8. Skill | Literacy rates | Schneider and Frey (1985) | Per capita investment on education | + |

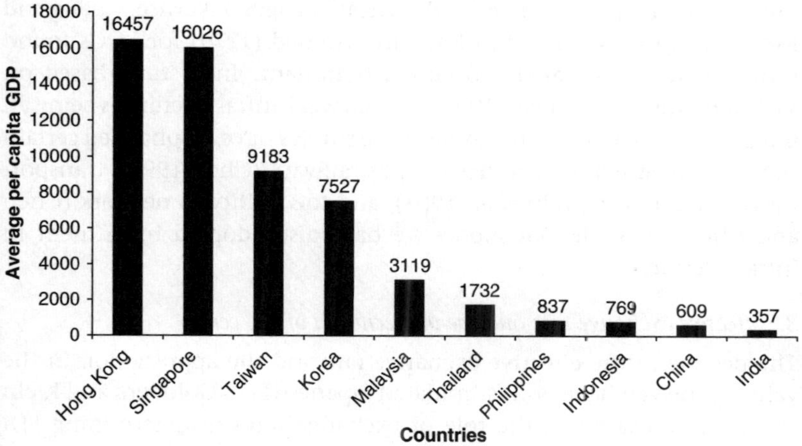


*Figure 5.2* Average per capita GDP, 1981–2005

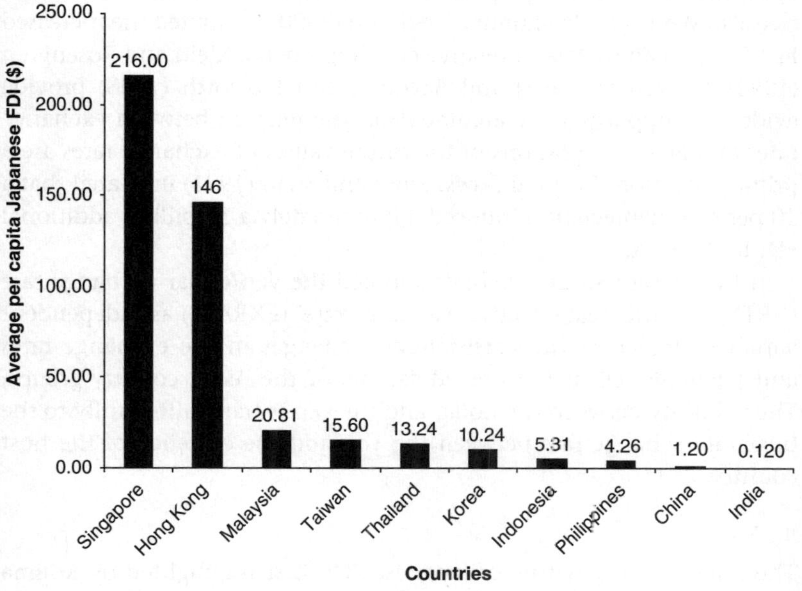


*Figure 5.3* Average per capita Japanese FDI, 1981–2005

important for Japanese MNEs' FDI vertical linkages. Likewise, Cheng and Kwan (2000) for China, and Root and Ahmed (1979) for LDCs found infrastructure to be an important determinant. In a study based on Vietnam, Kokko and Zejan (1996) stressed weak infrastructure as being an impediment to investment. Some of the studies have emphasized certain specific infrastructure facilities such as railways (Chen 1996), transport infrastructure (Coughlin *et al.* 1991), and the facility to network (Chen and Chen 1998). In our model we have also adopted investment in infrastructure.

*3. Effective exchange rate and the appreciation of the yen*

The decline in the effective exchange rate and the appreciation in the value of the yen have both stimulated Japanese FDI. Goldberg and Klein (1997) have examined the role of exchange rates in determining FDI flows from Japan and the USA to Southeast Asia and Latin America. Their empirical results indicate that the appreciation of the yen did boost direct investment from Japan to these areas. Japanese FDI to Asian countries has been stimulated by the decline in the East Asian real exchange rates (RER) and the sharp appreciation of the yen after the Plaza Accord (see also Wong and Yamamura 1996). Ito (2000) attributed the increased FDI from Japan to Asia to relative cost hypothesis. Klein and Rosengren (1994), Dewenter (1995) and Bayoumi and Lipworth (1998) provide evidences supporting the argument on the relation between exchange rates and FDI. Expectations of the future values of exchange rates are a prime generator of capital flows. Froot and Stein (1991) indicated that a 10 per cent depreciation induced approximately a $5 billion additional FDI to the USA.

In the present study, we have adopted the yen/dollar exchange rate (XRTY) and the 'real effective exchange rate' (EXRATE) as independent variables, to reflect the persistency of changes in the exchange rates and Japanese FDI in the pooled sample of the Asian country-groups. The volatility between the dollar and the yen is transmitted fully to the bilateral exchange rate between the yen and the currency of the host country.

*4. Trade*

The trade-creating nature of Japanese FDI, first highlighted by Kojima (1973), and extensively discussed by later researchers, even though it is considered to be static in approach, has led to a vast literature comparing various aspects of Japanese FDI. It continues to evoke interest in Japanese FDI–trade–FDI linkages according to which the dispersion of technology that influences the trade pattern is transmitted through FDI from the lead country to follower countries (Akamatsu 1960). Firms from the lead-country, that is, Japan, combine their technological advantage with the lower factor costs in follower countries; move production of 'second-tier' products offshore. The combination of foreign capital and cheaper production costs makes the follower country's products more competitive in the world market, leading to a higher volume of trade. This trade–FDI–trade interacting link has been discussed at length in a number of studies, including in the case of East Asia (for instance, Kreinin and Plummer 1994; UNCTAD 1996; Liu *et al.* 1997).

With its history of FDI-led export-oriented growth, East Asia is said to have ridden the crest of the 'third wave of integration (or globalization)'. The phenomenal growth of the 1980s and early 1990s has been attributed mainly to the linkages between Japan–East Asia's trade and FDI – both interacting in a mutually promoting way. In this dynamic context, regional agreements and regional production networks – involving the consolidation of facilities in a few locations and the building of suppliers' bases – is facilitating its efficient functioning. It has often been stated that there is a virtuous cycle at work between Japan and East Asia, with FDI contributing to greater levels of trade, which in turn creates pressures for further trade and investment, and leads to an even greater volume of FDI flows. Bilateral trade between Japan and the host East Asian countries has stimulated Japanese FDI as it has provided a good platform for business and also reflects its competitiveness. It is a dynamic process having led to greater business interactions between Japan and these host countries.

Taken as a whole, the region of East Asia has a considerably higher Japanese trade to GDP ratio; however, there are significant differences in the level of this ratio, with Singapore and Hong Kong at the higher end and Indonesia at the lower end, reflecting their relatively different economic positions (see Figure 5.4). Further, China is influencing the pattern of trade and FDI in the region while many MNCs are relocating their operations in China.

In view of the above, we have used the 'trade with Japan to GDP' ratio (FTJGDP) in the model in the present study.

### 5. *Human skills*

The creation of technological infrastructure expanding the domestic base of 'created' assets and human-resource creating activities has assumed great significance in the present Internet age. Comparative location advantage is not confined to tangible location factors, but also includes intangible assets such as human skills in addition to infrastructure and

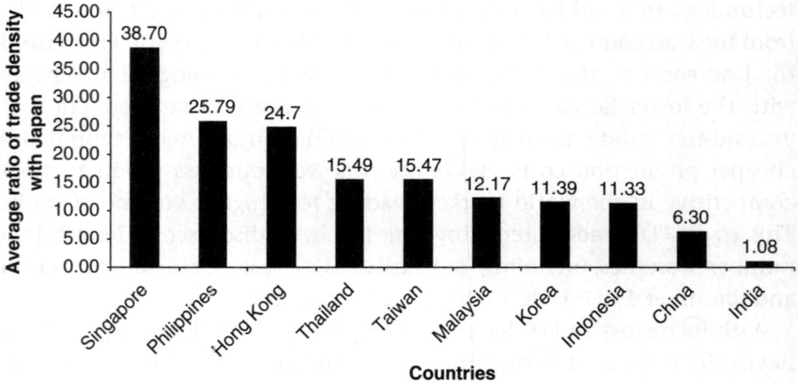


*Figure 5.4* Trade density with Japan: average from 1981 to 2005

the institutional framework which are the keys to competitiveness. A higher level of human capital is essential for absorbing technologies, managerial techniques such as JMT, and the spillover effects of FDI. Mody and Wang (1997), Ichniowski *et al.* (1997), MacDuffie and Krafcik (1992), Berthelemy and Demurger (2000) and Zhang (2001) have all found a positive relationship between human capital and FDI. We have adopted per capita investment in education (PCINVEDU) as one of the independent variables.

*6. Domestic investment*

Domestic investment invariably plays a key role in any economy and weighs heavily in the international location decisions made by MNEs. Studies (for instance, Sun *et al.* 2002) find a significant relationship between FDI and domestic investment. These economies witness very high ratios of domestic investment to GDP. We have, therefore, used the gross domestic capital formation/GDP ratio as one of the independent variables in our model (see Figure 5.5).

Foreign investment also results typically in increased levels of domestic investment. Bosworth and Collins (1999), through an analysis of panel data for 58 countries, found a significant relationship between capital inflows and domestic investment.

*7. Macroeconomic stability*

Macroeconomic stability is fundamental and enhances policy credibility. In its absence FDI will gain little traction. This is an important variable in the case of developing economies and particularly for East Asian

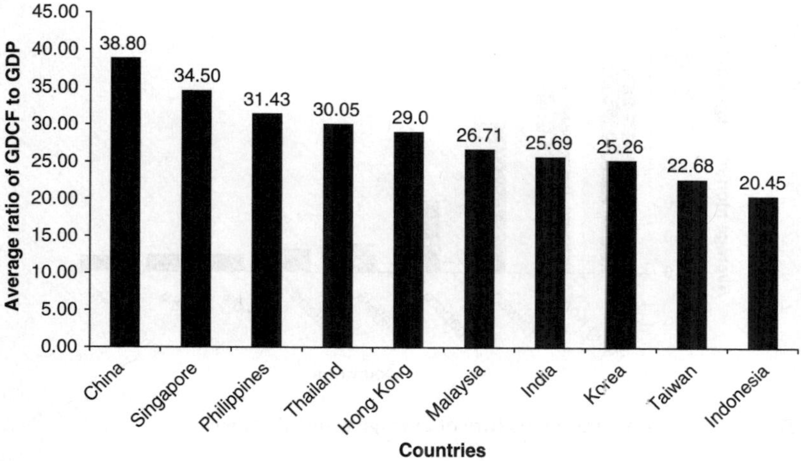


*Figure 5.5* Average ratio of gross domestic capital formation to GDP, 1981–2005

economies, which have witnessed a serious financial crisis during the 1990s.

In the present study we have used the overall ratio of budgetary deficit/surplus to GDP (BUGTDEF) as a measure of the overall economic stability of a country.

*8. Costs*

FDI is increasingly geared to more capital- and knowledge-intensive activities exhibiting a decline in labour-intensive FDI and Japanese FDI is no exception. Labour costs do not give any indication about the Japanese FDI location dimension. Apparently, with an increase in efficiency- and/or knowledge-based FDI, investors are not gaining cross-country competitive advantage through low wages, unless other conditions are also satisfied. This inference is also consistent with the findings of a number of studies (see Caves 1996; Dunning 1998a; Head and Ries 1996). Although Zhao and Zhu (2000) found a positive relationship but they had not examined it on a comparative cross-country basis.

Wages paid by the Japanese companies to workers bears testimony to the fact that wage rates are not statistical measures of significance to attract FDI. In other words, there is no substantive empirical evidence to support that lower wages attract higher FDI flows. For instance, even though cost-wise India figures among the relatively cheap but it had no advantage in FDI over others. This is borne out from the '15th survey of

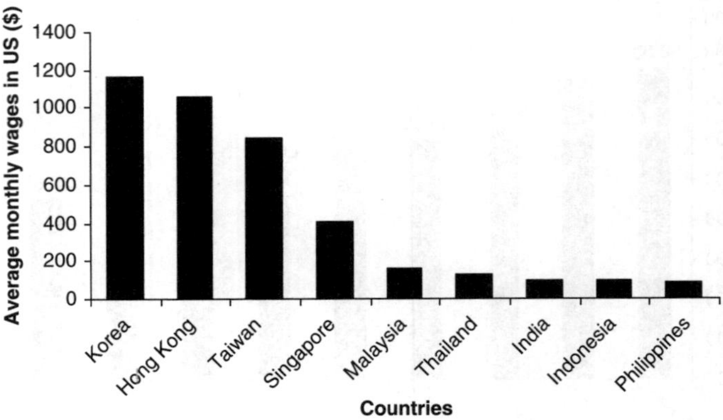


*Figure 5.6* A comparative picture of average monthly wages

the investment-related cost comparison in major regions in Asia' carried out by JETRO (Table 5A.2: End Notes) The study shows that the monthly wages paid to workers is 11 times more in Korea; ten times more in Hong Kong; eight times more in Taiwan; and four times in Singapore. In the case of the ASEAN, the wage rates are relatively higher in Malaysia and Thailand. Figure 5.6 presents a comparative picture of the average monthly wages paid by the Japanese companies during 2004.

Higher wages may be signifying higher skills, quality, efficiency and productivity. Besides, it is not just the costs but also a host of inflexible laws that have a negative effect on the incentive to work and productivity. After examining the data we have not hypothesized any particular relationship between the cost and location of FDI in these countries.

### 9. *Investment incentives*

Incentives are also important factors in the determination of investment decisions. Many studies (see, for instance, Boskin and Gale 1987; Grubert and Mutti 1991; Hines and Rice 1994; Lall and Mohammed 1983) have confirmed that fiscal and other incentives offer strong motivations for the location of foreign investments.

Schroath, Hu and Chen (1993) conducted an empirical test of some fiscal incentives in China and found a larger percentage of FDI in regions where there are tax and economic incentives. Wei (2000), based on a sample study of bilateral investment from 12 source countries to 45 host countries, found that an increase in either the tax rate or the corruption level in the host countries would reduce inward FDI.

*Method adopted*

For the country-groups we had no reliable data, unlike for other variables to examine the impact of these variables on Japanese FDI. Hence, we sought the information directly from the investors on the extent to which the selected incentives such as fiscal incentives, royalty, exchange-controls, exerted an influence on Japanese FDI outflows. In the questionnaires which were addressed to different groups of firms with investments in East Asian countries, China, and India, and also to firms with investments in other parts of the globe MNEs were also asked to give their grading on a five-point scale ranging from: −2 (very bad), −1 (bad), 0 (indifferent), +1 (good) and +2 (very good) in respect of the investment incentives. For this purpose, as for other variables (Chapter 3), four alternative systems of averaging, i.e., simple average and three weighted averages using three different systems of weighting, i.e., total assets, total capital stock and total number of employees as weights have been used. However, the weighted averages based on these three variables yielded similar results; we have presented a single weighted average based on 'Total Assets' in addition to the un-weighted one.

*Responses of investors*

Most of the responding companies asserted that the fiscal incentives, royalty, liberalized exchange system and the removal of restrictions are important in making investment decisions. The average ratings calculated from the responses given by the Japanese companies in the countries in which they have invested, confirms a positive relationship. The estimates are furnished in Table 5.3.

### 5.3.3 Cross-country FDI policies

Policy factors play a dominant role, but it is difficult to make a statistical examination of FDI-specific policies because they are often 'more implicit than explicit' (Globerman and Shapiro 1999). But there is a lot of literature about the enabling policy environment adopted by the East Asian countries to attract FDI (see, among others, Ozawa 1979; Phongpaichit 1990; Ramstetter 1991).

When the countries are competing for FDI, then cross-countries' location advantages to attract FDI have to be analysed in a comparative cross-national perspective as well as in terms of cross-national policy changes. The location-specific relative attractiveness of the countries may vitally affect both FDI decisions and also the several individual components of FDI flows. This holds true across the board – whether in

*Table 5.3* Average ratings of the economic incentives in the host countries by Japanese investors investing in Asia (five-point scale: +2, +1, 0, −1, −2)

| | **Un-weighted** | **Weighted** |
|---|---|---|
| 1. Fiscal incentives | | |
| Mean | (+) 0.78 | (+) 0.65 |
| S.D. | 0.42 | 0.48 |
| 2. Royalty | | |
| Mean | (+) 1.00 | (+) 1.04 |
| S.D. | 0.67 | 0.26 |
| 3. Liberailzed exchange system | | |
| Mean | (+) 1.44 | (+) 0.94 |
| S.D. | 0.68 | 0.73 |
| 4. Removal of restrictions | | |
| Mean | (+) 1.11 | (+) 1.28 |
| S.D. | 1.34 | 0.75 |

*Note*: It may be added that fiscal incentives are second best in nature, the first-best approach would be to address at source the unattractive features of the host economy environment.

terms of the system of incentives, entry–exit regulations, sectoral caps, bureaucratic procedures or other complexities for doing business.

*NIEs and the ASEAN-4*: NIEs and the ASEAN-4, with their economic dynamism and strong regional links with Japan in the lead, continue with their FDI policy reforms which include a further loosening of the restrictions on FDI – concerning ownership, sector allocation, and local employment, granting special FDI incentives, such as tax concessions, capital transfers and also making them more transparent Other major steps include: lifting or relaxing of limitations on stock shares; opening up of new fields of investment, services and trade in the main, diversifying modes of investment, which include greenfield investment and investment in mergers and acquisitions; simplifying approval formalities to the extent that in many fields FDI is registered merely for the record; the adoption of more preferential policies, including income tax reduction and exemption, incentives for expanding exports and allowing them to hire more foreign employees. Liberalization and pro-FDI policies on the one hand, and relatively well-developed infrastructure and other institutions, structural adjustment policies, and the creation of a single market through AFTA and AIA on the other, have placed these countries in a unique position (see Yusuf *et al.* 2003; ASEAN 2000). However, despite policy liberalization, the relatively more industrialized countries attracted larger amounts of FDI; other low-income ones continue to receive less.

*China*: China has been encountering tough challenges in its endeavour to attract more foreign investment. Its attempt to attract FDI forms a coherent mix of rigorous policy which forms a gradual and logical continuum moving faster in technology and innovation-driven FDI, even in a coercive manner. From the very beginning of the reform process, a driving force behind China's exceptional growth of FDI has been the adoption of the East Asian style of incentives, good location by creation of Special Economic Zones in southern China, joint venture (J.V.) status with 25 per cent foreign investment, including direct trading rights, the introduction of new technologies, and know-how, other logistics, increasing the openness of its economy, besides special privileges to foreign investors. Since 1998, China has further increased its efforts to encourage FDI in the development and innovation of technology by giving various fiscal incentives. Other inducing factors include its higher rate of economic growth, the reform of state-owned enterprises, the development of high-tech industries, and its accession to the WTO. The latter implies a further relaxation of the entry bans and a more open China in future: the opening up of new investment fields include its finance, insurance and securities, wholesale, retail, and intermediary services. These areas are highly attractive to Japanese investors (see also Huang 2003; Hatch and Yamamura 1996).

*India*: There is a paradigm shift in the attitude of India towards FDI since the decade of the 1990s after the liberalization of policies and removal of irritants. However, even when seeking to promote it, policy paradoxes still remain – for example, entry–exit barriers, labour market regulations, sectoral caps and operational gaps constitute important dimensions and work as disincentives in firms' location decision (see also the World Bank's study on *Doing Business in 2006*). FDI investors perceive a high degree of uncertainty in India owing to political complexities, bureaucratic delays which translate into a higher risk perception for which there is no risk–return trade-off for investors. India's structural inconveniences and the weak credibility of its regulatory systems is having an adverse impact on foreign investors. Secondly, there are sector policy issues whose elements and procedures still remain absent across the board – *viz.*, the power sector, the chemicals sector, food processing, services sectors, retail sector and Special Export Zones. Thirdly, the lack of coordination between the centre and the states, their duality and divide creates difficulties at the approval and implementation stages, leading not only to a cost and time overrun but also to the abandonment of the projects. Fourthly, policies remain more dispersed (in spite of the prioritization of recipient industries) and evolve by spurts depending upon the political complexion of the party in governance which constitutes an important factor jeopardizing the attainment of a coherent approach. In fact, entry bans and sectoral caps on FDI in different sectors make the FDI model more rent-seeking and also increase the political economy of dispensing patronage. Technology transfer is also rigorously pursued in India, *albeit* on paper in theoretical terms. Fifthly, the control systems are compounded by complex administrative procedures, lengthy approval procedures and formalities, delays, corruption, lack of transparency and accountability. Sixthly, there are frequent and sudden changes in policies, which make it difficult to prepare a business plan and have even resulted in many cases to changes in Memoranda of Understanding (MOUs). Policy shifts with changes in the political complexion of the governments constitute yet another major irritant in India. Institutions exist, but they lack accountability. One example of this is provided by the Special Export Zones (SEZs), which also exist in India but have yet to experience demonstrable success, in contrast to the position in China's coastal regions and other competing destinations. In India, the SEZs are still not fully at par with the Export Zones in China. In fact, when Japanese investors consider making any new investment decision, India often loses out at the screening stage.

Now we may sum up the cross-country FDI policies by giving a comparative perspective. We have basically the following three variants: First is the East Asian – NIEs and the ASEAN – variant adopting market-friendly and export-oriented policy relying on a combination of infrastructural support, tax concessions and so on accepting the rigours of international competition and willing to experiment with alternative policy instruments and to change them if found ineffective in building up a cost and efficiency based advantage. Second is the Chinese variant which essentially follows the East Asian model, making careful choices while departing from their belief system, getting the regime support and displaying an *adaptive efficiency*. And finally, third we have the Indian variant, still based on the *distrust* of FDI, lack of coordination, and a big gap in implementation. As between China and India some stylized facts about their FDI regime are given in Table 5A.4 at the end of the book.

### 5.3.4 China – India's differing perception

China has chosen to be hospitable to MNEs to secure the know-how for building up its own industry in the sunrise sectors. And the vision of the party leadership having a strong sense of national interest has influenced the kind of reforms that are pursued. This has helped China to emerge as a key player in the global market. The basic driving force behind China's efforts to attract FDI is to speedily modernise the economy and upgrade the technologies of its enterprises, including the small and medium-sized firms investing in joint ventures in village and town enterprises (see also Zhang and Van Den Bulcke 1995). It decentralized its decision-making process and even permitted individual cities to grant permission for FDI. The ubiquitous presence of firms established through FDI can be found in many industries and in many regions of the country. It has also established a dominant position in export production and the *de facto* operating control is substantial in its export-processing operation. A large number of Japanese MNEs have relocated production sites there. India compares weakly with China. The trends and patterns of Japanese FDI in India show that approximately 90 per cent of the total flows were in the four sectors of chemicals, electrical (including electronics), transport, and consultancy and R&D. By contrast, the sectors in which Japanese FDI is playing an important role in Asian countries including China are services, commerce, finance, insurance and real estate.

In a cross-country context the existing strategy for attracting FDI, including sectoral caps and entry barriers, needs to be refined in the light of new developments using information technology and modern marketing techniques. Secondly, the weak credibility of regulatory system and the multiple and conflicting roles of the players will have an adverse impact on foreign investors. It calls for the reforms of grass-roots – micro-micro reforms. In many cases, the regulatory reforms are stand-alone reforms and are neither mutually exclusive nor sequential in nature. There are policy paradoxes with adverse consequences.

## 5.4 The model – construction of variables and the method of estimation

The model – construction of variables and the method of estimation – is given in the technical annex at the end of this book. Here it is important to mention that in order to avoid the arbitrary choice of the explanatory variables in our analysis we began with a large number of independent variables, before narrowing these down to a few. This is a 'general to simple' modelling method like that suggested by Hendry and his associates (see Krishna 1997). Coming to the models, we have the general model and restricted models in the alternative specification.

*First,* the general model for ten countries in eight groups and *secondly* an alternative specification is presented.

In the general model, the variables are:

**Dependent variable**
FDI: Foreign direct investment outflows from Japan (in US dollars).

**Independent variables: the determinants**

1. GDP: Gross domestic product by industrial origin
2. GDCF/GDP: Ratio of gross domestic capital formation to gross domestic product
3. INVINFRA: Investment in infrastructure
4. XRTY: Change in the exchange rate of the yen
5. PCINVEDU: Per capita expenditure on education
6. BUGTDEF: Budget deficit to GDP ratio
7. EXRATE: Real effective exchange rate
8. FTJGDP: Ratio of trade with Japan to GDP
9. Time trend: The estimated equations also include 'time trend' variable.

Using the panel method, the general model has been estimated using the same number of independent variables for the following groups of countries:

- NIEs
- NIEs + China
- ASEAN-4
- ASEAN-4 + China
- ASEAN-4 + China + India
- China + India (together based on panel method)
- China and India separately using (OLS method)
- All the ten countries.

Secondly, in the alternative specification we have reduced not only the number of independent variables but also the number of groups to three – that is, and all the ten countries based on economic reasoning and the level of significance giving different specifications to different groups on the basis of their statistical significance and basic economic reasoning.

The determinants of FDI flows have been estimated with the help of balanced panel data techniques – namely, the Fixed (FE) and Random Effects (RE) models covering the periods 1981–90; 1991–2004 and 1981–2004. The Lagrange multiplier and Hausman test results indicate the

Random Effects model to be appropriate ones, even though both RE and FE models were estimated.

## 5.5 Econometric results and interpretation

As mentioned, the Lagrange multiplier statistic and Hausman test results indicate that Random Effects models are most appropriate for our analysis. Although the results remain qualitatively the same even in the Fixed Effects models, here we present only the results of the Random Effects models. Secondly, in order to avoid the problem of simultaneity between the explanatory variables and the dependent variable (that is, Log Japanese FDI), the independent variables are lagged by one year after observing the relationships. Thirdly, the results cover the period 1981–2004 and also two sub-periods, 1981–90 and 1991–2004, as the Japanese FDI to the country-groups was characterized by different waves over the period. To maintain comparability and consistency with the estimates of the entire period, panel application has also been undertaken for the sub-periods.

### 5.5.1 General model

*i(a) NIEs*

Infrastructure (INVINFRA) is a prominent determinant in terms of both the values of the coefficients and also the level of significance in attracting Japanese FDI even in the sub-periods. The decline in the effective exchange rate (EXRATE) stimulated Japanese FDI. This is consistent with Sazanami *et al.* (2003), who also found similar results. The estimates also reveal that the appreciation in the Japanese yen (XRTY) and 'economic stability' (BUGTDEF) have had positive effects. Trade with Japan (FTJGDP) is another significant variable taking the whole period into consideration. However, the coefficient of GDP is positive but not statistically significant.

*i(b) NIEs + China*

When China is included in the group of NIEs, the 'market' variable (here measured by GDP) also becomes a significant determinant (Table 5.5). In regard to the other variables, they remain the same, but become more prominent. The 'trade' variable (FTJGDP) becomes more prominent, with higher elasticity. The other variables which have become more significant are: the appreciation of the yen (XRTY), the decline in the effective exchange rate (EXRATE) and infrastructure (INVINFRA). They were also significant in the sub-periods.

*Table 5.4* Parameter estimates for Japanese FDI flows: NIEs

| Explanatory variables | 1981–90 | | 1991–2004 | | 1981–2004 | |
|---|---|---|---|---|---|---|
| | Coefficient | t-stat | Coefficient | t-stat | Coefficient | t-stat |
| 1 GDP | 0.523 | 0.9 | −0.039 | −0.13 | 0.398 | 1.51 |
| 2 GDCF/GDP | −1.845* | −2.38 | 0.357 | 0.87 | −0.391 | 1.17 |
| 3 FTJGDP | 0.912 | 0.98 | 0.355 | 0.94 | 0.732** | 1.94 |
| 4 PCINVEDU | 0.526** | 2.33 | −0.274** | −2.00 | 0.015 | 0.12 |
| 5 XRTY | 0.129 | 0.13 | 0.752* | 3.09 | 0.763* | 2.75 |
| 6 BUGTDEF | −0.004 | −0.10 | 0.037** | 1.76 | 0.055* | 3.14 |
| 7 INVINFRA | 0.951* | 2.17 | 0.523* | 2.23 | 0.6135* | 3.12 |
| 8 EXRATE | −1.546* | −2.34 | 1.22 | −1.52 | −1.428* | −2.66 |
| Time trend | −0.014 | −0.45 | −0.0005 | −0.06 | −0.0012*** | 0.09 |
| Constant | −4.632 | −0.50 | −2.059 | −0.61 | −4.261 | −1.46 |
| R-square | 0.766 | | 0.538 | | 0.527 | |
| Hausman statistic | 1.69 | | 8.96 | | 10.6 | |
| Lagrange multipliers | 1.68 | | 2.05 | | 1.26 | |
| Number of observations | 36 | | 56 | | 92 | |

*Note*: *Significant at 1 per cent; **Significant at 5 per cent; ***Significant at 10 per cent.

The results are consistent with the empirical results of other studies which relate to China. In particular, the results reported by Wei (1995), Liu *et al.* (1997), Dees (1998), Wei and Liu (2001), who have also used panel data to estimate the growth of FDI inflows into China indicate market size as having a significant and positive effect on inward FDI. The other factors which have motivated FDI to China are: trade (Wei *et al.* 1999); the appreciation of the yen (Wong and Yamamura 1996); and infrastructure (Head and Ries 1996).

### *ii(a) ASEAN-4*

In the case of ASEAN-4, the 'trade' variable (FTJGDP) shows higher elasticity. Japanese FDI-trade linkages are both efficiency-seeking and resource-seeking – the former creating trade while the latter one augments it. Decline in the effective exchange rate (EXRATE) also significantly stimulated Japanese FDI. Other variables found to be significant are: market size (GDP), except during the sub-period, i.e., 1991–2004. Infrastructure (INVINFRA) is significant except in the second period.

*Table 5.5* Parameter estimates for Japanese FDI flows: NIEs + China

| Explanatory variables | 1981–90 | | 1991–2004 | | 1981–2004 | |
|---|---|---|---|---|---|---|
| | **Coefficient** | **t-stat** | **Coefficient** | **t-stat** | **Coefficient** | **t-stat** |
| 1 GDP | 1.48* | 3.15 | 0.142 | 0.52 | 0.724* | 3.82 |
| 2 GDCF/GDP | 0.074 | 0.1 | 0.522 | 1.25 | −0.329 | −0.96 |
| 3 FTJGDP | 2.284* | 2.76 | 0.733* | 2.84 | 1.391* | 4.53 |
| 4 PCINVEDU | 0.105 | 0.47 | −0.217*** | −1.67 | −0.017 | 0.14 |
| 5 XRTY | 2.801* | 3.86 | 0.738* | 3.27 | 1.173* | 5.5 |
| 6 BUGTDEF | −0.052 | −0.95 | 0.032 | 1.52 | 0.062* | 3.38 |
| 7 INVINFRA | 0.797*** | 1.47 | 0.521* | 2.92 | 0.56* | 2.79 |
| 8 EXRATE | −1.989* | −4.72 | −2.641** | −5.31 | −1.989* | −4.72 |
| Time trend | −0.01 | −0.34 | −0.002 | −0.28 | −0.006 | −1.32 |
| Constant | −34.552 | −4.67 | −1.775 | −0.73 | −9.396* | −5.16 |
| R-square | 0.739 | | 0.692 | | 0.646 | |
| Hausman statistic | 13.77 | | 1.71 | | 1.03 | |
| Lagrange Multipliers | 1.79 | | 2.54 | | 2.52 | |
| Number of observations | 45 | | 70 | | 115 | |

*Note*: *Significant at 1 per cent; **Significant at 5 per cent; ***Significant at 10 per cent.

BUGTDEF, which is a measure of economic stability, is significant except during the first period 1981–90. But PCINVEDU is found to be significant only in the first period (Table 5.6).

### *ii(b) ASEAN-4 + China*

The determinants remain the same when China is added to the ASEAN-4. Only the values of the coefficients have changed. In other words, market size (GDP), trade with Japan (FTJGDP), decline in effective exchange rate (EXRATE), infrastructure (INVINFRA) and economic stability (BUGTDEF) show a significant influence on the level of Japanese FDI. Apparently, China exhibits the similar economic characteristics as that of ASEAN – closer to it than to the NIEs. The results are given in Table 5.7.

### *ii(c) ASEAN-4 + China and India*

When India is also included in the country-group ASEAN-4 + China, the coefficients of FTJGDP are at their highest – that is, trade plays an even more crucial role in attracting Japanese FDI. This is followed by 'market', 'economic stability' (BUGTDEF), and infrastructure (INVINFRA)

*Table 5.6* Parameter estimates for Japanese FDI flows: ASEAN-4

| Explanatory variables | 1981–90 | | 1991–2004 | | 1981–2004 | |
|---|---|---|---|---|---|---|
| | Coefficient | t-stat | Coefficient | t-stat | Coefficient | t-stat |
| 1 GDP | 2.469* | 3.3 | 0.429 | 1.34 | 0.847* | 3.83 |
| 2 GDCF/GDP | 0.388 | 0.54 | −0.164 | −0.70 | −0.0003 | 0.00 |
| 3 FTJGDP | 1.786* | 2.48 | 0.908* | 2.2 | 1.094* | 3.86 |
| 4 PCINVEDU | 1.307* | 2.85 | −0.122 | −0.31 | 0.158 | 0.57 |
| 5 XRTY | 0.322 | 1.27 | 0.153 | 1.18 | 0.072*** | 0.66 |
| 6 BUGTDEF | 0.055 | 1.26 | 0.129* | 3.4 | 0.101* | 4.00 |
| 7 INVINFRA | 1.098** | 2.66 | 0.132 | 0.68 | 0.719* | 2.3 |
| 8 EXRATE | −0.778 | −1.11 | −1.812** | −2.61 | −1.337** | −1.68 |
| Time trend | 0.049** | 2.00 | −0.010 | −1.20 | −0.004 | −1.16 |
| Constant | −16.288 | −1.92 | 4.016 | 1.17 | −2.567 | −1.14 |
| R-square | 0.795 | | 0.555 | | 0.661 | |
| Hausman statistic | 20.73 | | 17.62 | | 4.38 | |
| Lagrange multipliers | 1.25 | | 1.99 | | 1.98 | |
| Number of observations | 36 | | 56 | | 92 | |

*Note*: *Significant at 1 per cent; **Significant at 5 per cent; ***Significant at 10 per cent.

*Table 5.7* Parameter estimates for Japanese FDI flows: ASEAN-4 + China

| Explanatory variables | 1981–1990 | | 1991–2004 | | 1981–2004 | |
|---|---|---|---|---|---|---|
| | Coefficient | t-stat | Coefficient | t-stat | Coefficient | t-stat |
| 1 GDP | 1.566* | 2.83 | 0.478* | 2.91 | 0.755* | 7.3 |
| 2 GDCF/GDP | −1.201 | −1.16 | 0.932* | 2.52 | −0.037 | −0.17 |
| 3 FTJGDP | 4.291* | 5.33 | 1.142* | 2.99 | 1.591* | 5.36 |
| 4 PCINVEDU | 2.455* | 2.69 | 0.254 | −1.07 | 0.298 | 1.56 |
| 5 XRTY | 0.509 | 1.53 | 0.050 | 0.32 | 0.569* | 2.29 |
| 6 BUGTDEF | −0.116 | −1.61 | 0.109* | 2.45 | 0.121* | 5.2 |
| 7 INVINFRA | 0.220 | 0.40 | 0.133 | 0.85 | 0.561* | 2.79 |
| 8 EXRATE | −1.98* | −2.95 | −2.209** | −3.77 | −1.993* | −3.63 |
| Time trend | 0.132* | 2.99 | 0.00001 | 0.01 | 0.0015 | 0.42 |
| Constant | −31.916* | −2.43 | −661 | −0.36 | −4.708* | −2.89 |
| R-square | 0.789 | | 0.769 | | 0.661 | |
| Hausman statistic | 10.5 | | 11.86 | | 14.44 | |
| Lagrange multipliers | 2.14 | | 2.14 | | 0.84 | |
| Number of observations | 45 | | 70 | | 115 | |

*Note*: *Significant at 1 per cent; **Significant at 5 per cent; ***Significant at 10 per cent.

*Table 5.8* Parameter estimates for Japanese FDI flows: ASEAN-4 + China + India

| Explanatory Variables | 1981–90 | | 1991–2004 | | 1981–2004 | |
|---|---|---|---|---|---|---|
| | Coefficient | t-stat | Coefficient | t-stat | Coefficient | t-stat |
| 1 GDP | 0.649** | 2.00 | 0.781* | 5.73 | 0.771* | 7.17 |
| 2 GDCF/GDP | 0.048 | 0.05 | −0.038 | −0.19 | 0.009 | 0.04 |
| 3 FTJGDP | 1.766* | 4.69 | 1.248* | 8.23 | 1.292* | 7.86 |
| 4 PCINVEDU | 0.117 | 0.35 | 0.219 | 0.89 | 0.150 | 0.76 |
| 5 XRTY | 0.518*** | 1.6 | 0.151 | 1.25 | 0.217* | 1.76 |
| 6 BUGTDEF | 0.111* | 3.00 | 0.111* | 4.02 | 0.121** | 5.32 |
| 7 INVINFRA | 0.22 | 0.4 | 0.133 | 0.85 | 0.8104** | 3.37 |
| 8 EXRATE | −0.929** | −1.72 | −2.008* | −3.01 | −1.556* | −2.29 |
| Time trend | 0.005 | 0.3 | −0.002 | −0.33 | −0.001 | −0.31 |
| Constant | −6.859 | −1.22 | −0.944 | −0.54 | −5.743* | −3.36 |
| R-square | 0.796 | | 0.727 | | 0.732 | |
| Hausman statistic | 40.51 | | 7.45 | | 14.12 | |
| Lagrange multipliers | 0.50 | | 2.91 | | 0.99 | |
| Number of observations | 54 | | 84 | | 138 | |

*Note*: *Significant at 1 per cent; **Significant at 5 per cent; ***Significant at 10 per cent.

variables. Declines in the effective exchange rate (EXRATE) and the appreciation of the yen (XRTY) also appear as the other important determinants of Japanese FDI. The results are set out in Table 5.8.

### *iii China and India*

The estimates for China and India – taken together – show trade with Japan (FTJGDP) followed by the appreciation of the yen (XRTY) to be significant determinants of Japanese FDI at the 5 and 10 per cent levels, respectively. The coefficient of infrastructure was also significant at 10 per cent, but it relates only to China. The coefficient of GDP is positive, but not significant. The results are given in Table 5.9(a).

It can be argued, however, that since Japanese FDI to China is 17 times more than the flow to India, bracketing China and India together would mean subjecting Japanese FDI to the same forces – something which may not be tenable. Hence they have been examined separately also using the OLS method in view of the limited number of observations (Table 5.9(b)). We found the results for trade with Japan (FTJGDP) and infrastructure to be positive and significant at the 10 per cent level in the case of China. For India we did not obtain any significant results.

*Table 5.9a* Parameter estimates for Japanese FDI flows: China + India (1981–2004)

| Explanatory variables | Coefficient | t-stat |
|---|---|---|
| 1 GDP | 1.026 | 0.16 |
| 2 GDCF/GDP | 0.224 | 0.11 |
| 3 FTJGDP | **2.214**** | **2.98** |
| 4 PCINVEDU | 0.549 | 0.42 |
| 5 XRTY | **2.538***** | **1.69** |
| 6 BUGTDEF | −0.001 | −0.04 |
| 7 INVINFRA[(@)] | **0.001***** | **4.60** |
| 8 EXRATE | −0.163 | −0.05 |
| Constant | 1.956 | 0.06 |
| R-square | 0.904 | |
| Hausman statistic | 0.08 | |
| Lagrange multipliers | 1.05 | |
| Number of observations | 40 | |

*Note*: [(@)] Refers to China only. We did not have comparable data for India.
*Significant at 1 per cent; **Significant at 5 per cent; ***Significant at 10 per cent.

*Table 5.9b* Parameter estimates for Japanese FDI flows: China and India separately: OLS

| Explanatory variables | China | | India | |
|---|---|---|---|---|
| | Coefficient | t-stat | Coefficient | t-stat |
| 1 GDP | 52.324 | 1.12 | 2.466 | 0.06 |
| 2 GDCF/GDP | 7.828 | 1.87 | −3.195 | −1.41 |
| 3 FTJGDP | **1.09**** | **0.69** | 2.382 | 2.15 |
| 4 PCINVEDU | 1.332 | 0.81 | 0.865 | 0.36 |
| 5 XRTY | 0.349 | 0.14 | 5.609 | 2.26 |
| 6 BUGTDEF | −0.094 | −0.87 | 0.006 | 0.1 |
| 7 INVINFRA | **0.001***** | **4.60** | **$** | **$** |
| 8 EXRATE | 0.474 | 0.14 | −0.003 | −0.40 |
| Constant | −366.061 | −1.15 | −23.931 | −0.09 |
| R-square | 0.646 | | 0.885 | |
| Number of observations | 20 | | 18 | |

*Note*: $ We did not have comparable data for India. But investors have rated India's infrastructure as the worst of all the 10-countries (Chapter 4).
*Significant at 1 per cent; **Significant at 5 per cent; ***Significant at 10 per cent.

### *iv 10-countries*

Taking all the 10-countries together, the empirical results emerge as follows: The trade variable (FTJGDP) is the main driving force in attracting Japanese FDI. This is followed by market (GDP), infrastructure

*Table 5.10* Parameter estimates for Japanese FDI flows for all ten countries

| | Explanatory variables | 1981–90 | | 1990–2004 | | 1981–2004 | |
|---|---|---|---|---|---|---|---|
| | | Coefficient | t-stat | Coefficient | t-stat | Coefficient | t-stat |
| 1 | GDP | 0.976* | 4.87 | 0.455* | 3.39 | 0.5005* | 5.61 |
| 2 | GDCF/GDP | −0.516 | −1.11 | 1.066* | 4.15 | 0.514** | 2.07 |
| 3 | FTJGDP | 2.058* | 7.06 | 0.754* | 3.11 | 1.113* | 5.48 |
| 4 | PCINVEDU | 0.103 | 0.39 | −0.224 | −1.58 | 0.303** | 2.03 |
| 5 | XRTY | 0.711* | 2.97 | 0.062 | 0.56 | 0.369* | 3.53 |
| 6 | BUGTDEF | 0.046*** | 1.48 | 0.042* | 2.16 | 0.0609* | 3.61 |
| 7 | INVINFRA | 0.259*** | 0.90 | 0.417** | 3.11 | 0.491* | 4.17 |
| 8 | EXRATE | −1.943* | −2.94 | −1.366* | −3.62 | −0.972* | −3.22 |
| | Time trend | 0.018*** | 1.53 | −0.008** | −2.54 | 0.003 | 1.46 |
| | Constant | −13.150 | −3.38 | −1.015 | −0.63 | −7.105* | −5.11 |
| | R-square | 0.74 | | 0.615 | | 0.89 | |
| | Hausman statistic | 37.87 | | 88.73 | | 85.04 | |
| | Lagrange multipliers | 3.88 | | 1.01 | | 0.2 | |
| | Number of observations | 90 | | 140 | | 230 | |

*Note*: *Significant at 1 per cent; **Significant at 5 per cent; ***Significant at 10 per cent.

(INVINFRA), the appreciation of the yen (XRTY), the decline in the effective exchange rate (EXRATE), and economic stability (BUGTDEF). Bayoumi and Lipworth (1998), Sazanami *et al.* (2003), Lardy (1995), Henley *et al.* (1999), Chen (1996), Zhang (2001) and the others referred to earlier have also examined this situation, but have confined their analysis to one or two variables. The estimates are presented in Table 5.10.

### 5.5.2 Results of the restricted models

In the alternative specification, as mentioned, we have used a lesser number of variables mainly based on economic reasoning, taking into consideration only the three groups and the entire period. The results are given in Table 5.11.

*NIEs*

Japanese FDI flows in NIEs, which are also important intra-regional investors compared to other Asian countries, have relatively more factor-intensive, export-oriented and innovation-driven FDI. These countries are engaged in more knowledge activities and have also become more dominant players in the creation of skills and new technologies through the Japanese FDI efficiency-seeking route.

*Table 5.11* Restricted model: results

| | Explanatory variables | NIEs | ASEAN | All 10-countries |
|---|---|---|---|---|
| 1 | GDCF/GDP | 0.198<br>(0.78) | | |
| 2 | PCGDP | 0.603*<br>(6.4) | | |
| 3 | XRTY | 0.42**<br>(1.8) | | |
| 4 | EXRATE | −1.428*<br>(−2.66) | | |
| 5 | Time trend | −0.004***<br>(−1.62) | | |
| 1 | PCGDP | | 0.219***<br>(1.7) | |
| 2 | GDCF/GDP | | 1.875*<br>(5.59) | |
| 3 | XRTY | | 0.98*<br>(7.5) | |
| 4. | EXRATE | | −1.992*<br>(−3.63) | |
| 5 | INVINFRA | | 0.533*<br>(3.0) | |
| 1 | GDCF/GDP | | | 1.198*<br>(4.94) |
| 2 | FTJGDP | | | 1.112<br>(0.85) |
| 3 | BUGTDEF | | | 0.095*<br>(6.1) |
| 4 | XRTY | | | 0.631*<br>(6.14) |
| 5 | EXRATE | | | −0.638<br>(−3.73) |
| 6 | INVINFRA | | | 0.352*<br>(4.33) |

*Notes*: *Significant at 1 per cent; **Significant at 5 per cent; ***Significant at 10 per cent. Figures within parenthesis indicate the 't' test.

In the NIEs country-group, market variable (GDP) was not a significant determinant. However, in the restricted model when we replaced it by per capita income (PCGDP), it becomes significant. The other variable which is significantly positive is the appreciation of the yen (XRTY) while the decline in the effective exchange rate (EXRATE) is significantly negative.

*ASEAN-4*

Prominent variables in this group are infrastructure (INVINFRA), the appreciation of the Japanese yen (XRTY), the decline in the effective exchange rate (EXRATE) and the accumulation of capital (GDCF/GDP). They are all significant at the 1 per cent level.

*All 10-countries*

In the all-country group, trade with Japan (FTJGDP), domestic capital formation (GDCF/GDP), the appreciation of the yen (XRTY), the decline in the effective exchange rate (EXRATE) and infrastructure (INVFRA) are all significant at the 1 per cent level.

The results of the restricted models are given in Table 5.11.

## 5.6 Conclusions

Japanese FDI is characterized by strong waves in Asian NIEs, ASEAN-4, China and India. This chapter has assessed the significance of the economic determinants in attracting Japanese FDI to these country-groups using the balanced panel data set that comprises time series from 1981 to 2004.

To avoid the arbitrary choice of the determinants we began with a large number of independent variables before narrowing these down to a set of few which provided evidence of higher explanatory power. Even after doing this we were left with eight independent variables in the general model. We adopted this set of economic variables which played a dominant role in explaining the Japanese FDI flows to the country-groups. The Lagrange multiplier statistic and Hausman test results indicated the Random Effects models to be the appropriate one. Our estimation results are consistent with previous studies – even though they pertain to one or two variables – and have been extensively cited earlier. The most important results emanating from our empirical study are:

1. A statistically strong and robust relationship between Japanese FDI and host country trade (FTJGDP) is evident for all country-groups. Trade flows with Japan are a significant determinant of Japanese FDI flows, exerting a strong influence on it and may appear consistent with the Kojima hypothesis. This is true of all of the country-groups. Several empirical studies have shown a positive relationship taking specific country studies (in the case of China, see Chen 1999; Liu *et al.* 2001; Sun 1998 and many others cited earlier).

2. Infrastructure is another crucial determinant in every country-group which shows a positive and significant impact on Japanese FDI flows.
3. Market size (GDP) has a significant and positive effect on Japanese FDI flows. This is an important determinant in all of the country-groups, with the exception of the NIEs where it is PCGDP which turns significant in the restricted model. NIEs appear to be seeking technologically-intensive, innovation-driven FDI.
4. Estimates also reveal that Japanese FDI has been stimulated by the decline in the effective exchange rates of the host country while a positive relationship between FDI and appreciation of yen (XRTY) is evidenced in all the cases.
5. The budget deficit to GDP ratio, which measures macroeconomic stability, also turns out to be a significant variable in most country-groups.
6. Policy factors: The policy factors such as investment incentives by the host government to attract Japanese FDI also act as an important driving force. This is not in the model, but has been investigated separately (see Table 5.3).

## 5.7 Prospects

1. The prospects of Japanese FDI flows to NIEs, the ASEAN and China, as is evidenced above, are strongly positive. The flows are expected to rise further as most of the driving forces behind Japanese FDI growth are set to continue which includes its important role as a global production center, policy environment and significant regional integration.
2. Japan and ASEAN as a group or its member countries individually are expected to strengthen FDI relationships as in recent negotiations for a New Age Economic Partnership, in the course of which a broad range of provisions on investment, movement of personnel, intellectual property rights (IPRs), and competition policies have been discussed. This is expected to benefit their future business activities.
3. India, however, is an 'under-performer' in attracting Japanese FDI and may not reach the levels recorded by others. There are several operational gaps to be filled (Chapter 3). Unless the gaps are put in place, India's ability to attract Japanese FDI will remain as limited as it is today, however bold it may appear on paper. These also explain, among others, why the comparable China has managed to attract a much higher share of Japanese FDI than India despite the virtual absence of a well-established legal and judicial system. It calls

for many hard, but essential decisions which include infrastructure reforms in all its aspects and forms, strengthening trade relations with Japan, further reduction in tariff barriers notwithstanding their reduction over the period, reductions in the fiscal deficit, investment in human skills and taking efficient market-enhancing measures to achieve global standards in the provision of services.

4. From the policy angle significant initiatives are also needed to improve location-specific relative attractiveness for Japanese FDI in the cross-country context. This includes the opening up of the financial sector beyond the present foreign investment ceiling limit of 26 per cent in insurance and 74 per cent in the banking sector, and entry into the retail sector and real estate to improve their productivity and competitiveness. The major driving sectors of Japanese FDI are finance & insurance, commerce, services and real estate.
5. In India until recently a large number of items – numbering 114 – were reserved for the small-scale sector with a strong FDI ceiling limit of 24 per cent on equity. Recently, the Government of India has made an announcement to deserve 79 items, leaving 35 items still on the reserved list (Times of India, dated 9 February 2008). The problem with these units is that they are unable to face global competition due to technological obsolescence, low productivity, inferior quality and its negative fallouts. This is in sharp contrast with China where the policy is to upgrade the technologies of its enterprises, including the small and medium-sized firms investing in joint ventures in village and town enterprises (see also Zhang and Van Den Bulcke 1995). This emphasizes the fact that the driving force behind Chinese FDI is to speedily modernize the economy.

# 6
# Conclusions

## 6.1 The motivation

The dynamics of Japanese FDI over the decades since the 1970s – its rise and fall as well as shifts in the scale and direction – was unprecedented, as was its region-wise and sector-wise composition. There were waves triggered by a combination of factors that were medium term in nature and played out differently over the period for different regions and countries. In this, the Asia's emerging economies – the leading growth locomotive in the vanguard of economic globalization – are seen as an important motivating factor in revitalizing the internationalization of Japanese FDI.

Broadly speaking, while the rise in Japanese FDI in the 1970s was *'Asia-led'*, the subsequent waves in the 1980s and 1990s were *'US-led'*. During this period Japan had become the world's largest single foreign investor, reaching its peak in 1989 when it contributed about 30 per cent of the world flows. Such a growth in its FDI and the rise of its MNEs emanated mainly from an accelerated pace of technical and managerial changes, know-how and other ownership-specific advantages, which constituted an important landmark in the world economy. This was also Japan's most spectacular phase – the 'globalization' period. Even by virtue of its sheer size, Japanese FDI had important consequences – at both the macro and micro levels – for the economies of host countries, and in respect of international trade flows. For many countries – both developing and developed – the dramatic expansion of Japanese FDI represents a turnaround: improvement in the balance of payments, the provision of scarce foreign exchange resources, and the transfer of technology and skills – not available in the host country – to enhance the competitiveness and profitability of their local industries among others.

The spatial distribution of Japanese FDI between developed and developing regions is characterized by a near-cyclical pattern. The developed regions, which also registered high levels of economic growth, have been absorbing two-thirds of Japan's FDI outflows from the latter half of the 1980s almost till the end of the century, with a changing sector composition, from primary to manufacturing and then to the fast-growing services sector. More specifically, the developed countries – comprising North America, Europe, and Australia – witnessed a massive jump, reaching a peak of 79 per cent of the global total in 1990 from 41 per cent in 1981. The principal beneficiary among these was North America, which represented the largest export market, and received almost half of total Japanese FDI. As a natural corollary, the developing countries (including Asia) saw their share drop. Obviously at this time, the developed countries' gain was the developing countries' loss. Some of these trends were later partially reversed after the bursting of the asset-price bubble. If we focus on five-yearly average growth rates, notwithstanding the year-to-year fluctuations, the second half of the 1980s was the most attractive period for developed countries with an average share of over 73 per cent while for the developing countries the 1970s were on the whole more favourable, attracting over 55 per cent of the total.

Coinciding with these movements have been noticeable changes in the regional composition of FDI. Competitive pressures have been pushing Japanese firms to seek markets in different regions in order to strengthen their competitiveness and keep the economy both dynamic and productive. The ownership-specific advantages of firms, the location-specific advantages of countries and the internalization advantages to firms from direct investment abroad had all combined to determine the extent and pattern of their expansion.

The share of Japanese FDI received by developing countries and prominently that of Asia is of late witnessing an uptrend. At the same time, FDI flows to the West – particularly the United States – is recording a sharp decline. The decline in the level of Japanese investment in the United States coincides with the decline in Japanese investment in services, particularly real estate, while the increase in FDI outflows to countries in Asia is principally in manufacturing.

The ten countries – NIEs 4, ASEAN 4, China and India, though at different rungs in the economic ladder – are securing the major portion of Japanese FDI among the developing countries by varying magnitudes. Demonstrating a rapid growth in FDI and rapid economic expansion in many areas, these countries have undergone tremendous economic changes since the 1980s. However, within these ten countries, the geographical distribution of Japan's FDI has been changing significantly in volume from both within and between the NIEs, ASEAN-4, China and India and also over the period. However, the importance of India and China in the strategic planning of international investors, and of Japanese investors in particular, cannot be overemphasized. Judging on a per capita basis, their FDI is still relatively low, but they have ample absorptive capacity.

Location advantages are comparative in nature. When deciding on a location MNEs compare the relative advantages of suitable countries. For example, the location advantages of East Asia, China and India are not directly comparable with those of the USA and Western Europe, but they are comparable to other countries in this region. It is important to keep this factor in mind when investigating the location advantages. Furthermore, the economic characterization in attracting Japanese FDI differs greatly from country to country. The magnitude and nature of these FDI flows are influenced by the economic characteristics, social, institutional and political trajectories, and policy regimes of the countries relative to other competing countries. When an investor is planning to invest he has a number of competing candidate countries in which he can invest and optimize his returns. Therefore, investors' own perceptions about the location of the FDI climate assumes importance. While China is now taking the lion's share, NIEs are again witnessing an upsurge and the situation of India is looking up – *albeit* slowly.

## 6.2 Emerging trends in the environment for FDI

There is no predictive theory of FDI nor is the investment decision a one-shot algorithm. There are multiple stages, multiple players and factors – both exogenous and endogenous – which participate in this constant interplay. In the context of the current economic environment, when the economies are undergoing significant changes and there is a drastic reduction in tariff rates and a virtual disappearance of non-tariff barriers, MNEs are exploiting their ownership of intangible assets in third countries through efficiency-seeking investments. The determinants of efficiency-seeking investments could be different from those of market-seeking investments. MNEs could be motivated to go where knowledge is found and partnership with knowledge-intensive enterprises is formed. MNEs would invest in a third country if it were more efficient to produce goods in that country. The relative location advantages perceived by the investors will play a more crucial role in determining FDI inflows given the ownership advantages.

Another striking feature of the present emerging trend is the changing motivation and paradigm shift in the location hypothesis. This changing motivation consists mainly in the augmentation of the bundle of intangible assets – building own identities and brands; creating and managing the technology; raising resources through new instruments. A new social contract and networking is emerging that gives rise to new instruments of value addition and technology intermediation. When the MNEs examine the country-specific location advantages, they look not only for, say, the 'market-size' variable, but also the available amenities, its potential, quality and variety – for instance, now the 'size' variable may incorporate the culture and harmony while the presence of other 'amenities' will include its night life, recreation channels and the like. This is not to deny the relevance of conventional arguments for FDI. They still hold good and are also common to all – irrespective of the source of FDI.

Given the multiple motivations and risks involved, the investor will use complex investment algorithms in order to maximize the present value of the stream of net benefits accruing in the future within the shortest possible time. He will be concerned with not only the investment cost but also the operating expenses, both in terms of its magnitude and timing for it is well known that resources can be allocated in different ways to maximize the sum total of net benefits and these differ from country to country.

Further, different players and levels are constantly adding new dimensions. In respect of Japanese FDI the following deserve specific mention.

1. When Japanese investors consider making new investment decisions, they go through eight stages in the decision-making process and action cycle, namely: (i) Screening, (ii) Planning, (iii) Pre-feasibility study, (iv) Feasibility study, (v) Decision by the Board of Directors, (vi) Preparation of establishment, (vii) Implementation, and (viii) Operation. The screening stage is the most important part. Its major checkpoints are: (a) Political stability and security, (b) Sound economic fundamentals, market size and their trend, (c) Adequate infrastructure and living environment, (d) Economic policy and other laws, and (e) Incentives for foreign investment promotion law. Many investment proposals will actually lose out at the screening stage itself.
2. Location choices are multi-stage. For instance; first, the choice of the global region (for instance, East Asia, the USA, or Latin America) is made as the location advantages are not comparable at that level. In the second stage, choice is for location within the chosen region

of the first stage. The location determinants are different in the two stages. For example, for the first stage if the USA is selected it could be that the USA is a major market of their products. Likewise, for East Asia, it would be the availability of skilled labour, reduction in trade barriers, and overall lower costs. At the next stage, within East Asia if the NIEs have been chosen this may be due to efficiency considerations or to the fact that it may serve as an export base and provide an efficient investment environment from the viewpoint of risks and barriers. Likewise, if the ASEAN region is considered, it is a large regional grouping with market size, investment climate momentum and it plays an important role in knowledge spillover. The other important location factors appear to be the availability of a developed infrastructure, favourable government actions, including incentives, political climate and so forth. It is here that the economic determinants will be the major drivers of Japanese FDI.

3. Corporate governance of Japanese FDI – some sort of a social contract to networking and its institutions and instruments – has been a distinctive feature of Japan's business economy for decades. Having close, long-term business relationships between large corporations and a number of selected smaller firms they have been seen as rational effective systems presenting fewer risks, minimizing transaction costs and as a factor in its economic success. It has been observed that linkages among the firms' activities in technology, production and marketing has offered the *keiretsu* firms opportunities to exploit economies of scope while minimizing the disadvantages of internal diversification. This type of co-specialization helps to achieve minimizing transaction costs and maximize transaction value. It enables members to integrate market and technology information (Dyer and Ouchi 1993; Kodama 1995). *Keiretsu-specific* agglomeration, specifically those of vertically-linked firms, has attracted global attention, even though there is a continuing debate over their purpose and these have also been criticized as closed systems that exclude potential competitors. Some analysts even suggest that such groups are inconsistent with market forces, raising the possibility of long-term industrial decline and 'strategic failure' but many feel otherwise and they remain in one form or the other.
4. Efficiency-making production bases constitute an integral part of Japanese FDI. With 40 per cent of the world's population, China and India are potentially the world's largest markets and are therefore of considerable importance to Japanese investors. But India, despite having a large and growing market, has not been able to

attract Japanese FDI while China has. We have seen that there is a fundamental difference between India's profile and that of China. Japanese investors consider economic attractions to be stronger in China. The argument is broadly as follows: alongside the market demand, developed supply conditions, quality-services and other factors of production are also crucial. Besides, the notion of giving proper incentives or majority ownership also play an important role. The more favourable the demand conditions prevailing in the host country, the greater the attraction for inward market-seeking investment and the more favourable will be the response of foreign investors to commit to a higher level of investment with an intent of giving them a greater ownership in local operations. But if the host country is deficient in the quality of its factors of production, in providing an investor-friendly environment or in the development of supporting industries, the foreign investor will need to make good these deficiencies through other measures such as seeking greater involvement in ownership and control. When an investor is planning to invest and has a number of competing candidate countries where he can invest and optimize his benefits, he would look along multiple dimensions rather than a single one. The trade-off between multiple objectives is not a trivial one but may lead to a variety of outcomes. The MNE may invest in a high-cost but stable location, or invest an efficient amount in an unstable, low-cost location, but hold simultaneously excess capacity elsewhere or else the firm may invest only but too little in the less cost and unstable location. The last one arises only when upfront subsidies are available. Domestic conditions act as contingencies for the corporate governance of FDI. The factors are as portrayed in Porter's 'diamond' and are likely to have a bearing upon the preferences of the investors concerning the governance of their operations.

5. Japanese FDI excels in the use of international strategic alliances. It is not just confined to the export orientation of the firms, but is honed by extensive networks of alliances (Westney 1988). The genealogical tree of development of Japanese MNEs bears testimony to this.

At the core of the spread of Japanese FDI, however, remain sound economic determinants and country-specific advantages. Improvement in the investment climate is a continuous process to keep pace with the changing international economic environment to increase the speed of development, to enhance the inflow of technical know-how and management practices, and to improve productivity, efficiency and global competitiveness.

## 6.3 Results: investors' perceptions

### 6.3.1 Ratings of the critical parameters

The MNEs were asked to evaluate and rate location variables for the East Asian countries, China and India in a five-point scale ranging from (–) 2 to (+) 2. It was hypothesized that a better score would be positively related to their decision to invest. The results were quite revealing. The perception and preferences of the Japanese MNEs were consistent in respect of all their ratings. They were uniformly the same irrespective of the size of their investment.

### 6.3.2 Physical infrastructure

Infrastructure is the window through which one can judge the level of development of an economy. In the cross-country comparison, India's infrastructure gets the most adverse rating compared to East Asia and China – almost close to (–) 2 in the five grades ranging from (+) 2 to (–) 2. The weighted average grades have generally become worse in all of the cases where they were negative in the simple comparison. India is considered deficient in all of the areas of physical infrastructure – electricity, transport, water and telecommunications. In addition, those Japanese investors that have invested in other countries but not in India have all cited poor infrastructure as one of the basic reasons for not investing in India.

It is pertinent to mention that being in the nature of 'merit goods', most of the infrastructure facilities have historically been under government control and regulation and demand a very sound and accountable 'public administration' for implementation which is critically lacking in India. Infrastructure projects also involve the use of the 'networking' of existing facilities and in this sense; they need the 'unbundling' of activities and exploitation which remains difficult under the present dispensation. The success in attracting FDI depends largely upon the adequacy and efficiency of the system. India, with its large and growing population, increasing urbanization and crowded cities, aiming at accelerating the growth rate will make heavy demands on its infrastructure – the most important vehicle of growth – be it power, transport, telecom or water. Demand remains unsatisfied, even though the users are willing to pay a higher price for the services. Secondly, a sub-standard highways system means high fuel consumption, lower vehicle utilization, higher accident rates and higher costs of vehicle maintenance. The total economic costs of such a system can only be imagined. And where there are no highways, the economic costs are far more staggering. Power, telecommunications, railways and ports tell the same story. The poor infrastructure system in the country falls squarely on grossly inadequate policies and highly inefficient implementation.

### 6.3.3 Public administration – governance

India's public administration, that is, governance, also received a negative rating ranging between (–) 0.5 and (–) 0.8 using 'assets' and 'capital stock' respectively as weight while the simple average was (–) 0.8 compared to the other Asian countries under study. It has been perceived as poor, deficient, suffering from a lack of accountability and inordinate delays that ensured that it was unable to secure investors' confidence. This is principally because India followed 'a process which relies on systematic obfuscation about future intentions, if not outright deceit' Jenkins (1999).

This is also clearly evident that when there are critical bottlenecks and several operational gaps to be filled, an intense India shining campaign continues along with extravagant populist utterances which have no correlation with improvement in the ground realities. Given India's complex and formidable governance structure, the culture of publicity and 'road-show' approaches are decidedly shallow. It is no surprise that investors are lured in by the 'India shine campaign' only to be disappointed and give a poor rating to India compared to other countries.

### 6.3.4 Japanese Management Technique (JMT)

Japanese-style management, a vehicle of technology transfer, is like a human-ware technology, a set of production techniques and a system that takes full advantage of the motivation, responsibility, creativity of workers and places emphasis on teamwork and sharing of information, gaining more knowledge and new skills and enhancing the learning capacity of the organization. JMT has demonstrated its effectiveness in raising the quality, productivity, efficiency benefits, and its competitive advantages.

Japanese multinationals have pioneered JMT practices into the USA and western European economies. The USA has shown the highest rate of adoption of JMT, almost entirely accounted for by the exceptionally high adoption rate of quality circles and self managing teams, followed by France and then the UK.

FDI-led, Japanese manufacturing firms have implemented their management systems relatively more successfully. The main problems in the case of NIEs and ASEAN-4 were: maintaining business information, job-hopping and information-sharing drawbacks. In the case of China, problems were the same with an addition of government interference.

India records the lowest percentage level for the adoption of the technique. Only a few of them could introduce the technique into their companies. Investors feel that compared to East Asian countries, Indian labour is slow, not quality conscious, careless and lacking in team spirit and information sharing so vital for the application of the JMT. The other main reasons being: inability to understand the JMT, different value system, poor knowledge base of the labour force, gap between labour and management, poor quality maintenance, lack of inter-firm linkages, poor supplier capability compounded by poor physical infrastructure. Then they are work-specific and difficult to lay off. The Japanese management, however, prefers multi-skilled, soft and job-rotating type of labor. Further, relatively complex and bureaucratic procedures determining job classification and the structure of internal job ladders and labor force and lack of managerial commitment, lack of strict adherence to total quality control (TQC), just-in-time (JIT) procedures enabling rapid response to changes in the market conditions, substantially flatter organizational hierarchies, less rigid departmental boundaries, flexible job specifications and participatory management – enabling workers to understand the entire production processes, come up with suggestions for introducing process and product innovations – is not like one-shot algorithm but a continuous process of improvement involving social innovations is absent in the Indian environment.

This emphasizes the urgency of comprehensive labour reform in the country. The present-day labour laws, rules and procedures have led to a deterioration in the work culture. More flexible labour laws that improve work culture and enhance productivity will help to attract FDI inflows of the kind seen in Southeast Asia in the 1980s and in China since the 1990s.

The main system-level constraints to its adoption are the quality of human resources – the focal point of the Japanese management system of which core components are: quality circles, job rotation, self-managing teams and responsibility for quality by employees; intense human resource management systems, face-to-face information sharing and negotiation, and coordination based on a dense human network. If the labour has a different way of thinking about the job work, quality, or is job specific and militant then, firms face a 'dilemma' problem when applying the system – the problem of adapting to the local managerial and regulatory environment – the difficulties or even trade-offs that exist in the application–adaptation aspect of the transplanted production system. However, various applications and adaptations generate different patterns of 'hybrids' that blend Japanese elements and local influences within the subsidiary plants.

### 6.3.5 Controls and restrictions

The East Asian countries were rated more favourably. But the majority of the sample firms characterized India's control system as being either bad or very bad compared to East Asian countries. Likewise, the average ratings given by those Japanese investors investing abroad but not in India on different aspects of Indian policy regarding reasons for not investing in India, is uniformly negative. It views that India's policy shift is not fully reflected in operational procedures and in the attitude of the government personnel responsible for the implementation of the policy.

### 6.3.6 Administrative and other complexities

Controls are further compounded by the administrative and other complex formalities. Most of the regulations in India, whether relating to approvals or permissions or the legal system, tax laws, foreign exchange regulations, import duty and other formalities, are so complex that the companies could not understand them. In a number of cases the restrictive regulations and complexities have led to changes in MOUs. Added to this is the problem of lack of coordination between the centre and states, and the issue of non-standard regulations governing interstate commerce leading to further delays and complexities. India has perhaps substantially more state-level and secondary clearance requirements than most other countries in this region. India has also relatively much higher rates of corporate and individual taxes and the highest tariff barriers among the countries in which Japanese MNEs are investing.

An aggressive policy is followed by China and other East Asian countries to attract FDI by way of incentives and logistic support. In India, the policy stance is different on the ground from how it has been formulated on paper. For instance, according to the regulatory framework, automatic approval is stated to be available from the Reserve Bank of India (RBI) within two weeks of application. In actual practice, however, it has taken many companies as long as six months. Likewise, abrupt policy changes have also been cited by many investors as making it difficult for the companies to prepare their investment plans.

The regulatory framework must strive to reduce uncertainty, asymmetric information, and related transaction costs. At the core of this is the observation that neutral policies are better suited to attracting FDI than the interventionist method. Well-designed strategies should address the regulatory issues through effective management and strengthening government capabilities.

### 6.3.7 Developing the networks – social and economic

Japan has powerful networking with the East Asian region and as an investor is in a position to take a regional view of its investment decisions. But very few Japanese companies have network arrangements with Indian affiliates. The current technological revolution is very different from the earlier ones. The product life cycle is now short and for many products size advantages do not exist. The formation of a networking arrangement involving the exchange of information has become essential to enable companies to become significant players in technology creation and to be globally knowledge sharing. In the case of many East Asian countries, Japan has had this arrangement which is exchanging know-how, inducing local production and strengthening their interdependence. In this process, local companies are also acting as core or support industries and creating liaisons among themselves.

Similarly, strong social networking between Japan and East Asian countries has improved their bilateral affinities and influenced their investment decisions and strengthened the economic linkages. On the contrary, investors have mentioned about the social problems in India.

### 6.3.8 Rating of market size and labour

The two determinants, viz., market size and labour – even though considered important for location of investment – have been given the same rating, former as big, and latter as abundant, for India, China and the country-groups with no one scoring over the other.

## 6.4 Quantification of the ratings

The ratings were subjected to a quantitative analysis through a limited application of the logit model. The MNEs were asked to evaluate the location advantages in these countries. These were: infrastructure, the adoption of JMT, controls and restrictions, administrative complexities, networking, market and labour.

**6.4.1.** The results support the following location advantages, namely: 1. Infrastructure emerged as significant and supports the importance of infrastructure development in attracting FDI. 2. Japanese Management Technique (JMT) was also significant. Japanese MNEs appear to prefer to invest in countries where the adoption of JMT is easier. 3. The results also lend support to the liberalized economic regime.

**6.4.2.** 'Administrative complexities' did not turn out to be significant. The insignificance of this variable in the statistical analysis could be due to the presence of high levels of complexities and corruption in both India and China and the consequent inability of the Japanese MNEs to evaluate these scenes. Wei (1999) has also rated both China and India poorly.

**6.4.3.** As to the need for 'networking' all of the responses were positive, but the number was not enough to subject it to statistical testing.

**6.4.4.** Both India and China have been characterized by the MNEs having large markets and abundant labour. Hence in a cross-country comparison these have not turned out to be significant.

## 6.5 Econometric modelling of the determinants of Japanese FDI

**6.5.1.** The results of the model reveal a statistically strong and robust relationship between Japanese FDI and host country trade (FTJGDP). This is evident under all of the country-groups. Trade flows with Japan are a significant determinant of Japanese FDI flows, exerting strong influence on it and being consistent with the Kojima hypothesis. Several empirical studies have shown a positive relationship taking specific country studies (for instance, in the case of China, see Chen 1999; Liu *et al.* 2001; and Sun 2001). Our study shows that the same also holds good for the country-groups. This linkage between trade and FDI has emerged as one of the important explanatory variables.

**6.5.2.** Infrastructure (INVINFRA) is another crucial determinant in every country-group which shows a positive and significant impact on Japanese FDI flows. In fact, infrastructures appear to be the second most important variable to attract Japanese FDI after 'trade'.

**6.5.3.** Japanese FDI have been stimulated by the decline in the exchange rates (EXRATE) of the host country. At the same time, the appreciation of the yen (XRTY) has significantly stimulated FDI outflows from Japan. A positive relationship between FDI and XRTY is found in all cases.

**6.5.4.** Market size (GDP) has a significant and positive effect on Japanese FDI flows. This is an important determinant in all of the country-groups, with the exception of the NIEs, where it is PCGDP which is positively related in the restricted model. NIEs appear to be seeking technologically-intensive, innovation-driven FDI. This also emphasizes the importance of regional economic integration, which overcomes the market size constraint.

6.5.5. The budget deficit to GDP ratio captures the macroeconomic stability gives a wrong sign in the sub-periods in some cases, but turns out to be a significant variable in most country-groups when we consider the entire period.

6.5.6. Incentives: Investment incentives by host government to attract Japanese FDI are also a driving force, as was revealed through the investors' responses.

## 6.6 Prospects and challenges

Judging by the results of the study, the prospects appear positive as most of the driving forces behind Japanese FDI growth are set to continue. In addition, Japan's important role as a global production centre and regional integration factor will shape additional opportunities and incentives for further investment.

### 6.6.1 Asia revitalizing

The recent boost in Japanese FDI flows to these countries indicates that the Japanese 'globalization' strategy is being revitalized in Asia and this is shifting their emphasis from North America, mainly because of economic sluggishness and increasingly competitive global conditions. This signal of an investment boom in Asia – a return in Japanese FDI to NIEs after several years of declining flows; ASEAN, in particular Thailand and Philippines recording a rise and China surpassing all – shows it will serve not only as an export base in the medium term, but also continue as a supply base for the home market.

While Japanese investors' primary economic interests are clearly global, its economic activities in East Asia are heavily geared to its extra-regional interests, as many of the manufactures produced by the Japanese affiliates in the region are exported to North America and Europe. At the same time, Japanese regional activities have been systematically furthering East Asian economic integration, diverting a considerable portion of its regional affiliates 'exports' to its own market and accepting more manufactures from non-Japanese-affiliated regional firms in order to move the region forward. The emphasis of Japanese investors on cost, efficiency and quality are leading to such things as localizing product improvement, better R&D work, and the strengthening of support networks. The country-groups are already set in that economic environment, networks and alliances – both equity- and non-equity-based – that promise many challenges in the years ahead through trade and investment frameworks. The regional network component may become more dominant and transform the patterns of regional trade and investment.

### 6.6.2 Japanese FDI polarization between China and the ASEAN

We had estimated the 'country-effects' in the models while estimating the impacts of other variables. Interpreting the country-effects as measures of relative attractiveness for Japanese FDI the results implied the following (see Table 6.1):

- NIEs are far more attractive than China, with Singapore at the top. Taiwan, Hong Kong and Korea are equally attractive.
- More interesting is the comparison of China with the ASEAN-4. China is much more attractive than all of the four countries in this group. Indonesia is the least attractive, while Thailand and Malaysia have almost the similar ranking, but Philippines is revealed to be marginally inferior to China.

China is ahead of ASEAN in terms of its relative attractiveness for Japanese FDI. It is obvious that the above picture has to be seen in conjunction with all the other model results presented earlier and not independently. Results have demonstrated that China is a potential competitor to ASEAN-4 and an increase in Japanese FDI to China may lead

*Table 6.1* Measures of country attractiveness: NIEs-4, ASEAN-4 *vis-à-vis* China*

| | **NIEs-4 with China as benchmark** | **ASEAN-4 with China as the benchmark** |
|---|---|---|
| *NIEs-4* | | |
| 1. Singapore | 17.37 | |
| 2. Taiwan | 10.86 | |
| 3.Hong Kong | 10.51 | |
| 4. Korea | 10.36 | |
| *ASEAN-4* | | |
| 1. Philippines | | (–) 4.43 |
| 2. Malaysia | | (–) 10.48 |
| 3. Thailand | | (–)11.43 |
| 4. Indonesia | | (–)12.30 |

*Note*: *The implied measure for China is zero.

simultaneously to a decline of the same to the ASEAN-4. But ASEAN countries in general are undergoing fundamental changes in terms of both economic structure and through newcomers strengthening their position. The member countries are strengthening their ties further by lowering intra-regional trade barriers to rationalize productions fragmented within and attract FDI inflows. The reduction or elimination of restrictions will strengthen their linkages, consolidate it as a regional market, and enhance its competitiveness. New networks, alliances and fast 'catching-up' tendencies will have a great impact on Japanese FDI flows in these countries. As a 'single market' these countries will have greater intermediation with the world economy which is predicated in large part on value-added FDI. This will change the gear towards more innovation-driven growth and a reconfiguration of these countries' location-specific advantages generating dynamic effects and a cycle of increased attractiveness of the region as a location for foreign investment and motivation for MNEs. This interplay of new developments may affect the flow of investment between ASEAN and China, with the former forging further economic linkages and the latter, as a member of the WTO, also striving to achieve continuous improvement in its investment environment – further deregulation and market-opening measures on the one hand and Japanese firms accelerating the transplantation of production operations on the other.

### 6.6.3 India's position

The quality of basic economic FDI determinants is considered poor in India compared to that found in the NIEs, the ASEAN-4 and China. The ratings given by the MNEs in respect of the critical variables and the econometric model provide evidence of the gaps between India and these countries. It is a reflection of India's inability to live up to the investors' expectations which cause maximum damage to Japanese investment sentiments and explain why India is not a preferred destination, although it shares many common interests. In this context a few additional points deserve mention.

*First*, the prime drivers of Japanese FDI which make China and East Asian countries preferable locations are absent in India. It is not merely better infrastructure, or a better business climate or else a better policy and strategy but also India's cumbersome policy matrix, governance structure and implementation failures provide a plausible explanation why despite a lot of paperwork, tall promises and several meetings of India–Japan Business Cooperation Committees, it is not taking off to the required level.

*Secondly*, the conventional concepts of location-specific advantages are undergoing paradigm changes that call for a better quality of environment. In this context, illustratively, the need is not only for a world-class 'hard' infrastructure but also for a robust 'soft' infrastructure and improvement in the support system. India needs to tailor its policies to suit the current international business practice, and to improve its comparative advantages *vis-à-vis* the other candidate countries. The imperatives are both policy-related and operational ones and actions are to be directed to problematic areas.

*Thirdly*, Japan, as a global investor, would be interested in exploring new efficiency-making production bases. In view of its poor rating in terms of attracting efficiency-seeking FDI India does not fit into this frame. In addition, India is not a core member of the East Asian country-groups nor does it enjoy special treatment with the triad members (the USA, the EC and Japan). In the past, India enjoyed a preferred access to the Soviet Union under a rupee trade agreement. This had enabled the country to attract a number of MNEs to set up production bases for sourcing the Soviet market. Following the collapse of the Soviet Union, that advantage has now gone. It is imperative for India to make a serious attempt to secure preferential access to the EC. This will enable Japanese MNEs to set up production bases in the country for sourcing the European market.

*Fourthly*, Japan has a system of institutions and instruments and a unique sense of partnership motivated by the existence of conglomerates or corporate alliances – a set of long-term economic relationships among specific companies. Japanese investors maintain a stable and a relatively longer-term subcontracting relationship with their vendors and encourage the local firms to invest in new machinery for the modernization and introduction of more advanced technology. This maintains pressure on local vendors to perform well and drives them to ever-higher levels of efficiency. And, above all, the Japanese companies try to bring with them the Japanese style of management, with an emphasis on just-in-time delivery, quality circles and total quality control. These practices become integrated in the governance structure and provide coordination and incentives. Even though they succeed only partially, they have made an impact through greater microeconomic contribution to the host country's income, output and employment generation.

*Fifthly*, minimizing 'psychic distance' with Japan through a 'work culture' and networking is essential. Larger firms entail 'follow the leader' pattern wherein one firm induces others to follow. The Japanese possess a great advantage of unity with regard to language, lifestyle and even the basic philosophy of life. India, on the other hand, proclaims to have unity in diversity, but all too often it seems that the only language India has in common is the language of controversy. In Japan, so deep is the understanding between the government and industry that government can make industry do whatever is necessary in the national interest by a friendly chat across the table, without invoking any legal powers whatever. This is contrary to the Indian political system and governance.

*Finally*, it needs to be clearly stated that improvement in the quality of FDI determinants cannot be seen in isolation, but must be seen in the larger economic, social and political setting. India has a cumbersome institutional matrix and equally cumbersome are its political complexities which are rendered even murkier by the emergence of regional parties – a new class of rent-seekers with different perceptions – carrying populist radicalization to the extreme in order to achieve power. And the major casualty in this is structural adjustments, coordination and stabilization in the economic policies in accordance with changes in the world environment. The 1991 policy changes in India were undertaken 'by stealth' (Jenkins 1999) in the midst of many events – both external (such as the collapse of the erstwhile USSR and East European socialist regimes) and internal (the economic crisis) – broadly on the lines of the World Bank's structural adjustment programmes. But the country-specific advantages have not improved enough to counter the CSAs of China and East Asia. Now, following the field-level experience, India will be able to put the reforms into effect, tackle the internal constraints and improve its ability to attract efficiency-seeking foreign investment. FDI enters a country only if it is competitive and benefits both the investor and the host country.

To conclude: The vision of new Asia as a centre of economic power is emerging. China and India are attracting global attention as the world's fastest-growing economies. China is ahead of India in the FDI growth path. In fact, FDI flows from Japan are one of the most celebrated achievements of the reform era in China which has been hospitable to Japanese MNEs to secure know-how and build up its own industry. India is aiming to reach $50 billion of FDI by 2010, and it is anticipated that Japan will play an important role in the achievement of this goal. India is learning from the East Asian experiences – as did China – to attract Japanese FDI while charting its own independent path. We have identified the main barriers and the facilitators econometrically as well as through a direct survey of Japanese investors' perceptions of location advantages. This, it is hoped, will be helpful in the FDI policy formulation of the countries seeking to attract foreign investment and Japanese FDI in particular.

# End Notes

## 1

1. The 'ownership (O) advantages' change constantly in line with logistic and market demands through innovation and the deployment of new technologies, which constitute critical parts of FDI and competitiveness. As MNEs become more globalized and engage in more complex investment activity in a variety of environments that expose them to multiple stimuli to accumulate, integrate and control 'O' advantages, the importance of firm-specific factors in determining the FDI profile of a country becomes increasingly significant.

   Kogut (1983) argued that although the possession of superior intangible assets may give rise to the initial act of FDI, the sequential investment is related to sequential advantages, which accrue through governance in dispersed locations and their learning experiences in coordinating domestic and foreign production. In the same vein, Bartlett and Ghoshal (1988, 1989) later stated that MNEs' exposure to multiple stimuli enables them to develop competencies and learning opportunities.
2. The theory of internalization was first advanced by Coase (1937) in a domestic context and by Hymer (1976) in an international dimension. Later, Buckley and Casson (1976) synthesized it. For surveys of the FDI literature and their respective merits, see Ragazzi (1973), Dunning (1973, 1977, 1980, 2003), Stevens (1974), Hufbauer (1975), Casson (1979), Hood and Young (1980, 1988), Rugman (1980), Horst (1971, 1972).
3. Calvet (1980, 1981) speaks about the different taxonomy and distinguishes four main classes: (a) Market disequilibrium hypothesis, (b) Government-imposed distortions, (c) Market structure imperfections, and (d) Market failure imperfections. The other streams of the imperfection/diversification hypothesis include: financial market imperfections as against imperfections in markets for products and for knowledge – which argue that if a firm enjoys a stable stream of profits over time, it can lead to international diversification. Although the mechanics of diversification are well known, the application of international diversification to the MNEs has not always been substantiated. Originally, the international portfolio theorists had argued that variations in security returns across countries show less correlation than within a single country. However, the opinions differ. For a detailed analysis, see Agmon and Lessard (1977) and Errunza and Yalovsky (1978).
4. Dunning (2000) provides a brilliant synthesis of the key location advantages identified by different schools of thought as they apply to four main types of FDI – resource-seeking, market-seeking, efficiency-seeking or strategic-seeking. These schools include: (i) traditional location theories; (ii) theories related to the process of internalization; (iii) agglomeration theories; (iv) theories related to spatially specific transaction costs; (v) theories related to the presence of complementary assets; (vi) theories related to government-induced incentives; (vii) theories related to oligopolistic behaviour and product cycles; (viii) theories of risk diversification; (ix) exchange rate theories; and

(x) knowledge-enhancing theories of location. The relative importance of different determinants of FDI flows depends upon motives for investment; the type of investment – new or sequential; the sector of investment – for example, services or manufacturing; and the scale of investment, i.e., small and medium-sized or large MNEs.

5. By extending over borders MNEs make foreign direct investment and constitute one of the multinationals' many activities, *albeit* an essential one. Today they are at the heart of the development process. The contribution they make is determined mainly by the investment climate – the location-specific factors that shape the opportunities and incentives for MNEs to invest in the host countries. The World Bank's study of *Investment Climate* covering more than 26,000 firms in 53 countries highlights the primary constraints, including policy uncertainty, macroeconomic stability, problems of governance and infrastructure as the major obstacles to FDI (*World Development Report*, Chapter 1, Boxes 1&2, 2005).
6. Statistical results from several studies strongly buttress the argument that investors are inclined to favour such locations that could offer a variety of agglomeration economies (see Eaton, Lipsey and Safarian 1994; Braunerhjelm and Swenson 1996; Brianard 1997). As foreign firms face greater uncertainties than domestic firms in the host country, they may have strong incentives to follow previous investors because of the signals they send relating to the reliability of the host country location. In addition, it has been argued that firms increase their efficiency by locating close to each other because of: (a) knowledge spillovers between firms, (b) the advantages provided by thick markets in specialized factors, and (c) the scope for backward and forward linkages between customer and supplier firms (De Coster and Strange 1993; Krugman and Venables 1995, 1996; Krugman 1993, 1997). Even if there are no efficiency reasons to do so, firms may still find it rational to agglomerate spatially because investors locating in good locations may induce other investors. Localization of firms due to agglomeration economies – apart from demand, the low cost of abundant labour, technological capabilities, geographical and cultural proximity and the aggressive policy environment – can be an important factor in attracting FDI in to a host country. Illustratively, most of the Japanese FDI in India is concentrated in three geographical clusters. According to the latest available figures, there are some 231 Japanese firms operating in India. More than 93 per cent of these are located in three geographical clusters: Delhi and neighbourhood (80 units); Mumbai–Pune Belt (59); and the Bangalore–Chennai Belt (75). These three clusters account for 214 of the 231 Japanese firms.
7. A relatively small set of MNEs account for the majority of the world's trade and investment. Rugman and Verbeke (2004) have shown that the largest 500 MNEs account for over 90 per cent of the world's stock of FDI and they themselves conduct about half the world's trade and most of them have the vast majority of their sales within their home region. As a group they have been behaving differently from the non-MNE-affiliated local firms. These studies consider MNEs and their affiliates to be separate strategic groups (Dunning 1993; Caves 1996; Doremus *et al.* 1998).
8. Many studies have analysed the intra-MNE differences based on their home country characteristics. In particular, we refer to the differences in the

behaviour between the Japanese, European and the US MNEs (see Kojima 1973, 1986; Schroath, Hu and Chen 1993; Dunning 1994; Encarnation 1999; Ravenhill 1999).

9. Corporate groupings, also called *keiretsu*, have been a distinctive part of Japan's business economy for decades, a factor in its economic success and dominant players in the global economy. The Japanese *keiretsu*, specifically vertically linked firms, have attracted global attention, and there is continuing debate over their purpose. Branstetter (2000) observes that in Japanese economy vertical *keiretsu* groups tend to play an important role in most internationally competitive and technologically progressive industries. Such groups are now thought to be inconsistent with market forces. They have been criticized as closed systems that exclude potential competitors. However, during our discussion it was revealed that now the *keiretsu* organizations are undergoing changes and they have started sourcing materials and components outside their *keiretsu* groups – only economic variables playing a final role in their decision.

## 2

1. India's share in Japanese FDI is lower than all the others. There are a number of factors at work. Here it is felt important to mention a historical fact in passing that there has been an influential class of private capitalists in India that did not want FDI in competing areas, but advocated it mostly through the joint venture route which was non-competing and beneficial for domestic capitalists. This was not the case with the other countries. There is also a constant interplay of counteracting pressures exerted by different political parties in India which is not the case with China and the ASEAN.
2. The critics of Japanese FDI in India feel that in contrast to the NIEs, the ASEAN and China it is not coming to India to tap the third country export markets but rather to exploiting the domestic Indian market. But again India's investment climate provides a plausible explanation why most of the FDI has been domestic market-seeking in character rather than third-country export-seeking.

## 3

### 1. The Questionnaires

In devising the questionnaires, the basic consideration was that it should be simple and easy to answer while at the same time addressing our basic questions. Answers to most of the questions which were posed to the Japanese MNEs are based upon their actual experience as investors and although the answers were not of quantifiable varieties, they are most important in providing informed views about their preferences and reluctance to invest in different host countries – that is, India, China and East Asia The replies were on a five-point scale ranging from

(–) 2 to (+) 2 but some were in terms of the binary choice – yes/no – representing the willingness of the investors to invest.

## 2. Business objectives

Six business objectives were identified by the investors – each having more than one objective for investment in different scales. Theoretically, one can envisage as many as 63 combinations of business objectives:

$$\sum_{i=1}^{6} {}_6C_i = 63$$

Where:

$6$ = Total number of business objectives.
$i$ = Number of objectives in a combination.
${}_6C_i$ = Number of 6 objectives with $i$ objectives in a combination.

The results had shown that in actual practice 26 combinations of objectives had taken place. In the case of India, Japanese FDI was market-seeking.

*Table 3A.1* Market-seeking FDI: case of India-distribution of responses according to the objectives of investment

| Business objective | Percentage of responses |
|---|---|
| 1. Market as a single objective | 28.6 |
| Market with one more objective | |
| 2. Market + cheap labour | 14.3 |
| 3. Market + export to third country | 2.8 |
| 4. Market + presence of other Japanese firms | 8.6 |
| 5. Market + the presence of R&D | 2.8 |
| Market with multiple combination | |
| 6. Market + export to Japan + Export to third country | 2.8 |
| 7. Market + cheap labour + export to third country | 2.8 |
| 8. Market + cheap labour + presence of other Japanese firms | 5.7 |
| 9. Market + cheap labour + presence of R&D | 2.8 |
| 10. Market + export to Japan + export to third country + cheap labour + presence of other Japanese firms | 2.8 |
| | 74 |

*Note*: The remaining 26 per cent relates to other business combinations.

## 3. Sources of information

For undertaking investment, the normal sources of information which have been resorted to by Japanese investors are: (a) Official government sources; (b) the Internet; (c) Other Japanese enterprises; (d) Other sources, i.e., business papers, magazines, meetings etc. Sources of information also indirectly indicate the nature and level of relationship between the parent and the host country and the kind of knowledge-sharing that may be occurring between the countries. Continuous and complete information from the feasible sources maximizes the flow of FDI.

The source of information could be either one or a combination of more than one. Given the four sources of information, the total number of combinations that could theoretically occur is given by the following:

$$\sum_{i=1}^{4} {}_4C_i = 15$$

Where

$4$ = Total number of sources of information.
$i$ = Sources of information in a combination.
${}_4C_i$ = 4 sources of information with $i$ source in a combination.

The total number of possible combinations of alternative sources of information that could occur is 15. In the case of India the number of combinations that occurred was 11. And in most cases, it is the 'other sources' which has occurred. Most of the companies have learned of business opportunities in India through meetings, business papers or magazines, and so on. In the case of other countries all of the other combinations had occurred.

## 4. Transaction time

Transaction time in investment is an important determinant. It is reported to be relatively high in India compared to others. It is interesting to note that of all of the responses, the companies, which started their business operations subsequent to liberalization in India in 1991, 35 per cent reported that even to start their business operations, the time taken had ranged from 45 day to 180 days – with 80 per cent of them reporting more than 90 days.

## 5. Problems in investment environment – top five problems in India and the ASEAN

In its study entitled 'Japanese-Affiliated Manufacturers in Asia – ASEAN and India: Survey 2004' the Research Department of Japan External Trade Organization (JETRO) – have listed the top five problems in investment environment (p. 35). Although it does not speak about China – the major competitor for Japanese FDI – and also about the two other Asian Tigers – that is, South Korea and Taiwan – it gives a comparative picture of India *vis-à-vis* the ASEAN.

*Table 3A.2* Problems in investment environment – top five problems

| | | | | | |
|---|---|---|---|---|---|
| ASEAN | Troublesome and complicated tax practices | Troublesome and complicated administrative procedures | Insufficient conditions and maintenance of infrastructures | Uncertain and unclear policy management of local governments | Undeveloped economic legal system and arbitrary legal management and application |
| | (43.2)-I | (41.9)-II | (39.6)-III | (37.1)-IV | (34.5)-V |
| India | Insufficient conditions and maintenance of infrastructures | Troublesome and complicated tax practices | Troublesome and complicated administrative procedures | Undeveloped economic legal system and arbitrary legal management and application | Uncertain and unclear policy management of local governments |
| | (76.5)-I | (56.9)-II | (54.9)-III | (23.5)-IV | (11.8)-V |

*Note*: Figures within bracket indicate the percentages of the companies.

# 4

1. In the altered economic environment the small companies are scouring the world and becoming economic powerhouses, successful in technology creation and capable of taking quick, flexible and adaptable decisions, and having their own product-based websites. The choice for investment of the Japanese domestic firm falls on China and East Asia rather than India. The reasons are not confined solely to the business environment and proximity factors but also to the policy factors. For instance, China also aggressively invites FDI in the small sectors. It insists on larger foreign equity participation – a minimum of 25 per cent – while India imposes a 24 per cent ceiling on foreign equity. The small investors are increasingly motivated to invest and are becoming important players in technology creation and to spur growth dynamics in both China and East Asia. The large presence of small-scale investors is also one of the reasons why FDI is so substantial in this region.
2. India has not only to create an enabling environment but also liberate the small-scale sector, and build up cost- and efficiency-based systems to reach global standards. The existing strategy needs to be overhauled in the light of the perceived advantages and disadvantages to the country as an investment destination. The East Asian policy of adhering to performance and trying with alternative policy instruments and change them as soon as they are found to be ineffective with respect to the policy objective and accepting the rigours of international competition needs to be forged. China and India have also strikingly different perceptions with regard to FDI. One of the important driving forces behind FDI in China is to speedily upgrade the small and medium-sized firms while that of India is to treat them as reserve items.

## 5

### 1. Variables, Definitions and Data Sources

*Table 5A.1* Variables, definitions and data sources

| S.N. | Variables | Definition | Data sources |
|---|---|---|---|
| 1 | FDI | Log of Foreign direct investment | Website of the MoF Japan; JETRO publications over the period. |
| 2 | GDP | Gross Domestic product | Key Indicators of Developing Asian and Pacific Countries, ADB, various issues |
| 3 | GDCF/GDP | Gross domestic capital formation/GDP ratio | Key Indicators of Developing Asian and Pacific Countries, ADB, various issues |
| 4 | FTJGDP | Ratio of trade with Japan to GDP | Key Indicators of Developing Asian and Pacific Countries, ADB, various issues |
| 5 | PCINVEDU | Per capita investment in education | Key Indicators of Developing Asian and Pacific Countries, ADB, various issues |
| 6 | XRTY | Change in the exchange rate of yen to dollar | Key Indicators of Developing Asian and Pacific Countries, ADB, various issues |
| 7 | BUDTDEF | Budget deficit/GDP ratio | International Financial Statistics, Key Indicators of Developing Asian and Pacific Countries, ADB, various issues |
| 8 | INVINFRA | Investment in infrastructure | Key Indicators of Developing Asian and Pacific Countries, ADB, various issues |
| 9 | EXRATE | Real effective exchange rate | World Economic and Social Survey, UN, various issues; International Financial Statistics, Various issues |
| Restricted model* | | | |
| | PCGDP | Per capita GDP | For both population and GDP: Key Indicators of Developing Asian and Pacific Countries, ADB, various issues |

*Note*: *The other variables used in the restricted models have already been defined above.

## 2. Wages paid by the Japanese companies

The monthly wages of workers in the nine countries (China was not in JETRO's *Survey*) can be broadly divided into the following categories:

1. Between US$100 and US$200 in India, Indonesia, the Philippines and Thailand.
2. US$200 to US$1,000 in Singapore and Malaysia.
3. More than US$1,000 in Korea, Hong Kong and Taiwan.

The wage level is lowest for category 1, but the variables which the investors perceive as critical for the location of investment are mostly different. We have identified the variables representing location advantages that influence the Japanese MNEs' decision to invest in these countries (see Chapter 3 and Chapter 5).

Country-wise average monthly wages (in US$) paid by Japanese companies in the year 2004 are given in Table 5A.2.

*Table 5A.2* Monthly wages paid by the Japanese companies* (US$)

| S.N. | Country | Workers | Engineers | Middle-level managers |
|---|---|---|---|---|
| 1 | India | | | |
| | New Delhi | 124–146 | 250–408 | 845–1302 |
| | Bangalore | 134–166 | 387–424 | 825–1020 |
| 2 | Korea | | | |
| | Seoul | 984–2,159 | 1,337–2,033 | 2,069–2,894 |
| 3 | Hong Kong | 888–1,966 | 1,885–2,683 | 2,139–5,231 |
| 4 | Taiwan | 975–1,311 | 1,311–1,676 | 2,838–3,776 |
| 5 | Singapore | 469–622 | 1,719 | 2,916–3,250 |
| 6 | Thailand | | | |
| | Bangkok | 179 | 400 | 579 |
| 7 | Malaysia | 218 | 820 | 1,641 |
| 8 | Indonesia | | | |
| | Jakarta | 130 | 252 | 619 |
| | Belam | 95–112 | 391–559 | 335–1,117 |
| 9 | Philippines | | | |
| | Manila | 119 | 209 | 598 |
| | Cabu | 102 | 147 | 592 |

*Note*: *Average of the wages paid by the Japanese companies.
*Source*: JETRO (2005) 'The 15th Survey of Investment-Related Cost Comparison in Major Cities and Regions in Asia', March: 4–9.

## 3. Selected economic characteristics

*Table 5A.3* Selected economic characteristics: NIEs, ASEAN 4, China and India

NIEs

| Years | 1. Hong Kong | | | 2. Singapore | | |
|---|---|---|---|---|---|---|
| | Per capita Japanese FDI<br>1 | Ratio of Japanese FDI to GDP<br>2 | Trade density with Japan<br>3 | Per capita Japanese FDI<br>1 | Ratio of Japanese FDI to GDP<br>2 | Trade density with Japan<br>3 |
| 1981 | 64 | 1.1 | 23.0 | 105 | 1.9 | 52.7 |
| 1982 | 76 | 1.3 | 20.3 | 68 | 1.2 | 47.9 |
| 1983 | 105 | 2.0 | 23.4 | 120 | 1.9 | 40.7 |
| 1984 | 76 | 1.3 | 26.0 | 82 | 1.2 | 40.0 |
| 1985 | 24 | 0.4 | 23.2 | 124 | 1.9 | 37.5 |
| 1986 | 91 | 1.3 | 23.4 | 111 | 1.7 | 38.9 |
| 1987 | 192 | 2.3 | 24.9 | 178 | 2.4 | 44.8 |
| 1988 | 295 | 3.0 | 27.8 | 262 | 2.9 | 50.9 |
| 1989 | 334 | 3.0 | 25.8 | 649 | 6.3 | 47.6 |
| 1990 | 313 | 2.4 | 23.8 | 278 | 2.3 | 45.7 |
| 1991 | 161 | 1.1 | 26.7 | 198 | 1.4 | 45.0 |
| 1992 | 127 | 0.8 | 29.3 | 211 | 1.4 | 40.9 |
| 1993 | 210 | 1.2 | 27.9 | 198 | 1.1 | 42.1 |
| 1994 | 188 | 0.9 | 27.4 | 314 | 1.5 | 42.0 |
| 1995 | 186 | 0.8 | 27.7 | 336 | 1.4 | 42.3 |
| 1996 | 236 | 1.0 | 26.5 | 309 | 1.2 | 37.3 |
| 1997 | 108 | 0.4 | 24.7 | 488 | 1.9 | 33.8 |
| 1998 | 92 | 0.4 | 20.8 | 168 | 0.8 | 28.7 |
| 1999 | 148 | 0.6 | 18.9 | 250 | 1.3 | 32.8 |
| 2000 | 142 | 0.6 | 22.2 | 114 | 0.5 | 36.3 |
| 2001 | 52 | 0.2 | 20.9 | 278 | 1.3 | 29.6 |
| 2002 | 31 | 0.1 | 21.4 | 180 | 0.9 | 26.6 |
| 2003 | 58 | 0.3 | 25.3 | 77 | 0.3 | 27.2 |
| 2004 | 93 | 0.4 | 28.4 | 169 | 0.7 | 28.7 |
| 2005 | 258 | 1.0 | 27.2 | 128 | 0.5 | 27.2 |

*Table 5A.3* (Continued)

| Years | 3. Taiwan | | | 4. Korea | | |
|---|---|---|---|---|---|---|
| | Per capita Japanese FDI | Ratio of Japanese FDI to GDP | Trade density with Japan | Per capita Japanese FDI | Ratio of Japanese FDI to GDP | Trade density with Japan |
| | 1 | 2 | 3 | 1 | 2 | 3 |
| 1981 | 3.0 | 0.11 | 17.41 | 1.89 | 0.11 | 14.2 |
| 1982 | 3.0 | 0.11 | 14.7 | 2.62 | 0.11 | 11.7 |
| 1983 | 5.5 | 0.20 | 15.4 | 3.23 | 0.20 | 11.7 |
| 1984 | 3.4 | 0.11 | 16.3 | 2.65 | 0.11 | 11.9 |
| 1985 | 5.9 | 0.18 | 14.5 | 3.28 | 0.18 | 12.9 |
| 1986 | 15.0 | 0.39 | 17.0 | 10.58 | 0.39 | 15.0 |
| 1987 | 18.8 | 0.36 | 18.5 | 15.55 | 0.36 | 16.2 |
| 1988 | 18.8 | 0.30 | 19.1 | 11.49 | 0.30 | 15.3 |
| 1989 | 24.7 | 0.33 | 16.8 | 14.28 | 0.33 | 13.7 |
| 1990 | 21.9 | 0.28 | 15.2 | 6.62 | 0.28 | 12.4 |
| 1991 | 19.8 | 0.23 | 6.2 | 6.00 | 0.23 | 11.3 |
| 1992 | 14.1 | 0.14 | 14.5 | 5.14 | 0.14 | 9.9 |
| 1993 | 14.0 | 0.13 | 14.4 | 5.57 | 0.13 | 9.1 |
| 1994 | 13.2 | 0.12 | 14.5 | 8.96 | 0.12 | 9.7 |
| 1995 | 21.3 | 0.17 | 16.4 | 9.96 | 0.17 | 9.6 |
| 1996 | 24.4 | 0.19 | 15.1 | 9.13 | 0.19 | 9.1 |
| 1997 | 20.9 | 0.16 | 14.4 | 9.63 | 0.16 | 9.0 |
| 1998 | 10.3 | 0.09 | 13.9 | 6.55 | 0.09 | 9.2 |
| 1999 | 13.0 | 0.10 | 14.8 | 21.03 | 0.10 | 9.0 |
| 2000 | 22.9 | 0.17 | 17.9 | 17.38 | 0.16 | 10.22 |
| 2001 | 14.3 | 0.11 | 13.8 | 11.90 | 0.12 | 8.95 |
| 2002 | 16.7 | 0.13 | 13.9 | 13.15 | 0.11 | 8.23 |
| 2003 | 6.7 | 0.05 | 15.6 | 5.94 | 0.05 | 8.81 |
| 2004 | 21.1 | 0.16 | 18.8 | 17.57 | 0.12 | 10.11 |
| 2005 | 36.4 | 0.24 | 17.7 | 35.9 | 0.22 | 9.3 |

*ASEAN-4*

| Years | 1. Indonesia | | | 2. Thailand | | |
|---|---|---|---|---|---|---|
| | Per capita Japanese FDI | Ratio of Japanese FDI to GDP | Trade density with Japan | Per capita Japanese FDI | Ratio of Japanese FDI to GDP | Trade density with Japan |
| | 1 | 2 | 3 | 1 | 2 | 3 |
| 1981 | 16.09 | 2.65 | 16.7 | 0.65 | 0.09 | 9.8 |
| 1982 | 2.65 | 0.43 | 16.4 | 1.93 | 0.26 | 8.1 |
| 1983 | 2.37 | 0.44 | 15.8 | 1.45 | 0.18 | 9.4 |
| 1984 | 2.31 | 0.43 | 15.6 | 2.35 | 0.28 | 9.0 |
| 1985 | 2.51 | 0.47 | 12.9 | 0.93 | 0.12 | 8.7 |
| 1986 | 1.49 | 0.31 | 12.2 | 2.36 | 0.40 | 11.8 |
| 1987 | 3.17 | 0.72 | 14.5 | 4.68 | 0.49 | 10.1 |
| 1988 | 3.34 | 0.66 | 13.0 | 15.81 | 1.39 | 13.0 |
| 1989 | 3.52 | 0.62 | 12.9 | 23.11 | 1.77 | 15.4 |
| 1990 | 6.16 | 0.97 | 14.3 | 20.67 | 1.35 | 16.5 |
| 1991 | 6.52 | 0.93 | 13.3 | 14.27 | 0.82 | 16.5 |
| 1992 | 9.01 | 1.20 | 12.1 | 11.47 | 0.59 | 15.8 |
| 1993 | 4.30 | 0.51 | 11.0 | 9.96 | 0.46 | 16.2 |
| 1994 | 9.15 | 0.99 | 10.6 | 12.25 | 0.50 | 16.7 |
| 1995 | 8.24 | 0.79 | 10.6 | 20.88 | 0.74 | 18.5 |
| 1996 | 12.17 | 1.06 | 9.4 | 23.38 | 0.77 | 16.4 |
| 1997 | 12.49 | 1.17 | 9.6 | 30.81 | 1.21 | 16.2 |
| 1998 | 5.34 | 1.13 | 13.6 | 22.47 | 1.21 | 15.1 |
| 1999 | 4.50 | 0.68 | 9.5 | 13.41 | 0.68 | 16.7 |
| 2000 | 2.04 | 0.25 | 13.2 | 14.97 | 0.76 | 20.76 |
| 2001 | 3.01 | 0.38 | 12.4 | 14.11 | 0.77 | 20.64 |
| 2002 | 2.51 | 0.26 | 8.2 | 7.98 | 0.40 | 19.63 |
| 2003 | 3.03 | 0.27 | 7.5 | 9.88 | 0.44 | 20.75 |
| 2004 | 1.44 | 0.12 | 8.7 | 18.44 | 0.72 | 22.02 |
| 2005 | 5.4 | 0.42 | 10.4 | 32.8 | 1.20 | 23.3 |

*ASEAN-4* (Continued)

| Years | 3. Malaysia | | | 4. Philippines | | |
|---|---|---|---|---|---|---|
| | Per capita Japanese FDI | Ratio of Japanese FDI to GDP | Trade density with Japan | Per capita Japanese FDI | Ratio of Japanese FDI to GDP | Trade density with Japan |
| | 1 | 2 | 3 | 1 | 2 | 3 |
| 1981 | 2.19 | 0.12 | 21.3 | 1.45 | 0.20 | 8.00 |
| 1982 | 5.72 | 0.31 | 20.7 | 0.67 | 0.09 | 7.57 |
| 1983 | 9.40 | 0.46 | 20.2 | 1.25 | 0.20 | 7.00 |
| 1984 | 9.30 | 0.42 | 22.0 | 0.86 | 0.15 | 6.00 |
| 1985 | 4.97 | 0.25 | 21.2 | 1.12 | 0.20 | 5.29 |
| 1986 | 9.81 | 0.57 | 19.8 | 0.38 | 0.07 | 5.82 |
| 1987 | 9.86 | 0.52 | 19.8 | 1.25 | 0.22 | 6.41 |
| 1988 | 22.85 | 1.12 | 21.3 | 2.28 | 0.35 | 7.70 |
| 1989 | 38.79 | 1.78 | 25.0 | 3.36 | 0.47 | 8.82 |
| 1990 | 40.06 | 1.65 | 26.3 | 4.23 | 0.58 | 9.07 |
| 1991 | 47.44 | 1.83 | 31.2 | 3.19 | 0.45 | 9.44 |
| 1992 | 36.97 | 1.21 | 27.1 | 2.45 | 0.30 | 9.12 |
| 1993 | 40.90 | 1.25 | 29.1 | 3.09 | 0.38 | 10.73 |
| 1994 | 36.90 | 1.02 | 31.6 | 9.74 | 1.04 | 11.65 |
| 1995 | 27.80 | 0.65 | 34.2 | 10.20 | 0.97 | 12.20 |
| 1996 | 27.02 | 0.58 | 30.0 | 7.77 | 0.67 | 12.78 |
| 1997 | 36.50 | 0.81 | 27.9 | 7.13 | 0.64 | 14.79 |
| 1998 | 23.49 | 0.73 | 27.0 | 5.07 | 0.58 | 16.26 |
| 1999 | 23.02 | 0.67 | 29.7 | 8.27 | 0.84 | 14.18 |
| 2000 | 9.88 | 0.26 | 33.34 | 6.05 | 0.61 | 15.96 |
| 2001 | 10.70 | 0.29 | 29.52 | 10.08 | 1.11 | 16.41 |
| 2002 | 3.26 | 0.08 | 25.95 | 5.11 | 0.53 | 16.32 |
| 2003 | 18.48 | 0.45 | 24.59 | 2.40 | 0.25 | 16.93 |
| 2004 | 4.89 | 0.11 | 25.09 | 3.80 | 0.37 | 18.18 |
| 2005 | 20.1 | 0.40 | 20.90 | 5.20 | 0.45 | 16.7 |

| Years | 1. China | | | 2. India | | |
|---|---|---|---|---|---|---|
| | Per capita Japanese FDI | Ratio of Japanese FDI to GDP | Trade density with Japan | Per capita Japanese FDI | Ratio of Japanese FDI to GDP | Trade density with Japan |
| | 1 | 2 | 3 | 1 | 2 | 3 |
| 1981 | 0.026 | 0.009 | 3.80 | 0.004 | 0.009 | 0.87 |
| 1982 | 0.018 | 0.006 | 3.11 | 0.010 | 0.002 | 1.24 |
| 1983 | 0.003 | 0.001 | 3.33 | 0.019 | 0.004 | 1.14 |
| 1984 | 0.110 | 0.037 | 4.27 | 0.017 | 0.008 | 1.04 |
| 1985 | 0.094 | 0.033 | 6.97 | 0.014 | 0.006 | 1.13 |
| 1986 | 0.212 | 0.076 | 5.94 | 0.027 | 0.005 | 1.43 |
| 1987 | 1.131 | 0.381 | 5.13 | 0.030 | 0.009 | 1.29 |
| 1988 | 0.269 | 0.074 | 4.76 | 0.022 | 0.009 | 1.30 |
| 1989 | 0.392 | 0.098 | 4.21 | 0.036 | 0.007 | 1.44 |
| 1990 | 0.305 | 0.090 | 4.35 | 0.016 | 0.010 | 1.18 |
| 1991 | 0.503 | 0.143 | 4.99 | 0.141 | 0.006 | 1.24 |
| 1992 | 0.918 | 0.222 | 5.26 | 0.040 | 0.050 | 1.24 |
| 1993 | 1.435 | 0.281 | 6.50 | 0.107 | 0.013 | 1.16 |
| 1994 | 2.152 | 0.473 | 8.81 | 0.140 | 0.032 | 1.25 |
| 1995 | 3.697 | 0.639 | 8.21 | 0.233 | 0.039 | 1.32 |
| 1996 | 2.061 | 0.307 | 7.36 | 0.454 | 0.060 | 1.16 |
| 1997 | 1.615 | 0.220 | 6.74 | 0.267 | 0.110 | 0.94 |
| 1998 | 0.866 | 0.114 | 6.13 | 0.208 | 0.067 | 1.06 |
| 1999 | 0.605 | 0.078 | 6.67 | 0.165 | 0.051 | 1.03 |
| 2000 | 0.80 | 0.093 | 7.56 | 0.166 | 0.039 | 0.88 |
| 2001 | 1.14 | 0.124 | 7.48 | 0.140 | 0.033 | 0.94 |
| 2002 | 1.37 | 0.139 | 8.03 | 0.295 | 0.067 | 0.85 |
| 2003 | 2.43 | 0.222 | 9.43 | 0.081 | 0.016 | 0.77 |
| 2004 | 3.51 | 0.277 | 10.19 | 0.089 | 0.015 | 0.91 |
| 2005 | 5.03 | 0.30 | 8.3 | 0.24 | 0.03 | 0.09 |

| Features | China | India |
|---|---|---|
| FDI history | Closed till 1978; rapid increase since 1980s, especially in the south | Very restrictive prior to 1991, then gradual opening |
| FDI presence | Modest but rising | Modest, no clear trend |
| FDI regime in practice | Continuing; declining SOE preference; rapid decentralization; much corruption | Reforming, in context of dirigisme history; states are powerful; lack coordination; much corruption |
| Ownership structures | Dominant but declining SOEs, rapidly rising private and foreign firms | Still large SOE sectors reservations schemes for small firms |
| Trade regime | Closed till 1978; then progressively opening, especially for exports; 2002 WTO accession | Restrictive till 1991, then gradual opening |
| International connections | Hong Kong, China, important Diaspora | Large diasporas |
| Institutional quality | Uneven, though improving | Highly complex and cumbersome |
| Human capital | Pockets of excellence; uneven, rapid catch-up | Pockets of excellence; continuing high illiteracy |
| Openness | Heavy Government intervention; Permitted/encouraged/restricted/negative list; special incentives for FDI; case by case approach; approval system; ownership restrictions in many sectors; min. cap; free repatriability; M&A restrictive | Largely automatic; some negative list; 100% FDI in many sectors; ownership restrictions in a few sectors; no min. cap in most sectors; freely repatriable; M&A policy considered restrictive |
| EPZs/SEZs* | Incentives: Govt. infrastructure (road, ports, power), corporate tax 15% full refund of taxes on profits reinvested, duty free imports & exports<br>Labour laws: Flexible<br>Workers' organizations: Single trade union | Incentives: Basic infrastructure provided; enjoy relaxation in regard to Industrial Licensing, Small Scale reservation, Customs and Excise Acts; duty free import of capital goods and raw materials; retention of 100 per cent of export earnings etc. |
| FDI legislation | Separate legislation | Covered under FEMA |

*Sources*: 1. *Asian Development Outlook*, 2004, ADB.
2. *Asian Development Review*, 21(1): 2004, ADB.

## 4. Some stylized facts regarding FDI between India and China

Specific mention may be made of the SEZs of China and the EPZs of India. In China, SEZs are perceived as a major force in attracting FDI. They operate aggressively, providing the foreign investors with a choice of investment locations. The SEZs enjoy: (a) full freedom in allocation of developed plots on a purely commercial basis; (b) full authority to provide services like water, electricity, security, restaurants, recreation, etc. on commercial lines; (c) the facility to develop a township within SEZ with residential areas, markets, playgrounds, clubs, recreation centres, etc.; and (d) entitlements as provided in their Tax Act.

In India, the EPZ scheme was launched in April 2000 for manufacture, trading, re-conditioning, and repair or service activity and enjoys relaxation with regard to industrial licensing, small-scale reservation, excise, customs, duty-free import of capital goods and raw materials. But it is widely held that they are not on a par with the Export Zones of China where the government has been able to insulate foreign investment from domestic policy issues and foreign investment receives special treatment in wide-ranging areas of capital, labour and tax rates. This would require many legal and bureaucratic changes for businesses operating within the EPZs.

# Technical Annex

## 2

### Estimation of the growth rates of Japanese FDI

The growth rates of Japanese FDI have been calculated by using the least-squares regression method. This method also takes into account all observations in a period, hence the resulting growth rates reflect general trends that are not unduly influenced by exceptional values, particularly at the end points. The least-squares growth rate is estimated by fitting a least-squares linear regression trend line to the logarithmic annual values of the variable, i.e., FDI, in the relevant period. More specifically, the trend growth rate has been estimated from a semi-log equation which has the general form:

$$\ln Y = \alpha + \gamma t + e_t$$

Where $t$ represents time and $e$ is the error term. From this equation growth rate of FDI can be obtained by taking exp.$(\gamma) - 1$

## 3

### Logit model

To identify the relative importance of the variables representing location advantages from the viewpoint of Japanese investors, the logit model has been used, even though the number of observations in the estimation of the model is rather small. A larger sample would have produced more significant results. This became evident from a smaller sample, as only INFST was significant but as the number of observations increased, JMT and CONTROL variables also turned out to be significant with their + and – sign as expected. The response from MNEs to variables like 'partnership' and 'networking' relationship was limited. In a number of cases it was reported that the chemistry of joint partnership did not work well. In regard to networking, wherever the investor has intention to invest he wants networking to be developed otherwise they have remained silent. In view of this both the variables were not included in the model.

The binary logit model used is:

$$\mathrm{DII} = \alpha_0 + \alpha_1\,ADCOM + \alpha_2\,CONTROL + \alpha_3\,INFST$$
$$+\alpha_4\,JMT + \alpha_5\,LABOR + \mu$$

The expected sign of $\alpha_1$ and $\alpha_2$ is negative while that of $\alpha_3$, $\alpha_4$, and $\alpha_5$ is positive.

The variables are explained below.

*Dependent variable*

DII 'Are you interested in investing in India compared to China and East Asian countries?' The obvious assumption is that this is a conscious decision on the part of the investors. Value one was given to a 'yes' answer and zero to a 'no' answer. This is a binary variable taking the value zero or one.

*Independent variables*

The Japanese MNEs were asked to mark their opinion on the Indian situation compared to China and East Asian countries on a five point scale: −2, −1, 0, +1, +2. A zero score would indicate that in the opinion of the firm, the Indian situation is not very different from that of China and other East Asian countries; a positive score would indicate that the Indian situation is better or preferred, while a negative score would indicate that the Indian situation is worse compared to other Asian countries. The variables included in the estimation are:

INFST, Infrastructure. In the case of infrastructure the firms were asked to rate separately telecommunications, electricity and transport. INFST is an overall infrastructure variable and as the three responses were highly correlated ranging from 0.97 to 0.99 providing significant explanatory power, an average of the three scores representing the three constituents of infrastructure has been adopted.

CONTROLS: as explained in the text, this variable refers to controls and restrictions on foreign exchange conversion, the repatriation of profits, dividend payments, and imports.

ADCOM, Administrative complexities: It mainly deals with public administration, delays, the prevalence of corruption, the transparency of rules and the accountability of decision makers.

JMT refers to the adoption of Japanese Management Techniques.

*Table 3A.1a* Logit model for interest to invest in India (excluding labour as an explanatory variable)

Dependent Variable: DII
Method: ML – Binary Logit
Convergence achieved after 6 iterations
Covariance matrix computed using second derivatives

| Variable | Coefficient | Std. Error | z-Statistic | Prob. |
|---|---|---|---|---|
| C | 2.194049 | 1.446152 | 1.517164 | 0.1292 |
| **CONTROL** | **−1.247000*** ** | **0.737194** | **−1.691551** | **0.0907** |
| **INFST** | **3.288871*** | **1.145953** | **2.869989** | **0.0041** |
| **JMT** | **2.422409** ** | **1.032928** | **2.345188** | **0.0190** |
| ADCOM | −1.021710 | 0.835842 | 1.222372 | 0.2216 |
| Mean dependent var | 0.620000 | S.D. dependent var | 0.490314 | |
| Log likelihood | −17.93414 | Akaike info criterion | 0.917365 | |
| Restr. log likelihood | −33.20321 | Schwarz criterion | 1.108568 | |
| LR statistic (4 df) | 30.53814 | Hannan-Quinn criter. | 0.990176 | |
| Probability (LR stat) | 3.80E-06 | Avg. log likelihood | −0.358683 | |
| McFadden R-squared | 0.459867 | | | |

*Notes*: *Significant at 1 per cent; **Significant at 5 per cent; ***Significant at 10 per cent.

*Table 3A.1b* Logit model for interest to invest in India (including labour as an explanatory variable)

Dependent Variable: DII
Method: ML – Binary Logit
Convergence achieved after 6 iterations
Covariance matrix computed using second derivatives

| Variable | Coefficient | Std. Error | z-Statistic | Prob. |
|---|---|---|---|---|
| C | 2.311264 | 1.492254 | 1.548841 | 0.1214 |
| **CONTROL** | **−1.600532*** ** | **0.874952** | **−1.829280** | **0.0674** |
| **INFST** | **4.006040*** | **1.331743** | **3.008119** | **0.0026** |
| **JMT** | **2.671648** ** | **1.144994** | **2.333330** | **0.0196** |
| LABOR | 1.622918 | 1.137964 | 1.426159 | 0.1538 |
| ADCOM | −0.966440 | 0.884185 | −1.093030 | 0.2744 |
| Mean dependent var | 0.620000 | S.D. dependent var | | 0.490314 |
| Log likelihood | −16.72899 | Akaike info criterion | | 0.909160 |
| Restr. log likelihood | −33.20321 | Schwarz criterion | | 1.138602 |
| LR statistic (5 df) | 32.94843 | Hannan-Quinn criter. | | 0.996533 |
| Probability (LR stat) | 3.85E-06 | Avg. log likelihood | | −0.334580 |
| McFadden R-squared | | | | 0.496163 |

*Notes*: *Significant at 1 per cent; **Significant at 5 per cent; ***Significant at 10 per cent.

LABOR: relates to the availability of cheap and abundant labour. However, companies' responses were almost the same between India and China with only a few differences between them. Hence, estimates have been attempted both with and without labour.

Tables 3A.1(a) and (b) present the maximum likelihood estimates of the binary logit model, first excluding labour and then including it.

## 4

### 1. Determinants in the international orientation of Japanese firms – the case of the electronics industry

### The model

The principal determinants of the international orientation of Japanese firms are found to be: the 'size' – captured here by sales turnover; level of technology; R&D; and ownership. The variables thus identified are given in the equation below.

$$\text{DOI} = \alpha_0 + \alpha_1 \log(\text{sales}) + \alpha_2 \text{ KL} + \alpha_3 \text{ R\&D} + \alpha_4 \text{ FOR} + \mu$$

*Dependent variable*

DOI: Degree of international orientation – that is, here the ratio of exports to total sales.

*Independent variables*

KL: Capital–labour ratio as a measure of the level of technology.
Size: Captured by sales turnover – here log of sales is taken as a measure of size.
RD: Research and development.
FOR: Foreign ownership.

DOI is having a positive relationship with the capital–labour (C–L) ratio, log of sales, and research and development. FDI undertaken by firms with high R&D, high sales levels and higher C–L ratio characterizes the market structure of these firms.

The model results are set out in Table 4A.1.

*Table 4A.1* Japanese electronics industry (214 firms)

| Variables | Coefficient | Std. Error | z-Statistic | Probability |
|---|---|---|---|---|
| *Results of the binary logit* | | | | |
| C | −13.48032 | 2.288335 | −5.890886 | 0.0000 |
| KL | 0.009733 | 0.005193 | 1.874171 | 0.0609 |
| L. Sales | 1.264798 | 0.215647 | 5.865132 | 0.0000 |
| RD | 10.85607 | 6.459311 | 1.680685 | 0.0928 |
| FOR | 0.009130 | 0.015621 | 0.584454 | 0.5589 |
| *Results of the Normal Tobit* | | | | |
| C | −114.2535 | 18.30066 | −6.243135 | 0.0000 |
| KL | 0.146984 | 0.038279 | 3.839781 | 0.0001 |
| L. Sales | 11.43938 | 1.680938 | 6.805355 | 0.0000 |
| RD | 40.52031 | 83.44703 | 0.485581 | 0.6273 |
| FOR | 0.232519 | 0.185378 | 1.254294 | 0.2097 |

## Model results

### 2 Japanese domestic companies' reasons for not investing outside

The principal reasons given by the domestic companies are five – either single or in combination which can be as many as:

$$\sum_{i=1}^{5} {}_5C_i = 31 \text{ Combinations could occur}$$

where:
5 = Total number of reasons for not investing outside Japan.
$i$ = Number of reason(s) in a combination.

Thus the reasons for not investing outside Japan there can be as many as 31 combinations.

### 3 Business goals of the domestic companies

The domestic companies have given seven goals and technically there can be as many as:

$$\sum_{i=1}^{7} {}_7C_i = 127 \text{ combinations}$$

where 7 = Total number of objectives and $i$ = Number of business objective(s) in a combination.

# 5

## Econometric model – determinants of Japanese FDI

Hendry and his associates have suggested the strategy of 'general to simple' modelling as an alternative to the traditional 'simple to general modelling'. This methodology is particularly relevant to studies using time series data as adopted here (see Krishna 1997). To avoid the arbitrary choice of the explanatory variables in our analysis we began with a large number of independent variables, before narrowing these down to a few. Even after that we were left with eight independent variables (excluding the 'time' trend). Using the panel method, we have proceeded as follows:

### General model

First, a general model has been estimated using the same number of independent variables for all of the groups of countries. The model formulated and the variables specified in the general model are given below.

$$\begin{aligned} \text{FDI} = {} & a_0 + a_1\, GDP + a_2\, (GDCF/GDP) + a_3\, FTJGDP + a_4\, PCINVEDU \\ & + a_5\, XRTY + a_6\, BUGTDEF + a_7\, INVINFRA + a_8\, EXRATE \\ & + a_9 \text{ Time trend} \end{aligned}$$

*Dependent variable*

FDI: Foreign direct investment outflows from Japan in US dollars.

*Independent variables: the determinants*

1. GDP: Gross domestic product by industrial origin
2. GDCF/GDP: Ratio of Gross domestic capital formation to Gross domestic product
3. INVINFRA: Investment in infrastructure
4. XRTY: Change in the exchange rate of the yen
5. PCINVEDU: Per capita expenditure on education
6. BUGTDEF: Budget deficit to GDP
7. EXRATE: Real effective exchange rate
8. FTJGDP: Ratio of trade with Japan to GDP
9. Time trend: The estimated equations also include a 'time trend' variable.

## Restricted models

In the alternative specification we have reduced not only the number of independent variables but also the number of groups – that is, NIEs, the ASEAN, and the ten countries – giving different specification to different groups on the basis of their statistical significance and basic economic reasoning covering the period 1981–2004. The model estimated for each group is given below.

*NIEs*

$$\text{FDI} = a_0 + a_1\, PCGDP + a_2\,(GDCF/GDP) + a_3\, XRTY + a_4\, EXRATE + \text{Time trend}$$

*ASEAN-4*

$$\text{FDI} = a_0 + a_1\, PCGDP + a_2\,(GDCF/GDP) + a_3\, XRTY - a_4\, EXRATE + a_5\, INFRA + \text{Time trend}$$

*Ten countries*

$$\text{FDI} = a_0 + a_1\,(GDCF/GDP) + a_2\, FTJGDP + a_3\, BUGTDEF + a_4\, XRTY + a_5\, EXRATE + a_6\, INFRA$$

## Construction of variables

Dependent and independent variables were constructed using the available sources. In regard to the dependent variable, that is, Japanese FDI outflows to the host countries, we have used the data compiled by Ministry of Finance (MoF) of Japan from its website and JETRO publications compiled over a period of time. MoF data are given in yen. These were converted into dollars by using the corresponding year's yen–dollar exchange rates. These compiled FDI flows over a long period, attempted in the present study, provide information in determining the trends.

With regard to the independent variables – namely, GDP, GDCF, investment in infrastructure, education and other variables – the sources are listed in Table 5A.1 in the Annex. Here it may be mentioned that in most of the cases the figures were given in the host country's own national currencies. These were converted in dollars using the respective year's exchange rate.

The period taken is 1981–2004. The long time series data has given us enough degrees of freedom compared to many of the early studies relying on relatively short time series data and consequently suffering from too few degrees of freedom.

**Panel data models**

Panel methods have become popular as they provide greater power than individual country studies and hence give greater efficiency and more degrees of freedom. Hence, the determinants of FDI flows have been estimated with the help of balanced panel data techniques – namely, the fixed and random effects models covering the period 1981–90, 1991–2004 and 1981–2004. The Lagrange multiplier and Hausman test results indicate the Random Effects model to be appropriate ones even though both RE and FE models were estimated.

# References


Abegglen, James C. and George, Stalk, Jr. (1985) *Kaisha: The Japanese Corporation*, New York: Basic Books, Inc.

ADB (1998 to 2006 Year-wise issues) *Key Indicators*, Manila: Asian Development Bank.

ADB (2004) *Asian Development Outlook*, Hong Kong, China: Oxford University Press for the ADB.

ADB (2004) *Asian Development Review*, 21(1), Asian Development Bank.

Agarwal, J. (1980) 'Determinants of Foreign Direct Investment: A Survey', *Weltwirtschaftliches Archiv*, 116, 739–73.

Agenor, Pierre-Richard (2001) 'Benefits and Costs of International Financial Integration: Theory and Facts', Working Paper 2699, International Economics, Trade, Capital Flows, Washington, DC: World Bank.

Agmon, T.B. and D.R. Lessard (1977) 'Investor Recognition of Corporate International Diversification', *Journal of Finance*, September, 1049–55.

Aharoni, Yair (1966) *The Foreign Investment Decision Process*, Boston, MA: Harvard Business School.

Aitken, Brian, Harrison, Ann and Lipsey, Robert E. (1996) 'Wages and Foreign Ownership: A Comparative Study of Mexico, Venezuela, and the United States', *Journal of International Economics*, 40(3–4): 345–71.

Akamatsu, K. (1960) 'A Theory of Unbalanced Growth in the World Economy', *Weltwirtschaftliches Archiv*, 86(2): 196–217.

Alvarez, Roberto and Holger Gorg (2005) 'Multinationals and Plant Exit: Evidence from Chile', GEP Research Paper 05 16, University of Nottingham.

Anderson, O. (1993) 'On the Internationalisation Process of Firms: A Critical Analysis', *Journal of International Business Studies*, 24(2): 209–33.

Aoki, M. (1984) 'Aspects of Japanese Firm', in M. Aoki (ed.), *The Economic Analysis of the Japanese Firm*, Amsterdam: North-Holland, pp. 3–43.

Aoki, M. (1988) *Information, Incentives and Bargaining in the Japanese Economy*, Cambridge: Cambridge University Press.

Aoki, M. (1990) 'Towards an Economic Model of the Japanese Firm', *The Journal of Economic Literature*, 28: 1–27.

Aoki, M. and R. Dore (1994) *The Japanese Firm: The Sources of Competitive Strength*, Oxford: Oxford University Press.

ASEAN (2000) *ASEAN Investment Report 2000: Challenges and Development*, Jakarta: ASEAN Secretariat.

Balasubramanyam, V.N., M. Salisu and D. Sapsford (1999) 'Foreign Direct Investment as an Engine of Growth', *Journal of International Trade and Economic Development*, 8: 27–40.

Barkema, H., J. Bell and J. Pennings (1996) 'Foreign Entry, Cultural Barriers, and Learning', *Strategic Management Journal*, 17(2): 151–66.

Barrell, Ray and Nigel Pain (1999) 'Trade Restraints and Japanese Direct Investment Flows', *European Economic Review*, 43(1): 29–45.

Bartlett, C.A. and S. Ghoshal (1988) 'Managing Innovations in the Transnational', in C.A. Bartlett, Y. Doz and G. Hedlund (eds), *Research on Multinational Management*, London: Addison-Wesley.

Bartlett, C.A. and S. Ghoshal (1989) *Managing Across Borders – The Transnational Solution*, Boston: Harvard Business School Press.

Bayoumi, Tamim and Gabrielle Lipworth (1997) 'Japanese Foreign Direct Investment and Regional Trade', IMF Working Paper: WP/97/103, August. (Also in the *Journal of Asian Economics*, 9(4) (1998): 581–607).

Belderbos, Rene (2001) 'Overseas Innovation by Japanese Firms: An Analysis of Patents and Subsidiary Data', *Research Policy*, 30: 313–32.

Belderbos, Rene, Giovanni Capannelli and Kyoji Fukao (2001) 'Backward Vertical Linkages of Foreign Manufacturing Affiliates: Evidence from Japanese Multinationals', *World Development*, 29(1): 189–208.

Belderbos, Rene and Martin Carree (2002) 'The Location of Japanese Investments in China: Agglomeration Effects, Keiretsu, and Firm Heterogeneity', *Journal of the Japanese and International Economies*, 16(2): 194–211.

Bende Nabende, A., J.L. Ford, S. Sen and J. Slater (2000) 'FDI Locational Determinants and the Linkage between FDI and other Macroeconomic Factors: Long-run Dynamics in Pacific Asia', Discussion paper 11, Department of Economics, University of Birmingham.

Benjamin, Tan and Vertinsky, Ilan (1996) 'Foreign Direct Investment by Japanese Electronics Fims in the United States and Canada: Modeling the Timing of Entry', *Journal of International Business Studies*, 27(4): 655–81.

Berthelemy, J.C. and S. Demurger (2000) 'Foreign Direct Investment and Economic Growth: Theory and Application to China', *Review of Development Economics*, 4(2): 140–55.

Bos, Antonio, and William E. Cole (1994) 'Management System as Technology: Japanese, US and National Firms in the Brazilian Electronic Sector', *World Development*, 22(2): 225–36.

Boskin, M.J. and W.G. Gale (1987) 'New Results on the Effects of Tax Policy on the International Location of Investment', in M. Feldstein (ed.), *The Effects of Taxation on Capital Accumulation*, Chicago: University of Chicago Press, pp. 201–19.

Bosworth, B.P. and S.M. Collins (1999) 'Capital Flows to Developing Economies: Implications for Saving And Investment', *Brookings Papers on Economic Activity*, 1: 143–69.

Branstetter, Lee (2000) 'Vertical Keiretsu and Knowledge Spillovers in Japanese Manufacturing: An Empirical Assessment', *Journal of the Japanese and International Economies*, 14(2): 73–104.

Braunerhjelm, Pontus and Roger Swenson (1996) 'Host country Characteristics and Agglomeration in Foreign Direct Investment', *Applied Economics*, 28: 833–40.

Brewer, T. (1993) 'Government Policies, Market Imperfections and Foreign Direct Investment', *Journal of International Business Studies*, First Quarter 24(1): 101–21.

Brianard, S. Lael (1997) 'An Empirical Assessment of the Proximity-Concentration Trade-Off Between Multinational Sales and Trade', *The American Economic Review*, 87(4): 520–44.

Buckley, P.J. and M. Casson, M. (1976, 1991) *The Future of Multinational Enterprise*, London: Macmillan.

Buckley, P.J. and M. Casson, M. (1981) 'The Optimal Timing of a Foreign Direct Investment', *The Economic Journal*, 91: 75–87.

Calof, J.L. and P.W. Beamish (1995) 'Adapting to Foreign Markets: Explaining Internationalisation', *International Business Review*, 4(2): 115–31.

Calvet, A.L. (1980) 'Markets and Hierarchies: Towards a Theory of International Business', Doctoral dissertation, Sloan School of Management, MIT.

Calvet, A.L. (1981) 'A Synthesis of Foreign Direct Investment Theories And Theories of Multinational Firm', in Alan M. Rugman (ed.), *International Business*, vol. I, New York: Routledge.

Casson, M.C. (1979) *Alternatives to the Multinational Enterprise*, London: Macmillan.

Casson, M.C. (1987) *The Firm and the Market*, Oxford: Basil Blackwell.

Caves, Richard E. (1971) 'International Corporations: The Industrial Economics of Foreign Investment', *Economica*, NS(38): 1–27.

Caves, Richard E. (1974) 'Causes of Direct Investment: Foreign Firms' Shares in Canadian and United Kingdom Manufacturing Industries', *Review of Economics and Statistics*, 56: 279–93.

Caves, Richard E. (1996) *Multinational Enterprise and Economic Analysis*, 2nd edition, Cambridge: Cambridge University Press.

Chen, C. (1996) 'Regional Determinants of Foreign Investment in Mainland China', *Journal of Economic Studies*, 23: 8–30.

Chen, C., L. Chang and Y. Zhang (1995) 'The Role of Foreign Direct Investment in China's Post 1978 Economic Development', *World Development*, 23(4): 691–703.

Chen, Homin and Tain Jy Chen (1998) 'Network Linkages and Location Choice in Foreign Direct Investment', *Journal of International Business Studies*, 29(3): 445–67.

Chen, Chien Hsun (1996) 'Regional Determinants of Foreign Direct Investment in Mainland China', *Journal of Economic Studies*, 23(2): 18–30.

Chen, Chunlai (1999) 'The Impact of FDI and Trade', in Y. Wu (ed.), *Foreign Direct Investment and Economic Growth in China*, Cheltenham: Edward Elgar.

Cheng, Leonard K. and Yum K. Kwan (2000) 'What Are the Determinants of the Location of Foreign Direct Investment? The Chinese Experience', *Journal of International Economics*, 51(2): 379–400.

Cheng, L.K. and H. Zhao (1995) *Geographical Pattern of Foreign Direct Investment in China: Location, Factor Endowments, and Policy Incentives*, Department of Economics, Hong Kong University of Science and Technology, February.

Cleeve, Emmanuel (2000) 'Why Do Japanese Firms Locate in Particular British Regions?', *Asia Pacific Journal of Economics & Business*, 4(1): 112–24.

Coase, Ronald H. (1937) 'The Nature of the Firm', *Economica*, NS(4).

Contractor, F.J. (1990) *Do Government Policies Toward Foreign Investment Matter?*, GSM Working Paper, Newark, NJ, Rutgers University.

Coughlin, Cletus C., V. Joseph and Terza Vachira Arromdee (1991) 'State Characteristics and the Location of Foreign Direct Investment within the United States', *Review of Economics and Statistics*; 73(4): 675–83.

Cyert, Richard and James March (1963) *A Behavioral Theory of the Firm*, Englewood Cliffs, NJ: Prentice Hall.

Davidson, William (1980) 'The Location of Foreign Direct Investment Activity: Country Characteristics and Experience Effects', *Journal of International Business Studies*, 11(2): 9–22.

D'Costa, Anthony P. (1995) 'The Restructuring of the Indian Automobile Industry: Indian State and Japanese Capital', *World Development*, 23(3): 485–502.

De Coster, G.P. and W.C. Strange (1993) 'Spurious Agglomerations', *Journal of Urban Economics*, 33(3): 273–304.

Dees, S. (1998) 'Foreign Direct Investment in China: Determinants and Effects', *Economics of Planning*, 31(2/3): 175–94.

Delery, J.E. and D. Harold Doty (1996) 'Modes of Theorizing in Strategic Human Resources Management', *Academy of Management Journal*, 39(4): 802–35.

Dewenter, K.L. (1995) 'Do Exchange Rate Changes Drive Foreign Direct Investment?', *Journal of Business*, 68(3): 405–33.

Dickens, W.T., L. Katz and K. Lang (1986) 'Are Efficiency Wages Efficient?', NBER *Working Paper* No. 1935.

Doeringer, B. Peter, Edward Lorenz and David G. Terkla (2003) 'The Adoption and Diffusion of High-performance Management: Lessons from Japanese Multinationals in the West', *Cambridge Journal of Economics*, 27: 265–86.

Doeringer, P., C. Evans-Klock and D. Terkla (1998) 'Hybrids or Hodgepodges? Workplace Practices of Japanese and Domestic Startups in the United States', *Industrial and Labour Relations Review*, 51(2): 171–86.

Doremus, Paul N., William W. Keller, Louis W. Pauly and Simon Reich (1998) *The Myth of the Global Corporation*. Princeton: Princeton University Press.

Doyle, P., J. Saunders and V. Wong (1992) 'Competition in Global Markets: A Case Study of American and Japanese Competition in the British Markets', *Journal of International Business Studies*, 23(3): 419–42.

Drabek, Zdenek and Warren Payne (1999) 'The Impact of Transparency on Foreign Direct Investment', *Staff Working Paper*, ERAD-99-02, Geneva: WTO.

Dunning, John H. (1958) *American Investment in British Industry*, London: George Allen & Unwin.

Dunning, John H. (1973) 'The Determinants of International Production', *Oxford Economic Papers*, 25(3): 289–336.

Dunning, John H. (1977) *United Kingdom Transnational Manufacturing and Resource Based Industries and Trade Flows in Developing Countries*, Geneva: UNCTAD.

Dunning, John H. (1980) 'Toward an Eclectic Theory of International Production: Some Empirical Tests', *Journal of International Business Studies*, 11(1): 9–31.

Dunning, John H. (1981a) *International Production and the Multinational Enterprise*, London: George and Unwin.

Dunning, John H. (1981b) 'Explaining the International Direct Investment Position of Countries: Towards a Dynamic or Developmental Approach', *Weltwirtschaftliches Archiv/Review of World Economics*, 117(1): 30–64.

Dunning, John H. (1986) 'The Investment Cycle Revisited', *Weltwirtschaftliches* Archiv, 122: 667–77.

Dunning, John H. (1988) *Explaining International Production*, London: Unwin Hyman.

Dunning, John H. (1990) 'The Eclectic Paradigm of International Production: A Personal Perspective', in C.N. Pitelis and R. Sugden (eds), *The Nature of the Transnational Firm*, London: Routledge.

Dunning, John H. (1991) 'The Eclectic Paradigm of International Production: A Personal Perspective', in C.N. Pitelis and R. Sugden (eds), *The Nature of the Transnational Firm*, London: Routledge, pp. 117–36.

Dunning, John H. (1992) 'The Competitive Advantages of Nations and TNC Activities: A Review Article', *Transnational Corporations*, 1: 135–68.

Dunning, John H. (1992a) 'The Governance of Japanese and US Manufacturing Affiliates in the UK: Some Country-Specific Differences', in B. Kogut (ed), *Country Competitiveness: Technology and the Organization of Work*, Oxford: Oxford University Press.

Dunning, John H. (1993) *Multinational Enterprises and the Global Economy*, New York: Addison-Wesley Publishing Company.

Dunning, John H. (1995) 'Reappraising the Eclectic Paradigm in an Age of Alliance Capitalism', *Journal of International Business Studies*, 26: 461–91.

Dunning, John H. (1998a) 'Changing Geography of Foreign Direct Investment: Explanations and Implications', in Nagesh Kumar *et al.* (eds), *Globalization, Foreign Direct Investment and Technology Transfer: Impacts on and Prospects for Developing Countries*, London and New York: Routledge, pp. 43–90.

Dunning, John H. (ed.) (1998b) *Globalization, Trade and Foreign Direct Investment*, New York: Elsevier.

Dunning, John H. (1998) 'Location and the Multinational Enterprise: A Neglected Factor?', *International Business Review*, 9: 163–90.

Dunning, John H. (2000) 'The Eclectic Paradigm as an Envelop for Economic and Business Theories of MNE Activity', *Journal of International Business* Studies, 9: 163–90.

Dunning, John H. (2003) *Global Capitalism, FDI and Competitiveness*, Cheltenham: Edward Elgar.

Dyer, J.H. and W. Ouchi (1993) 'Japanese-Style Partnerships: Giving Companies a Competitive Edge', *Sloan Management Review*, Fall.

Eaton, B. Curtis, Richard G. Lipsey and A. Edward Safarian (1994) 'The Theory of Multinational Plant Location: Agglomeration and Disagglomerations', Economic Growth and Policy Program, Canada Institute of Advanced Research, Canada.

Eaton, Jonathan and Tamura, Akiko (1996) 'Japanese and American Exports and Investment As Conduits of Growth', National Bureau of Economic Research, NBER Working Paper Series, Working Paper 5457, Cambridge, MA, USA.

Elger, T. and C. Smith (1998) 'Exit, Voice and "Mandate": Management Strategies and Labour Practices of Japanese Firms in Britain', *British Journal of Industrial Relations*, 36(2): 185–207.

Encarnation, D.J. (1999) *Japanese Multinationals in Asia: Regional Operations in Comparative Perspective*, New York: Oxford University Press.

Errunza, V.R. and M. Yalovsky (1978) 'International Diversification and the Multinational Corporation', Working paper, McGill University, Montreal.

Ferrantino, Michael J. (1993) 'The Effect of Intellectual Property Rights on International Trade and Investment', *Weltwirschaftliches Archiv*, 129: 300–31.

Flamm, Kenneth (1984) 'The Volatility of Offshore Investment', *Journal of Development Economics*, 16: 231–48.

Florida, Richard (1997) 'The Globalisation of R&D: Results of a Survey of foreign Affiliated R&D laboratories in the USA', *Research Policy*, 26(1): 85–103.

Ford, Stuart; Strange, Roger (1999) 'Where Do Japanese Manufacturing Firms Invest Within Europe, and Why?', *Transnational Corporations*. 8(1): 117–42.

Forsgren, M. (1989) *Managing the Internationalisation Process – The Swedish Case*, London: Routledge.

*Foreign Collaborations*, (1980 to 2001 – annual publication): Department of Scientific and Industrial Research, Ministry of Science & Technology, Govt. Of India.

Froot, Kenneth A. and Jeremy C. Stein (1991) 'Exchange Rates and Foreign Direct Investment: An Imperfect Capital Markets Approach', *Quarterly Journal of Economics*, 106(4): 1191–217.

Ghemawat, Pankaj (2001) 'Distance Still Matters: The Hard Reality of Global Expansion', *Harvard Business Review*, October: 2–3.

Gibbons, R. and M. Waldman (1999) 'Careers in Organizations: Theory and Evidence', in O. Ashenfelter and D. Card (eds), *Handbook of Labor Economics*, Amsterdam and New York: Elsevier.

Giddy, Ian H. (1978) 'The Demise of the Product Cycle Model in International Business Theory', *Columbia Journal of World Business*, 13: 90–7.

Giddy, Ian H. and Alan M. Rugman (1979) 'A Model of Trade, Foreign Direct Investment and Licensing', Research Working Paper No. 274A, New York: Columbia University Graduate School of Business.

Globerman, S. and D. Shapiro (1999) 'The Impact of Government Policies on Foreign Direct Investment: The Canadian Experience', *Journal of International Business Studies*, 30(3): 513–32.

Goldberg, L.S. and M.W. Klein (1997) 'Foreign Direct Investment, Trade and Real Exchange Rate Linkages in Southeast Asia and Latin America', NBER Working Paper, No. 6344.

Gorg, Holger and Eric Strobl (2003) 'Footloose Multinationals?', *The Manchester School*, 71: 1–19.

Graen, G.B. and M. Wakabayashi (1994) 'Cross-cultural Leadership-making: Bridging American and Japanese Diversity for Team Advantage', in H.C. Triandis, M.D. Dunnette and L.M. Hough (eds), *Handbook of Industrial and Organizational Psychology*, New York: Consulting Psychologist Press.

Grosse, Robert and Len Trevino (1996) 'Foreign Direct Investments in the United States: An Analysis by Country of Origin', *Journal of International Business Studies*, 27(1): 139–55.

Gruber, W., R. Mehta and R. Vernon (1967) 'The R&D Factor in International Trade and International Investment of the United States', *Journal of Political Economy*, 75: 20–37.

Grubert, H. and J. Mutti (1991) 'Taxes, Tariffs and Transfer Pricing in Multinational Corporate Decision Making', *Rev. Econ. Statist.* 73 (May): 285–93.

Habib, Mohsin and Zurawicki, Leon (2002) 'Corruption and Foreign Direct Investment', *Journal of International Business Studies*, 33(2): 291–307.

Harriss, John (1995) 'Japanization: Context and Culture in the Indonesian Automotive Industry', *World Development*, 23(1): 117–28.

Hatch, Walter, and Yamamura, Kozo (1996) *Asia in Japan's Embrace*, Cambridge: Cambridge University Press.

He Canfei (2002) 'Information Costs, Agglomeration Economies and Location of Foreign Direct Investment in China', *Regional Studies*, 36(9): 1029–36.

Head, K. and J. Ries (1996) 'Inter-City Competition for Foreign Investment: Static and Dynamic Effects of China's Incentive Areas', *Journal of Urban Economics*, 40: 38–60.

Henley, J., C. Kirkpatrick and G. Wilde (1999) 'Foreign Direct Investment in China: Recent Trend and Current Policy Issues', *World Economy*, 22(2): 23–43.

Hennart, J.F. (1982) *A Theory of Multinational Enterprise*, Ann Arbor, MI: University of Michigan Press.

Hennart, J.F. (1986) 'What is Internalisation?', *Weltwirtschaftliches Archiv*, 122: 791–806.

Hennart, J.F. (1991) 'The Transaction Costs Theory of Joint Ventures: An Empirical Study of Japanese Subsidiaries in the United States', *Management Science*, 37: 483–97.

Hines, J.R. and E.M. Rice (1994) 'Fiscal Paradise: Foreign Tax Havens and American Business', *Quarterly Journal of Economics*, 109 (February): 149–83.

Hong, Mao and Luoshou Chen (2001) 'Quantitative and Dynamic Analysis of the OLI Variables Determining FDI in China', *Review of Urban and Development Studies*, 13(2): 163–72.

Hood, N. and S. Young (1980) *European Development Strategies of US Owned Manufacturing Companies Located in Scotland*, Edinburgh: HMSO.

Hood, N. and S. Young (1988) chapter in J.H. Dunning and P. Robson (eds), *Multinational Corporate Integration and Regional Economic Integration*, Oxford: Basil Blackwell.

Horst, T. (1971) 'The Theory of the Multinational Firm: Optimal Behavior under Different Tariff and Tax Rates', *Journal of Political Economy*, 79(5): 1059–72.

Horst T. (1972) 'Firm and Industry Determinants of the Decision to Invest abroad: An Empirical Study', *Review of Economics and Statistics*, 54 (August): 258–66.

Horstman, I. and Markusen, J.R. (1987) 'Strategic Investments and the Development of Multinationals', *International Economic Review*, 28: 109–21.

Hu, Yao-Su. (1992) 'Global or Stateless Corporations are National Firms with International Operations', *California Management Review*, 34 (2, Winter): 107–26.

Huang, Yasheng (2003) *Selling China: Foreign Direct Investment During the Reform Era*, Cambridge: Cambridge University Press.

Hufbaur, G.C. (1975) 'The Multinational Corporation and Direct Investment', in P.B. Kenen (eds), *International Trade and Finance*, Cambridge: Cambridge University Press.

Humphrey, John (1995) 'Industrial Reorganization in Developing Countries: From Models to Trajectories', *World Development*, 23(1): 149–62.

Husted, Bryan (1999) 'Wealth, Culture, and Corruption', *Journal of International Business Studies*, 30(2): 339–60.

Hymer, Stephen H. (1976) *The International Operations of Multinational Firms: A Study of Foreign Direct Investment*, Boston, MA: MIT Press.

Ichniowski, C., K. Shaw and G. Prennushi (1997) 'The Effects of Human Resource Management Practices on Productivity: a Study of Steel Finishing Lines', *American Economic Review*, 87(3): 291–313.

IMF (2000) *Capital Controls: Country Experiences With Their Use and Liberalisation*, Washington, DC: IMF.

IMF (2004) *World Economic Outlook*, Washington, DC: IMF.

*International Financial Statistics* (different issues), Washington, DC: IMF.

*Investment Guide* (1999) Ministry of Commerce and Industry, Government of India.

Ito, Takatoshi (2000) 'Capital Flows in Asia', in Sebastian Edwards (ed.), *Capital Flows and the Emerging Economies*, Chicago and London: University of Chicago Press, pp. 255–96.

*Japan Company Handbooks*, Volumes 1 and 2, 2000 and 2004, Tokyo: Keizai Inc.

Jenkins, Rob (1999) *Democratic Politics and Economic Reforms in India*, Cambridge: Cambridge University Press.

JETRO (1995 to 2006). *White Papers on Foreign Direct Investment*, Tokyo.

JETRO (2004) *Japanese-Affiliated Manufacturers in Asia – ASEAN and India: Survey*, Tokyo.

JETRO (2005) *The 15th Survey of Investment-Related Cost Comparison in Major Cities and Regions in Asia*, March: 4–9.

Johanson, Jan and Jan-Erik Vahlne (1977) 'The Internationalization Process of the Firm – A Model of Knowledge Development and Increasing Foreign Market Commitments', *Journal of International Business Studies*, 8(1): 22–32.

Jianping, Ding (1999) 'Agglomeration Effects in manufacturing Location-Are There Any Country's Preferences?', *Economia Internazionale*, 52(1): 59–78.

Johanson, Jan and Jan-Erik Vahlne (1990) 'The Mechanism of Internationalization', *International Marketing Review*, 7(4): 11–24.

Johanson, Jan and Finn Wiedersheim-Paul (1975) 'The Internationalization of the Firm – Four Swedish Cases', *Journal of Management Studies*, 12(3): 305–22.

Johnson, Harry G. (1970) 'The State of Theory in Relation to the Empirical Analysis', in Raymond Vernon (ed.), *Technology Factor in International Trade*, New York: NBER, pp. 9–21.

Kaplinsky, Raphael (1994) *Easternization: The Spread of Japanese Management Techniques to LDCs*, London: Frank Cass.

Kaplinsky, Raphael (1995) 'Technique and System: the Spread of Japanese Management Techniques to Developing Countries', *World Development*, 23(1): 57–71.

Kaufmann, Daniel, Aart Kraay and Pablo Zaido Lobaton (1999) 'Aggregating Governance Indicators', Working Paper 2195, Washington, DC: World Bank.

Kaufmann, Daniel, Aart Kraay and Massimo Mastruzzi (2004) 'Governance Matters III: Governance Indicators for 1996, 1998, 2000 and 2002', *The World Bank Economic Review*, 18(2): 253–86.

Kawabe, Nobuo and Tatsuo Kimbara (1991) 'Review of Studies on Japanese-Style Management', in S. Yamashita (ed.), *Transfer of Japanese Technology and Management to the ASEAN Countries*, Tokyo: University of Tokyo Press, pp. 123–33.

Kenney, M. and R. Florida (1993) *Beyond Mass Production: The Japanese System and its Transfer to the U.S.*, New York: Oxford University Press.

Kevin Zhang Hongli (2001) 'How Does Foreign Direct Investment Affect Economic Growth in China?', *Economics of Transition*, 9(3): 679–93.

Kim, S. (1995) 'Expansion of Markets and the Geographic Distribution of Economic Activities: The Trends in US Manufacturing Structure, 1860–1987', *Quarterly Journal of Economics*, 110: 881–908.

Kimura, Y. (1989) 'Firm-Specific Strategic Advantages and Foreign Direct Investment Behavior of Firms: The Case of Japanese Semiconductor Firms', *Journal of International Business Studies*, 20(Summer): 296–394.

Kindleberger, C.P. (1969) *American Business Abroad: Six Lectures on Direct Investment*, New Haven: Yale University Press.

Klein, M.W. and E. Rosengren (1994) 'The Real Exchange Rate and Foreign Direct Investment in the United States: Relative Wealth vs. Relative Wage Effects', *Journal of International Economics*, 36: 373–89.

Knickerbocker, F.T. (1973) *Oligopolistic Reaction and Multinational Enterprise*, Cambridge, MA: Harvard University Press.

Kobrin, Steven. (1976) 'The Environmental Determinants of Foreign Direct Manufacturing Investment: An Ex-post Empirical Analysis', *Journal of International Business Studies*, 7(1): 29–42.

Kodama F. (1995) *Emerging Patterns of Innovation: Sources of Japan's Technological Edge*, Boston: Harvard Business School Press.

Koechlin, Timothy (1992) 'The Determinants of the Location of USA Direct Foreign Investment', *International Review of Applied Economics*, 6(2): 203–16.

Kogut, B. (1983) 'Foreign Direct Investment as a Sequential Process', in C.P. Kindleberger and D.B. Audretsch (eds), *The Multinational Corporation in the 1980s*, Cambridge, MA: MIT Press.

Koike, K. (1994) 'Learning and Incentive Systems in Japanese Industry', in M. Aoki and R. Dore (eds), *The Japanese Firm: Sources and Competitive Strength*, Oxford: Oxford University Press.

Kojima, K. (1973) 'A Macroeconomic Approach to Foreign Direct Investment', *Hitotsubashi Journal of Economics*, 14: 1–21.

Kojima, K. (1975) 'International Trade and Foreign Investment: Substitutes or Complements', *Hitotsubashi Journal of Economics*, 16: 1–12.

Kojima, K. (1978a) *Japanese Foreign Direct Investment*, Tokyo: Charles E. Tuttle.

Kojima, K. (1978b) *Direct Foreign Investment: A Japanese Model of Multinational Business Operations*, London: Croom Helm.

Kojima, K. (1982) 'Macroeconomic Versus International Business Approach Direct Foreign Investment', *Hitotsubashi Journal of Economics*, 23: 1–10.

Kojima, K. (1985) 'Japanese and American Direct Investment in Asia: A Comparative Analysis', *Hitotsubashi Journal of Economics*, 26 (June): 1–35.

Kojima, K. (1986) 'Japanese Style Direct Foreign Investment', *Japanese Economic Studies*, 14(3) (Spring): 52–82.

Kokko, Ari and Zejan, Mario (1996) 'Planned and Failed Foreign Direct Investment in Vietnam', *Asia Pacific Development Journal*; 3(1): 37–54.

Kreinin M.E. and Plummer, M.G. (1994) 'Natural Economic Blocs: An Alternative Formulation', *The International Trade Journal*, 8(2): 193–205.

Krishna, K.L. (ed.) (1997) *Econometric Applications in India*. New Delhi: Oxford University Press.

Krugman, P. (1993) 'Regionalism vs Multilateralism: Analytical Notes', In J. de Melo and A. Panagariya (eds), *New Dimensions in Region Integration*, New York: Cambridge University Press.

Krugman, P.R. (1997) 'Good News from Ireland: A Geographical Perspective', in A.W. Gray (ed.), *International Perspectives on the Irish Economy*, Dublin: Indecon.

Krugman, P.R. and A.J. Venables (1995) 'Globalization and the Inequality of Nations', *Quarterly Journal of Economics*, 110(4): 857–80.

Krugman, P.R. and A.J. Venables (1996) 'Integration, Specialization, and Adjustment', *European Economic Review*, 40(3): 959–67.

Kuemmerle, W. (1999) 'The Drivers of Foreign Direct Investment into Research and Development: An Empirical Investigation', *Journal of International Business Studies*, 30(1): 1–24.

Kujawa, D. (1983) 'Technology Strategy and Industrial Relations: Case Study of Japanese Multinationals in the United States', *Journal of International Business Studies*, Winter: 92–122.

Lall, S. and S. Mohammed (1983) 'Multinationals in Indian Big Business: Industry Characteristics of Foreign Investment in a Heavily Regulated Economy', *Journal of Development Economics*, 13 (August): 143–57.

Lardy, N. (1995) 'The Role of Foreign Trade and Investment in China's Economic Tranformation', *China Quarterly*, 144: 1065–82.

Lazear, E.P. (1998) *Personal Economics for Managers*, New York: John Wiley.

Lecraw, D.J. (1984) 'Bargaining Power, Ownership and the Profitability of Transnational Corporations', *Journal of International Business Studies*, 15: 27–43.

Levinthal, A.D. and J.G. March (1993) 'The Myopia of Learning', *Strategic Management Journal*, 14: 95–112.

Levis, M. (1979) 'Does Political Instability in Developing Countries Affect Foreign Investment Flows? An Empirical Examination', *Management International Review*, 19: 59–68.

Lipsey, R.E. and M.Y. Weiss (1969) 'The Relations of US Manufacturing Abroad to US Exports Framework for Analysis', *Business and Economics Section Proceedings*, American Statistical Association.

Lipsey, R.E. and M.Y. Weiss (1972) 'Analyzing Direct Investment and Trade at the Company Level', *Business and Economics Section Proceedings*, American Statistical Association.

Liu, X.H. Song, Y. Wei and P. Romilly (1997) 'Country Characteristics and Foreign Direct Investment in China: A Panel Data Analysis', *Weltwirtschaftliches Archiv*, 133(2): 313–27.

Liu, X., C. Wang and Y. Wei (2001) 'Causal Links Between Foreign Direct Investment and Trade in China', *China Economic Review*, 12(2): 190–202.

Loree, David W. and Stephen E. Guisinger (1995) 'Policy and Non-Policy Determinants of U.S. Equity Foreign Direct Investment', *Journal of International Business Studies*, 26(2): 281–300.

MacDuffie, J.P. and J. Krafcik (1992) 'Interacting Technology and Human Resources for High Performance Manufacturing: Evidence from the International Auto Industry', in T. Kochan and M. Useem (eds), *Transforming Organisations*, New York, Oxford University Press.

Magee, Stephen P. (1977) 'Information and Multinational Corporations: An Appropriability Theory of Direct Foreign Investment', in Jagdish Bhagwati (ed.), *The New International Economic Order*, Cambridge, MA: MIT Press, pp. 317–40.

Markusen, James R. (1995) 'The Boundaries of Multinational Firms and the Theory of International Trade', *Journal of Economic Perspectives*, 9: 169–89.

Markusen, J.R. and A.J. Venables (1998) 'Multinational Firms and the New Trade Policy', *Journal of International Economics*, 46(2): 183–203.

Melin, L. (1992) 'Internationalization as a Strategy Process', *Strategic Management Journal*, 13: 99–118.

Mody, Ashoka, Dasgupta, Susmita and Sinha, Sarbajit (1999) 'Japanese Multinationals in Asia: Drivers and Attractors', *Oxford Development Studies*, 27(2): 149–64.

Mody, Ashoka and Fang-Yi Wang (1997) 'Explaining Industrial Growth in Coastal China: Economic Reforms and What Else?', *World Bank Economic Review*, 11: 293–325.

Munday, M. (1990) *Japanese Manufacturing Investment in Wales*, Cardiff: University of Wales Press.

Nordstrom, K.A. (1991) *The Internationalisation of the Firm Searching for New Patterns and Expectations*, Stockholm: IIB.

Nordstrom, Kjell and Jan-Erik Vahlne (1992). *Is the Glove Shrinking? Psychic Distance and the Establishment of Swedish Sales Subsidiaries During the Last 100 Years*, International Trade and Finance Association's Annual Conference, Laredo, Texas, 22–5 April.

Ozawa, T. (1979) *Multinationalism: Japanese Style*, Princeton, NJ: Princeton University Press.

Ozawa, T. (1990) *Multinational Corporations and Flying Geese Paradigm of Economic Development in the Asian Pacific*. A paper presented at the 20th Anniversary World Conference on Multinational Enterprises and the 21st Century Scenarios, Tokyo, 4–6 July.

Phongpaichit Pasuk (1990). *The New Wave of Japanese Investment in ASEAN*, Singapore: Institute of Southeast Asian Studies.

Porter, Michael E. (1990) *The Competitive Advantage of Nations*, New York: The Free Press.

Porter, M., H. Takeuchi, and Sakakibara, M. (2000) *Can Japan Compete?* Cambridge, MA: Basic Books.

Ragazzi, G. (1973) 'Theories of the Determinants of Direct Foreign Investment', IMF Staff Papers, July 1973: 471–98.

Ramstetter, Eric O. (1991) *Regional Patterns of Japanese Multinational Activities in Japan and Asia's Developing Countries*, Osaka: Kansai University, Institute of Economic and Political Studies.

Ravenhill, J. (1999) 'Japanese and US subsidiaries in East Asia: Host Economy Effects', in D.J. Encarnation (ed.), Japanese Multinationals in Asia: Regional Operations in Comparative Perspective, New York: Oxford University Press, pp. 261–84.

Reich R.B. (1990) 'Who is us', *Harvard Business Review*, January/February, 53–64.

Reich R.B. (1991) 'Who is them', *Harvard Business Review*, March/April: 77–88.

Rivoli, Pietra and Eugene Salorio (1996) 'Foreign Direct Investment and Investment Under Uncertainty', *Journal of International Business Studies*, 27: 335–57.

Root, Franklin and Ahmed, Ahmed (1979) 'Empirical Determinants of Manufacturing Direct Foreign Investment in Developing Countries', *Economic Development and Cultural Change*, 27(4): 751–61.

Rugman Alan M. (1980) 'Internalization as a General Theory of Foreign Direct Investment: A Reappraisal of the Literature', *Weltwirtschaftliches Archiv*, 116: 365–79.

Rugman Alan M. (ed.) (2002) *International Business*, vol. I, Theory of the Multinational Enterprise, London: Routledge.

Rugman Alan M. and Alain Verbeke (2004) 'A Perspective on Regional and Global Strategies of Multinational Enterprises', *Journal of International Business Studies*, 35(1): 3–18.

Sakakibara, E. and S. Yamakawa (2003a) *Regional Integration in East Asia: Challenges and Opportunities. Part One: History and Institutions*, Washington, DC: World Bank.

Sakakibara, E. and S. Yamakawa. (2003b). *Regional Integration in East Asia: Challenges and Opportunities. Part Two: Trade, Finance and Integration*, Washington, DC: World Bank.

Sazanami, Yoko (1992) 'Determinants of Japanese Foreign Direct Investment: Locational Attractiveness of European Countries to Japanese Multinationals', *Revue Economique*, 43: 661–9.

Sazanami, Yoko, Seiji Yoshimura and Kozo Kiyota (2003) 'Japanese Foreign Direct Investment to East Asia and Exchange Rate Policies – Some Longer Term Policy Implications After the Crisis', *Keio Economic Studies*, 40(1): 1–26.

Schneider, Friedrish and Bruno S. Frey (1985) 'Economic and Political Determinants of Foreign Direct Investment', *World Development*, 13: 161–75.

Schroath, F.W., M.Y. Hu and H. Chen (1993) 'Country of Origin Effects of Foreign Investment in People's Republic of China', *Journal of International Business Studies*, Second Quarter: 277–90.

Scott, Bruce R. (1985) 'National Strategies: Key to International Competition', in Bruce R. Scott and George C. Lodge (eds), *U.S. Competitiveness in the World Economy*, Boston: Harvard Business School Press.

Stevens, G.V. (1974) 'Determinants of Investment', in John H. Dunning (ed.), *Economic Analysis and the Multinational Enterprise*, London; Allen & Unwin.

Sun, H. (1998) 'Macro-Economic Impact of Direct Foreign Investment in China, 1979–96', *The World Economy*, 21(5): 675–94.

Sun, Haisun and Ashok Parikh (2001) 'Exports, Inward Foreign Direct Investment (FDI) and Regional Economic Growth in China', *Regional Studies*, 35(3): 187–96.

Sun, Q., W. Tong and Q. Yu (2002) 'Determinants of Foreign Direct Investment Across China', *Journal of International Money and Finance*, 21(1): 79–113.

Syamwil, Indra Budiman and Paul Hidehiko Tanimura (2000) 'The Spatial Distribution of Japanese Manufacturing Industries in Indonesia', *Review of Urban and Regional Development Studies*, July, 12(2): 120–36.

Teece, D.J. (1977) 'Technology Transfer by Multinational Firms', *The Economic Journal*, 87: 242–61.

Teece, D.J. (1981) 'The Market for Know-how and Efficient International Transfer of Technology', *Annals of American Academy of Political and Social Science*, 458: 81–96.

Teece, D.J. (1983) 'Technological and Organisational Factors in the Theory of the Multinational Enterprise', in Mark C. Casson (ed.), *The Growth of International Business*, London: Macmillan, pp. 51–62.

Teece, D.J. (1986) 'Profiting from Technological Innovation: Implication for Integration, Collaboration, Licensing and Public Policy', *Research Policy*, 15: 286–305.

Tejima, S. (1994) 'Prospects for Japanese Foreign Direct Investment (FDI) in the 1990s: Towards a New Globalization of the 1990s and the 2000s', in K. Ohno and Y. Okamoto (eds), *Regional Integration and Foreign Direct Investment: Implications for Developing Countries*.

Terry, Edith (1996) 'An East Asian Paradigm?', *Atlantic Economic Journal*, 24: 183–98.

Trevino, L.J. and J.D. Daniels and H. Arbelaez (2002) 'Market Reform and FDI in Latin America: An Empirical Investigation', *Transnational Corporations*, 11(1).

Tuan, Chyau and F.Y. Linda (2003) 'FDI Facilitated by Agglomeration Economies: Evidence from Manufacturing and Services Joint Ventures in China', *Journal of Asian Economics*, January 13(6): 749–65.

Tuman, John P. and Craig Emmert, F. (1999) 'Explaining Japanese Foreign Investment in Latin America', *Social Science Quarterly*, 80(3): 539–55.

Twomey, M.J. (2001) 'A Century of Foreign Investment in Mexico', UM Deardon Economic Working Paper 98, University of Michigan, Deardon.

Tyson, Laura (1991) 'They are not Us: Why American Ownership Still Matters', *American Prospect*, 4(Winter): 36–49.

Urata, S. (1998) 'Japanese Foreign Direct Investment in Asia: Its Impact on Export Expansion and Technology Acquisition of the Host Countries', in Nagesh Kumar *et al.*, *Globalization, Foreign Direct Investment and Technology Transfer: Impact on and Prospects for Developing Countries*, London and New York: Routledge, pp. 146–74.

Urata, Shujiro (1993) 'Japanese Foreign Direct Investment and Its Effect on Foreign Trade', in Takatoshi Ito and Anne O. Krueger (eds), *Trade and Protectionism NBER: East Asia Seminar on Economics*, vol. 2, Chicago: University of Chicago Press.

UN (1995 to 2003) *World Economic and Social Survey*, New York.

UN (2006) *World Economic Situation and Prospects*, New York.

UNCTAD (1998 to 2006) *World Investment Reports*, United Nations.

UNCTAD (1996) *Incentives and Foreign Direct Investment*, Current Studies, Series A (30), New York and Geneva: UN.

UNCTC (1992) *The Determinants of Foreign Direct Investment – A Survey of the Evide*nce, New York: United Nations.

UNDP (2003–06) *Human Development Report*, New York: Oxford University Press, New York.

Vernon, R. (1966) 'International Investment and International Trade in the Product Cycle', *Quarterly Journal of Economics*, 80: 190–297.

Vernon, R. (1979) 'The Product Cycle Hypothesis in a New International Environment', *Bulletin of Economics and Statistics*; 41: 255–67.

Vernon, R. and Louis T. Wells (1981) *Manager in the International Economy*, Fourth Edition Englewood Cliffs, NJ: Prentice Hall.

Veugelers, Reinhilde (1991) 'Locational Determinants and Ranking of Host Countries: An Empirical Assessment', *Kyklos*; 44(3): 363–82.

Wakabayashi, Mitsuru and George B. Graen (1991) 'Cross-cultural Human Resource Development: Japanese Manufacturing Firms in Central Japan and Central US States', in Malcolm Trevor (ed.), *International Business and Management of Change*, Brookfield, VT: Avebury, pp. 147–69.

Wang, Zhenquan and Nigel J. Swain (1995) 'The Determinants of Foreign Direct Investment in Transforming Economies: Empirical Evidence from Hungary and China', *Weltwirtschaftliches Archiv*, 131(2): 359–82.

Wei, Y. and X. Liu, (2001) *Foreign Direct Investment in China: Determinants and Impact*, Cheltenham: Edward Elgar.

Wei, Shang-jin (2000) 'How Taxing Is Corruption On International Investors?', *The Review of Economics and Statistics*, 82(1): 1–11.

Wei, Shang-jin (1995) 'Attracting Foreign Direct Investment: Has China Reached its Potential?', *China Economic Review*, 6(2): 187–99.

Wei, Yingqi, X. Liu, D. Parker and K.Vaida (1999) 'The Regional Distribution of Foreign Direct Investment in China', *Regional Studies*, 33(9): 857–67.

Wei, Shang-jin (1999) 'Can China and India Double their Inward Foreign Direct Investment', A Paper presented at the *NBER Conference on India*, Neemrana (December 1999). Accessed at http://www.nber.org/-confer/99/indiaf99/India-China-FDI.PDF.

Welch, L.S. and R. Luostorinen (1988) 'Internationalization: Evolution of a Concept', *Journal of General Management*, 14(2): 34–55.

Wells, L.T. and A.G. Wint (1991) 'The Public–Private Choice: The Case of Marketing a Country to Investors', *World Development*, 19(7): 749–61.

Westney, D.E. (1988) 'Domestic and International Learning Curves in Managing International Competitive Strategies', in Farok Contractor and Peter Lorange (eds), *Cooperative Strategies in International Business*, Lexington, MA: Lexington Books.

Wheeler, David and Ashoka Mody (1992) 'International Investment, Location Decisions: The Case of U.S. Firms', *Journal of International Economics*, 33: 57–76.

Williamson, O.E. (1975) *Markets and Hierarchies: Analysis and Antitrust Implications*, New York: The Free Press.

Williamson, O.E. (1979) 'Transaction Cost Economics: The Governance of Contractual Relations', *Journal of Law and Economics*, 22: 223–61.

Williamson, O.E. (1981) 'The Modern Corporation, Origins, Evolution, Attributes', *Journal of Economic Literature*, 19: 1537–68.

Williamson, O.E. (1989) 'Transaction Cost Economics', in R. Schmalensee and R.D. Willing (eds), *Handbook of Industrial Organization*, vol. 1, pp. 135–82.

Williamson, O.E. (1985) *The Economic Institutions of Capitalism*, New York: Free Press.

Wong, K. and K. Yamamura (1996) 'Japan's Direct Investment in the United States: Causes, Patterns, and Issues', in L. Hollerman and R.H. Myers (eds), *The Effect of Japanese Investment on the World Economy*, Stanford, CA: Hoover Institute Press, Stanford University, pp. 1–46.

World Bank (1994) *World Development Report, 1994: Infrastructure for Development*, Oxford University Press, New York.

World Bank. (2002 to 2007) *World Development Indicators*, Washington, DC: World Bank.

World Bank (2005) 'A Better Investment Climate for Everyone', *World Development Report*, New York: A co-publication of the World Bank and the Oxford University Press.

World Bank (2006) *Doing Business in 2006*, Washington, DC: World Bank.

*World Economic and Financial Surveys* (different issues), Washington DC: IMF.

Yamamura, K. (1994) 'Comment. Does Ownership Matter?', in Mark Mason and Dennis Encarnation (eds), *Japanese Multinationals in Europe*, Oxford: Clarendon Press, pp. 87–90.

Yamazawa Ippei and Imai Ken-ichi (ed.) (2001) 'China Enters WTO: Pursuing Symbiosis with the Global Economy', Institute of Developing Economies, Japan External Trade Organization.

Yuan, Lee Tsao (ed.) (1991) 'Growth Triangle: The Johore–Singapore–Rau Experience', Singapore Institute of Policy Studies, Institute of Southeast Asian Studies.

Yusuf, Shahid, M.Anjum Altaf, Barry Eichengreen, Sudarshan Gooptu, Kaoru Nabeshima, Charles Kenny, Dwight H. Perkins and Marc Shotten (2003) *Innovative East Asia*, New York: World Bank and Oxford University Press.

Zhang, H. and D. Van Den Bulcke (1995) 'Rapid Changes in the Investment Development Path in China', *Discussion Paper*, 1996/E/21, University of Antwerp, Centre for International Management and Development, pp. 1–59.
Zhang, K. (2000) 'Foreign Direct Investment and Economic Growth in Developing Countries', Illinois State University; Paper presented at the ASSA Conference.
Zhang, K.H. (2001) 'What Attracts Foreign Multinational Corporations to China?', *Contemporary Economic Review*, 11: 385–96.
Zhao, Hongxin and Gangti Zhu (2000) 'Location Factors and Country of Origin Difference: an Empirical Analysis', *Multinational Business Review*, 8(1): 60–73.

# Index

*Note*:
The following abbreviations have been used in the compilation of this index
*en* end notes
*f* figure
*t* table
*ta* technical annex